Counselling Individuals:
A Rational–Emotive Handbook

Second edition

This book is dedicated to:

Sheila Chown who taught me (W.D.) what it means to be a dedicated academic psychologist. Enjoy your retirement, Sheila.

Counselling Individuals: A Rational–Emotive Handbook

Second edition

Windy Dryden

Department of Psychology, Goldsmiths' College,
University of London

Joseph Yankura

Institute for Rational-Emotive Therapy, New York

Foreword by Albert Ellis
President, Institute for Rational-Emotive Therapy,
New York

Whurr Publishers Ltd
London

First published 1987 by Taylor & Francis Ltd
All rights acquired by Whurr Publishers Ltd 1990
19b Compton Terrace, London N1 2UN, England

Second edition published 1993 by Whurr Publishers Ltd

British Library Cataloguing in Publication Data

A catalogue record for this book
is available from the British Library.

ISSN 1-870332-78-4

Phototypeset by Computape (Pickering) Ltd, Pickering, North Yorkshire
Printed and bound in the UK by Athenaeum Press Ltd, Newcastle upon Tyne

Foreword

Albert Ellis

I have read quite a number of books explaining what rational-emotive therapy (RET) is and how therapists and counsellors can effectively use it, and this book by Windy Dryden and Joseph Yankura is easily one of the very best. It is accurate, clear, comprehensive and well written. It includes excellent illustrations, case materials and verbatim transcripts of counselling sessions. It is up to date and it covers a number of different RET styles; it also incorporates some useful techniques from other therapies which are often used with standard RET procedures. All told, authors Dryden and Yankura have done a fine job of describing the main theories and practices of RET, and have produced a book that is remarkably good for counsellors and therapists who have not extensively used it before; they have also made it quite useful for many of its seasoned practitioners.

The expanded ABCs of RET

I originally pointed out in *Reason and Emotion in Psychotherapy* that rational-emotive counselling sees cognition, emotion and behaviour not as disparate aspects of human functioning but as integrated and interactive processes (Ellis, 1962). I have recently expanded this concept and shown how the ABCs of RET inevitably interact with each other and how all of them include cognitive, emotive and behavioural elements (Ellis, 1991a). In the original RET, I showed how unfortunate activating events or adversities (As) in people's lives rarely directly cause them to feel and to behave in a disturbed manner and thereby create dysfunctional consequences (Cs). Instead people largely (but not completely) disturb themselves with their self-defeating beliefs (Bs) about their As (Ellis, 1957, 1962; Ellis and Harper, 1961a). In my revised ABCs of emotional disturbance, I show that even people's unfortunate activating events (As) are normally seen in the biased and influential light of their beliefs (Bs) and in the light of their reactions or consequences (Cs). Also, their beliefs (Bs) and their consequences (Cs) are strongly influenced by the activating events (As) of their lives. Similarly, people's cognitions affect their feelings but the latter also significantly affect the former, and their behaviours largely follow from their thoughts and feelings, but these thoughts and feelings are also significantly affected by people's behaviours.

The ABCs of RET, therefore, as explained in this book, are still at the core of RET theory and practice; however, they include some complex interactions which affect people's relationships with themselves and with others, and which often have to be examined and dealt with in effective counselling.

RET was always concerned with individuals and their cognitive–behavioural problems, as this book efficiently shows, but it also has specialised in interpersonal relationships, as indicated in my first book on RET, *How to Live with a 'Neurotic'* (Ellis, 1957) and in many other RET writings (Ellis, 1960; Ellis and Harper, 1961b). The ABCs have been extended to show how one partner's emotional consequences (C_1) often serve as activating events (As) for the other partner, who then may upset herself in regard to these As and create her own disturbed consequences (C_1) about them. But then the other partner may easily make these Cs into his own activating events (A_2) and may upset himself at his own consequences (C_2) about them. The ABCs of interpersonal relationships, therefore, may again become quite complex (Ellis et al., 1989; Ellis, 1991a, 1992).

Self-actualisation and counselling

Like most other therapies, RET usually first focuses on clients' emotional and behavioural problems and tries to help them work on their presenting symptoms, to overcome them, and – as this book accurately shows – to attempt to make a profound philosophical change; through this clients can effect an *elegant* solution so that they rarely disturb themselves in the future and, when they do so, they are able fairly quickly to see what they are doing to upset themselves again and to work at un-upsetting themselves. However, RET also assumes that once they are on the road to becoming less disturbable, clients also can use their innate self-actualising tendencies to create for themselves a more fulfilling and more enjoyable life than they would otherwise lead. RET, therefore, with a good many clients, helps in reassessment of basic goals and values and an attempt to lead a more self-actualising existence (Dryden, 1991; Ellis 1991b; Bernard, 1992). Ideally, it is not only therapeutic but also attempts to help people fulfil more of their growth potential.

Constructivism and RET

As Windy Dryden and Joseph Yankura show in this book, RET was first positivistic and therefore a bit on the overly rational side, even though it was always humanistic and existentialist (Ellis, 1962, 1973). I was apprised of the critical realism of Karl Popper (1962) and W. W. Bartley (1962) in 1976, however, by Michael Mahoney's book, *Scientist as Subject* (1976) and have been non-positivistic ever since. Instead, RET for the last two decades has to some extent followed, and even gone beyond, George Kelly's (1955) pioneering ideas about constructivism. Kelly belived that people do not merely react to situations and to their social learning, but that they creatively construct their individualised and often highly unique responses to the situations they encounter (Neimeyer, 1992). This is what RET basically says when it points out that people take the activating events (As) of their lives and formulate beliefs (Bs) about them, which in turn significantly affect their consequences (Cs) that follow their As and Bs.

RET, however, adds to Kelly's constructivist formulations the notion that people's belief systems (Bs) have two main parts when they are neurotic. First, they have *preferential* beliefs – 'I like *x* and I dislike *y*' – which are derived from: (1) their biological tendencies (e.g. to prefer sugar rather than salt in their coffee); (2) their learned goals and values (e.g. to wear certain styles of clothing), which they tend to [gullibly] accept from their parents, teachers and culture; and (3) the idiosyncratic tastes or habits which they tend to create or construct themselves (e.g. 'I like brandy and three spoonfuls of sugar in my coffee').

People's desires and preferences, as this book shows, rarely make them emotionally disturbed, because they include flexible *buts* and *neverthelesses*. For example: 'I very much prefer to succeed at work and at love *but* I never *have to* do so. Too bad if I fail, but the world won't come to an end.' 'I really dislike working hard to earn a living; *nevertheless* I'll be worse off if I don't, so I damned well better do it!'

People's absolutist *demands* and *commands*, says RET, do often produce dysfunctions and disturbances because they are unrealistic, illogical and often impossible to achieve. Thus, they may imperatively believe, 'Because I very much prefer to succeed at work and love, I always *have to*, else I am a *rotten person!*' or 'Because I really dislike working hard to earn a living, I *must not* have to do so, and other people *should* always take care of me!' With these *demands* and *commands* they are in real trouble!

Like many other counselling methods, RET holds that people may learn their absolutist shoulds and musts from their families and culture but even then they *choose* to accept and act on them. For they *could* see through the self-defeating *musts* of their families, *not* agree with them, and keep their socially imbibed *preferences* as *only* that – mere wishes and desires. But they very often have, says RET, a powerful *innate* tendency to take almost any of their *strong* desires, no matter *how* they acquired or developed them, and *make them, construct them* into inflexible demands.

RET, then, agrees with Kelly and other constructivists that humans have strong, innate tendencies to change their environment and themselves and to creatively go for self-improvement and self-fulfilment (Maslow, 1954; Kelly, 1955; Rogers, 1961). It is even more constructivist than most other therapies in that it hypothesises that, in addition to being inherently self-actualising, the vast majority of humans have a biological tendency to take their strong preferences, goals and values, and to *devise* and *construct* absolutist, inflexible *shoulds* and *musts* about them. Finally, by thinking about their thinking, and by thinking about thinking about their thinking, both of which are again their natural constructivist tendencies, they can *re*construct their self-defeating musturbatory constructions and use their human potentials to (1) un-upset themselves, (2) train themselves (after a while) to be much less upset*able*, and (3) use their cognitive, emotive and behavioural abilities to construct happier, more self-actualised lives. RET, then, realistically acknowledges the three main sides of human constructiveness: first, people's innate tendancies to *construct* healthy, fulfilling goals, desires, purposes, meanings and ideals that enable them to survive and to lead creative, happy lives. Second, their strong human propensities to *de*construct their healthy preferences by raising them into unhealthy, self-defeating imperative demands, commands and 'necessities'. Third, their innate potential consciously to observe, think about and reassess their disturbed thoughts, feelings and behaviours, and to use a number of cognitive, emotive and behavioural methods to *re*construct and *re*actualise their lives. RET helps clients (and other people) to see their constructive, deconstructive and reconstructive tendencies more clearly and to work more constructively on themselves and their environment than they often do without using effective counselling methods.

   Counselling Individuals: A Rational–Emotive Handbook, by Windy Dryden and Joseph Yankura, presents the RET theory and practice of counselling so clearly and thoroughly that therapists who study it can truly understand and efficiently apply it, and so that many lay individuals can also appreciably benefit from its lucid and helpful pages. Good reading like this can nicely lead to good therapy!

Albert Ellis

References

BARTLEY, W. W., III (1962). *The Retreat to Commitment*. Peru, IL: Open Court.

BERNARD, M. E. (1992) *Staying Rational in an Irrational World*. New York: Carol Publishing.

DRYDEN, W. (1991). *A Dialogue with Albert Ellis: Against Dogma*. Milton Keynes, England: Open University.

ELLIS, A. (1957). *How to Live with a 'Neurotic'*. North Hollywood, CA: Wilshire. Revised edition, 1975

ELLIS, A. (1960). *The Art and Science of Love*. New York: Lyle Stuart.

ELLIS, A. (1962) *Reason and Emotion in Psychotherapy*. Secaucus, NJ: Citadel.

ELLIS, A. (1973). *Humanistic Psychotherapy: The Rational-Emotive Approach*. New York: McGraw-Hill.

ELLIS, A. (1991a). The revised ABCs of rational-emotive therapy. *Journal of Rational-Emotive and Cognitive-Behavior Therapy* 9, 139-172.

ELLIS, A (1991b). Achieving self-actualization: The rational–emotive approach. *Journal of Social Behavior and Personality* 6(5), 1-18.

ELLIS, A. (Speaker). (1992) *The Rational-Emotive Approach to Marriage and Family Therapy*. Two cassette recordings. Norcross, GA: The Resource Link.

ELLIS, A. and HARPER, R. A. (1961a). *A Guide to Rational Living*. New York: Prentice-Hall.

ELLIS, A. and HARPER, R. A. (1961b). *A Guide to Successful Marriage*. North Hollywood, CA: Wilshire.

ELLIS, A., SICHEL, J., YEAGER, R., DiMATTIA, D. and DiGIUSEPPE, R (1989). *Rational-Emotive Couples Therapy*. New York: Pergamon.

KELLY, G. (1955). *The Psychology of Personal Constructs*. New York: Norton.

MAHONEY, M. M. H. (1976) *Scientist as Subject*. Cambridge, MA: Ballinger.

MASLOW, A. H. (1954). *Towards a Psychology of Being*. New York: Van Nostrand Reinhold.

NEIMEYER, G. J. (1992) Back to the future with the psychology of personal constructs. *Contemporary Psychology* 37, 994-997.

POPPER, K. R. (1962). *Objective Knowledge*. London: Oxford.

ROGERS, C. R. (1961). *On Becoming a Person*. Boston: Houghton Mifflin.

Preface

We are pleased to present this newly revised and expanded second edition of *Counselling Individuals: The Rational–Emotive Approach*. Like the first edition, this book is primarily intended for those who work in a counselling role with individuals who are *not* severely psychologically disturbed. Here we adopt a pragmatic definition of counselling by which we mean 'a mode of helping designed to encourage people to overcome their emotional and behavioural problems and thence to lead satisfying lives'. Since counselling (as defined here) is deemed to be most suitable for clients who are *not* severely disturbed, it is likely to be a relatively shorter-term intervention than psychotherapy, which is more appropriate for clients with more severe psychological problems. Thus, this book is designed for counsellors, from a broad range of professional groups, whose clients are likely to have non-severe problems of anxiety, shame and embarrassment, depression, guilt, anger, hurt, jealousy and self-discipline (e.g. procrastination).

The distinction we have made between counselling and psychotherapy raises issues that focus on the assessment of the severity of clients' psychological problems. Some counselling agencies ask all potential clients to attend for an 'intake' assessment interview to determine whether or not the 'applicant' is suitable for counselling (as defined here). In such cases, intake interviewers usually carry out detailed appraisals of: (a) the client's history of psychological disturbance, and (b) his or her current functioning. This assessment may indeed be carried out by counsellors themselves before offers of help are considered. If the present working definition of counselling is used as the criterion, then clients most likely to benefit from this mode of helping are those who have emotional and behavioural problems in the neurotic range of disturbance; who do not have a long history of poor psychological functioning; and who can demonstrate evidence of having experienced good interpersonal relationships in their lives. This book then is designed specifically for use with this clientèle.

This book is definitely not designed for use with clients whose problems are in the psychotic range of disturbance, although it should not be forgotten that such individuals do have neurotic difficulties and counselling can be appropriate for such problems when the individuals are not actively psychotic.

This leaves clients who have severe personality problems, a long history of poor psychological functioning and impaired interpersonal relationships – the so-called 'personality disorders'. While this book can be used to inform therapeutic work with such individuals, it has not been written with this clientèle in mind, and thus needs to be supplemented by such books as Albert Ellis's (1985) *Overcoming resistance: Rational-emotive therapy with difficult clients*.

Not all counsellors carry out a detailed assessment-based intake interview before offering assistance to people seeking their help. Such helpers tend to assume that they can help a client unless evidence exists to the contrary, at which point they would seek to refer the client concerned to a more appropriate helping agent. For such counsellors we reiterate the above remarks concerning this book's proposed usage.

This book is best used as a supplement to training courses in rational-emotive counselling and should not be regarded as a training resource in its own right. The book is divided into two parts. Part One is devoted to outlining rational-emotive therapy. Here we discuss: (1) some of the major theoretical concepts that underpin rational-emotive counselling: (2) the role of cognition and action in rational-emotive theory; (3) the rational-emotive view of psychological disturbance and health; and (4) the determinants of the major dysfunctional emotions and behaviours for which clients seek counselling help. Part Two is devoted to the practice of rational-emotive counselling. Here we present: (a) a discussion of the indications and contraindications for individual counselling and the counsellor–client relationship; (b) strategies for inducting clients into rational–emotive counselling and assessing their major problems; (c) methods for promoting intellectual insight into rational concepts; (d) methods for promoting emotional insight into rational concepts; (e) the rational–emotive counselling sequence; (f) the rational–emotive counselling process; (g) a review of obstacles to client change and how to deal with them; (h) a client's account of her experience within rational–emotive counselling; (i) a discussion of the distinctive features of rational-emotive counselling as compared with other approaches to cognitive-behavioural counselling.

Rational-emotive counselling is one of the major approaches to counselling based on cognitive-behavioural principles. Whilst rational-emotive practitioners primarily use methods derived from rational-emotive counselling, they also use methods derived from these other approaches to cognitive-behavioural counselling (see Dryden and Golden, 1986). The present book outlines the major strategies and techniques that are most closely associated with rational-emotive counselling and does not seek to cover other cognitive-behavioural methods. In the final chapter we suggest several references that deal with these other methods.

Acknowledgements

We wish to thank the following:

The Institute for Rational-Emotive Therapy, New York for granting us permission (a) to reproduce: the Biographical Information Form © 1968; the Personality Data Form © 1968; the RET Self-help Form © 1984; and the pamphlet entitled 'How to Maintain and Enhance Your Rational-Emotive Therapy Gains' © 1984 and (b) to use extracts in original and modified form from W.D.'s articles on Vivid RET first published in: *Rational Living*, 1983, **18**(1), 7-12; *Journal of Rational-Emotive Therapy*, 1983, **1**(1), 9-14 and *Journal of Rational-Emotive Therapy*, 1984, **2**(1), 27-31.

Guilford Press for granting us permission to use and modify material published in a chapter entitled 'Rational-emotive therapy' by Windy Dryden and Albert Ellis in K. S. Dobson (Ed.), *Handbook of Cognitive-Behavioral Therapies*. New York: Guilford Press, 1987.

Harper & Row for granting us permission to use and modify material published in a chapter entitled 'Rational-emotive therapy' by Windy Dryden and Albert Ellis, in W. Dryden and W. L. Golden (Eds), *Cognitive-Behavioural Approaches to Psychotherapy*. London: Harper & Row, 1986.

Plenum Press for granting us permission to reproduce material (page 7, line 18 – page 9, line 6) from a chapter entitled 'What is rational-emotive therapy (RET)' by Albert Ellis and Michael Bernard, in A. Ellis and M. E. Bernard (Eds), *Clinical Applications of Rational-Emotive Therapy*. New York: Plenum Press, 1985.

Contents

Chapter 7

Chapter 8

Chapter 9

Chapter 10

Chapter 11

Chapter 12

Chapter 13

Part I
Theory

Chapter 1
The Basic Theory of Rational–Emotive Counselling

Overview

In this opening chapter, we trace the historical development of rational-emotive counselling and outline some of its predominant philosophical and psychological influences. Then we cover the following major theoretical concepts of rational-emotive counselling: rationality, hedonism and enlightened self-interest versus selfishness. We point out that rational-emotive counselling has a decided humanistic emphasis and also highlight the role of activity in human happiness. We continue by outlining the rational-emotive view that humans have two biologically based tendencies (i.e. relevant to their psychological problems): a tendency to think irrationally, and a tendency to work towards changing such thinking. This leads on to a discussion of the two fundamental human disturbances put forward by rational-emotive theory: ego disturbance and discomfort disturbance. We conclude the chapter by stating briefly the rational-emotive position on *thought*, *emotion* and *action*, emphasising the interactional view it takes of these three processes.

The Historical Development of Rational–Emotive Counselling and Psychotherapy

Albert Ellis founded rational-emotive therapy (RET) in 1955 when he was a New York clinical psychologist, having begun his career in the helping professions in the early 1940s. As a result of research he was doing at that time for a massive work to be entitled *The Case for Sexual Liberty*, he gained a local reputation for being an authority on sexual and marital relationships. He was consulted by his friends on their sexual and relationship problems and discovered that he could be successful in helping them with these problems in a short period of time. He decided to pursue formal training in clinical psychology after discovering that there were no formal training possibilities then offered in sex and marital counselling. After getting a PhD degree in clinical psychology, he chose to be trained in psychoanalysis, believing, then, that it was the deepest and most effective form of psychotherapy available. He decided on this course of action because his experiences as an informal sex-marital counsellor had taught him that disturbed relationships were really a product of disturbed persons, 'and that if people were truly to be helped to live happily with each other they first had better be shown how they could live peacefully with themselves' (Ellis, 1962, p. 3).

Ellis initially enjoyed working as a psychoanalyst partly because it allowed him to express both his helping and problem solving interests. However, he became increasingly dissatisfied with psychoanalysis as an *effective* and *efficient* form of treatment. In the early 1950s, Ellis began to experiment with different forms of therapy, including psychoanalytically oriented psychotherapy and eclectic-analytic therapy. But although he became more effective with his clients, he remained dissatisfied about the efficiency of these methods. During this period of experimentation, he returned to his lifelong hobby of reading philosophy to help him with his search for an effective and efficient form of therapy. One of the major influences on his thought at that time was the work of the Greek and Roman Stoic philosophers (e.g. Epictetus and Marcus Aurelius). They emphasised the primacy of philosophic causation of psychological disturbances – a viewpoint which was not popular in America in the 1950s – and de-emphasised the part played by psychoanalytic and psychodynamic factors. In essence the Stoic viewpoint, which stated that people are disturbed not by things but by their view of things, became the foundation of RET in particular, and this perspective (following Ellis' pioneering formulations) remains at the heart of present-day cognitive-behavioural approaches to psychotherapy.

Major philosophical influences

Apart from Stoicism, present-day RET owes a philosophical debt to a number of other sources that have influenced its development. Immanuel Kant's writings on the power (and limitations) of cognition and ideation strongly impressed Ellis (Ellis, 1981a) and the work of Spinoza and Schopenhauer was also important in this respect. Philosophers of science, such as Popper (1959, 1963), Reichenbach (1953), and Russell (1965), were influential in helping Ellis see that all humans develop hypotheses about the nature of the world. Moreover, these philosophers stressed the importance of testing the validity of such hypotheses rather than assuming that they are necessarily correct; the practice of RET is synonymous, in many respects, with the logico-empirical methods of science (Ellis, 1962, 1979a). RET also stresses the flexibility and antidogmatism of the scientific method and holds that rigid absolutism is the very core of human disturbance (Ellis, 1983a).

Although the philosophy of RET is at variance with devout religiosity, there is one respect in which Christian philosophy has been most influential. RET's theory of human value (which will be discussed later) is similar to the Christian viewpoint of condemning the sin but forgiving the sinner (Ellis, 1983a; Hauck, 1972; Powell, 1976). Due to its stand on self-acceptance and its bias against all forms of human rating, RET allies itself with the philosophy of ethical humanism (Russell, 1930, 1965) which opposes the deification and devilification of humans. Since RET considers that humans are at the centre of their universe (but not of *the* universe) and have the power of choice (but not of unlimited choice) with regard to their emotional realm, it has its roots in the existential philosophies of Heidegger (1949) and Tillich (1977). Indeed, RET has a pronounced humanistic-existential outlook (Ellis, 1973).

Ellis was influenced, particularly in the 1960s, by the work of the general semanticists, (e.g. Korzybski, 1933). These theorists outlined the powerful effect that language has on thought and the fact that our emotional processes are heavily dependent on the way we, as humans, structure our thought by the language we employ.

Major psychological influences

In developing RET, Ellis was similarly influenced by the work of a number of psychologists. He received a training analysis from an analyst of the Karen Horney school, and Horney's (1950) concept of the 'tyranny of the shoulds' was certainly an early influence on his emphasis on the primacy of absolute, dogmatic evaluative thought in the development and maintenance of much psychological disturbance. The work of Adler was important to the development of RET in several respects:

> Adler (1927) was the first great therapist to really emphasize inferiority feelings – while RET similarly stresses self-rating and the ego anxiety to which it leads. Like Adler and his Individual Psychology, RET also emphasizes people's goals, purposes, values and meanings. RET also follows Adler in regard to the use of active-directive teaching, the stress placed on social interest, the use of a holistic and humanistic outlook, and the employment of a highly cognitive-persuasive form of psychological treatment. (Ellis, 1981b)

Although RET was originally termed 'rational psychotherapy', it has always advocated the use of behavioural methods as well as cognitive and emotive techniques in the practice of counselling and therapy. Indeed, Ellis utilised some of the methods advocated by several of the earliest pioneers in behaviour therapy (Watson and Rayner, 1920; Jones, 1924; Dunlap, 1932), first in overcoming his own early fears of speaking in public and of approaching women, and second in the active-directive form of sex therapy which he practised in the early 1950s. This behavioural active-directive emphasis remains prominent in present-day rational-emotive counselling and psychotherapy.

In its 38 years' existence, RET has been practised in various therapeutic modalities (individual, group, marital and family), by many kinds of helping professionals (e.g. psychologists, psychiatrists, social workers) with a variety of client populations (e.g. adults, children, the elderly) suffering from a wide range of psychological disorders. Apart from their use in counselling and psychotherapy, rational-emotive principles have been applied in educational, industrial, and commercial settings. A recent development has been the application of RET to public education in the form of 9-hour intensive workshops. In this respect, it is playing a significant role in the field of preventive psychology. RET is practised throughout the world and there are RET 'institutes' in the USA, Israel, Italy, Germany, Holland, Australia, England and Mexico. It is thus a well-established form of cognitive-behavioural therapy.

Major Theoretical Concepts

Rational-emotive counselling is based on a set of assumptions which stress the complexity and fluidity of human beings. Given this fundamental view of human nature, the RET approach to counselling rests on the following theoretical concepts.

Rationality

In our experience, when counsellors are first introduced to rational-emotive counselling, they often become preoccupied with the term 'rational'. Their initial reaction to this term is usually negative because they think, erroneously, that it means 'unemotional' and conclude, again wrongly, that RET counsellors seek to help their clients by encouraging them to become unemotional. 'Rationality' *does* play a central role in rational-emotive theory but it has a very specific meaning within this theory.

To understand the specific RET meaning of 'rationality' it is first important to realise that within rational-emotive theory humans are seen as having two basic goals - to stay alive and to be happy. While there are shared methods of pursuing the former basic goal (e.g. seeking adequate shelter from the elements, maintaining a proper diet, etc.) there are a myriad different ways of pursuing the latter. Humans are remarkably idiosyncratic in what they find personally meaningful or fulfilling.

Given the above considerations, the term 'rational' means *that which helps people to achieve their basic goals and purposes*. Furthermore, in rational-emotive theory, people are seen as having primary (but not exclusive) control over their major psychological processes (i.e. thoughts, emotions and actions). Given that we use these processes in the pursuit of our basic goals, it follows that our thoughts, feelings and actions are deemed to be 'rational' when they help us in the pursuit of these goals. Conversely, the term 'irrational' in rational-emotive theory means *that which prevents people from achieving their basic goals and purposes*. Much RET counselling is spent helping clients to identify and change their 'irrational' (or self-defeating) thoughts, emotions and actions, given that such processes impede goal achievement.

There are no absolute criteria of 'rationality' in rational-emotive theory. These criteria need to be seen as *relative to* the goals and purposes that the individual deems to be important. RET counsellors endeavour to help their clients remove the obstacles to goal attainment that clients themselves construct, and do not seek to impose an absolute standard of 'rationality' as some people, new to RET counselling, incorrectly think.

Responsible hedonism

We have seen how rational-emotive theory considers that humans are basically hedonistic - in the sense that they seek to stay alive and to achieve a reasonable degree of happiness. Again, counsellors new to rational-emotive counselling wrongly consider that the rational-emotive concept of responsible hedonism implies urging clients to pursue a life based on the 'pleasures of the flesh', rather than encouraging them to pursue their personally meaningful goals. Thus, people whose goal is to raise money for starving children in Ethiopia, and who involve themselves in activities directed towards this end, are acting 'hedonistically' in the sense that it is meaningful for them and that they are happy doing so. This responsibly hedonistic decision - based on the principle of social interest (Adler, 1964) - is a far cry from the 'pleasures of the flesh' connotation of hedonism.

Rational-emotive theory makes an important distinction between short-term and long-term hedonism. For example, it is important to us to write this book. It represents a personally meaningful project we have set for ourselves, i.e. to encourage counsellors to offer what we have found to be an effective, brief method of psychological counselling. As such, writing this book is an example of long-term hedonism, since it will take time for us to complete, and a longer time for it to have an effect on the counselling community. We might also enjoy watching television which, as it is immediately available to us, constitutes an example of short-term hedonism. Pursuing our short-term interests to the extent that it significantly interferes with our long-term hedonistic project is irrational according to the definition of 'rationality' provided above, since the book is more personally meaningful to us than is watching television. Pursuing our long-term hedonistic interests to the exclusion of our more immediately available interests may also be irrational in the sense that we might become stale; a condition that would probably affect our creativity. Therefore counselling individuals involves not only encouraging them to become aware of their short- and long-term goals, but also helping them to achieve a healthy balance between the two. What represents a healthy balance for a given individual is ultimately best judged by that person, and not by his or her counsellor.

Enlightened self-interest versus selfishness

At this point, the reader may consider that rational–emotive theory advocates selfishness. This is not so, if by selfishness is meant the exclusive pursuit of one's own goals while cynically disregarding the goals of others. Rather, rational–emotive theory recommends that people act according to the principle of enlightened self-interest, which is deemed to be the healthy alternative to selfishness. By enlightened self-interest is meant putting oneself first most of the time, while putting others (particularly significant others) a close second. It thus includes an important dimension of what Adler (1964) calls 'social interest'. It is recognised that decisions concerning whose interests to serve at a given moment – self or others – are complex and depend on (1) the context, (2) the importance of one's own goals versus the importance that others attribute to their goals, and (3) the likely consequences of making such decisions.

Enlightened self-interest means that from a long-term perspective we will give priority to pursuing our most important goals, since as Ellis (1979a) notes, it is likely that other people will do the same. Thus, if we do not give priority to our own goals it is unlikely that others will put our interests before theirs. In this respect, Ellis (1979a) notes that 'those people who spend their lives sacrificing themselves for others tend to get less than their share of happiness' (p. 55). However, if a given client genuinely considers that one of his basic goals is to put the interests of others before his own, and can provide good evidence that this stance will bring him happiness, then good RET counsellors will respect this decision and will not try to dissuade the client from pursuing this goal.

In summary, it can be seen from the above that in counselling individuals RET counsellors strive to help their clients to be mindful of the balance between their own short- and long-term goals, and the balance between their own interests and the interests of others who live in their social world.

Philosophic and scientific emphases

As noted earlier, Ellis's formulation of RET was heavily influenced by the work of a number of ancient and contemporary philosophers. Rational–emotive theory recognises that all human beings are implicit philosophers, in the sense that we attempt to gain insight into and understanding of ourselves, other people, and the environment in which we exist. Typically, we utilise whatever understandings we achieve to impose a sense of order upon the world around us, and to develop guidelines which are used in the service of survival and goal-attainment. In essence, each of us formulates our own personal philosophy of life.

Our personal philosophies can be viewed as consisting of a constellation of self-generated hypotheses about the world and our place within it, and we are capable of applying our thinking skills to the process of testing and revising these hypotheses. In this sense, RET agrees with George Kelly's (1955) view that human beings are also scientists. Often, however, we tend to be rather poor scientists, insofar as we may fail to test and reject hypotheses which lead us to think, feel, and act in self-defeating ways. With its philosophic and scientific emphases, RET attempts to help clients to become 'better scientists' by showing them how they can identify, test and revise (as necessary, in order to function more effectively) the hypotheses which comprise their personal philosophies.

Humanistic emphasis

Rational–emotive counselling does not pretend to be 'purely' objective, scientific, or technique-centred but takes a definite *humanistic-existential approach* to human problems and their basic solutions. It deals primarily with disturbed human evaluations, emotions and behaviours. As noted above, it is highly rational and scientific, but uses rationality and science in the service of humans in an attempt to enable them to live and be happy. It is hedonistic, but, as has been shown, espouses long-range instead of short-range hedonism; so that people may achieve the pleasures of the moment and those of the future, and may arrive at maximum freedom *and* discipline. It hypothesises that probably nothing superhuman exists and that devout belief in superhuman agencies tends to foster dependency and increase emotional disturbance. It assumes that no humans, whatever their antisocial or obnoxious behaviour, are damnable nor subhuman. It particularly emphasises the importance of *will* and *choice* in human affairs, even though it accepts the likelihood that some human behaviour is at least partially determined by biological, social and other forces (Ellis, 1976; Bandura, 1986). In addition, rational–emotive theory emphasises the important role played by activity in human happiness. It acknowledges that humans have a better chance of being happy when they *actively* strive towards their goals, and that they are less likely to be successful in this regard if they are passive or half-hearted in their endeavours (Dryden, 1984a). It also stresses the important role played by activity in the change process. Clients who translate their counselling-derived insights into action in their daily lives usually achieve better results from counselling than clients who do not take such action.

Two basic biologically based tendencies

Unlike most other theories of counselling which stress the impact of significant life events on the development of psychological disturbance, rational–emotive theory hypothesises that the biological tendency of humans to think irrationally has a notable impact on such disturbance. Its view that irrational thinking is heavily determined by biological factors (always interacting with influential environmental conditions) rests on the seeming ease with which humans think crookedly, and the prevalence of such thinking even among people who have been rationally raised (Ellis, 1976). While Ellis has acknowledged that there are social influences operating here, he has also noted '. . . even if everybody had had the most rational upbringing, virtually all humans would often irrationally escalate their individual and social preferences into absolutistic demands on (a) themselves, (b) other people, and (c) the universe around them' (Ellis, 1984a, p. 20).

The following ten points constitute evidence in favour of the rational–emotive hypothesis of the biological basis of human irrationality:

1. Virtually all humans, including intelligent and competent people, show evidence of major human irrationalities.
2. Virtually all the disturbance-creating irrationalities (absolutist 'shoulds' and 'musts') that are found in our society are also found in just about all social and cultural groups that have been studied historically and anthropologically.
3. Many of the irrational behaviours that we engage in, such as procrastination and lack of self-discipline, go counter to the teachings of parents, peers and the mass media.
4. Humans – even intelligent and competent people – often adopt other irrationalities after giving up former ones.
5. People who vigorously oppose various kinds of irrational behaviours often fall prey to these very irrationalities. Atheists and agnostics exhibit zealous and absolutist philosophies and even highly religious individuals act immorally.
6. Insight into irrational thought and behaviours helps only partially to change them. For example, people can acknowledge that drinking alcohol in large quantities is harmful, yet this knowledge does not necessarily help them abstain from heavy drinking.
7. Humans often return to irrational habits and behavioural patterns even though they have often worked hard to overcome them.
8. People often find it easier to learn self-defeating than self-enhancing behaviours. Thus, people very easily overeat but have great trouble following a sensible diet.
9. Psychotherapists, who presumably should be good role models of rationality, often act irrationally in their personal and professional lives.
10. People frequently delude themselves into believing that certain bad experiences (e.g. divorce, stress, and other misfortunes) will not happen to them.

However, rational–emotive theory holds that humans have a second basic biological tendency, namely, to exercise the power of human choice and to work towards changing their irrational thinking. Thus, they have the ability to see that they make themselves disturbed by the irrational views they bring to situations, the ability to see that they can change their thinking and, most importantly, the ability to actively and continually work towards changing this thinking by the application of cognitive, emotive and behavioural methods. While rational–emotive theory asserts that humans have a strong biological tendency to think irrationally (as well as rationally), it holds that they are by no means slaves to this tendency and can transcend (although not fully) its effects. In the final analysis the rational–emotive image of the person is quite an optimistic one (Ellis, 1973; Ellis and Bernard, 1985).

Two fundamental human disturbances

According to rational–emotive theory, humans can make absolute demands on self, other people and the world. However, if these demands are more closely investigated they can be seen to fall into two major categories of psychological disturbance: *ego disturbance* and *discomfort disturbance* (Ellis, 1979b, 1980a).

In ego disturbance, a person makes demands on self, others and the world, and if these demands are not met in the past, present or future, the person becomes disturbed by damning 'self'. As one of us has shown (Dryden, 1984a), self-damnation involves the process of giving my 'self' a global negative rating, and 'devil-ifying' my 'self' as being bad or less worthy. The rational and healthy alternative to self-damnation is self-acceptance, which involves *both* refusing to give one's 'self' a single rating (because it is an impossible task, due to one's complexity and fluidity; and because it normally interferes with attaining one's basic goals and purposes) *and* acknowledging one's fallibility.

In discomfort disturbance, the person again makes demands on self, others and the world which are related to dogmatic commands that comfort and comfortable life conditions must exist. When these demands are not met in the past, present or future, then the person becomes disturbed. Tolerating discomfort in order to aid goal attainment and long-range happiness is the healthy and rational alternative to demands for immediate gratification.

Thus, as will be shown later, self-acceptance and a high level of frustration tolerance are two of the main cornerstones of the rational–emotive image of the psychologically healthy being (Ellis, 1979a).

Psychological interactionism: thoughts, emotions and actions

As discussed earlier in this chapter, RET counsellors are interested in helping their clients to stay alive and to pursue happiness. During the counselling process this involves the counsellor and client working as a team to identify and change aspects of the client's functioning which are irrational. Both client and counsellor seek to answer the question: 'How is the client stopping him or herself from pursuing his or her personally defined meaningful goals?' As counsellor and client investigate the factors concerned, the search normally involves close scrutiny of the *thoughts* that the client has about him or herself, others and the world in relation to the goal at hand; the relevant *emotions* he or she has about him or herself, others and the world; and his or her *actions* in the area of concern.

It is important to stress here that rational–emotive theory states that a person's thoughts, emotions and actions cannot be treated separately from one another. Rather they are seen as overlapping or interacting processes – an example of what psychologists call 'psychological interactionism'. For instance, let us take the case of one of our (W.D.'s) clients, Helen, who has just moved to London. She wants to go out and make friends but does not do so because she is 'scared of meeting new people'. Her feelings of anxiety encourage her to brood on 'horrific' thoughts and images of rejection and loneliness and help to influence her tendency to withdraw from people. So, she stays within the 'safe' but lonely confines of her bed-sitting room. Her thoughts (predictions of rejection and consequent attitude of self-loathing) help to create her anxiety and help to reinforce her inactivity – 'Why go out and expose myself to those outside risks?' Finally, her inactivity seems to encourage her negative thoughts about herself: 'I'm no good for being so gutless!' – and gives her ample opportunity for anxious brooding, even though withdrawal protects her from the greater anxiety of meeting new people.

RET and rationalism

Almost from its inception, RET has mistakenly been identified by a number of its critics as representing a form of philosophical rationalism. Classical rationalists subscribe to the view that human reason and intellect are the true source of knowledge; as such, they negate the role played by the senses, experience and everyday data-gathering in helping us to understand the world in which we live. Ellis, however, has made it clear (even in some of his earliest writings) that he does not subscribe to this anti-empirical perspective, and that RET is not a rationalist system (Ellis, 1962, 1968).

Despite Ellis's attempts to delineate the distinctions between RET and rationalism, some cognitive–behavioural theorists with stature in the field have recently attempted to categorise the various cognitive therapies as to whether they fall into 'rationalist' or 'constructivist' camps. They have expressed the opinion that RET can be clearly identified with the former orientation (Guidano, 1988; Mahoney, 1988).

Ellis (1990) has offered a rebuttal to this contention, and has suggested that RET is actually more 'constructivistic' in its theory and practice than the forms of cognitive therapy espoused by his constructivist critics. As noted earlier, RET does not posit absolutist and invariant criteria of rationality;

rather, it adopts a relativistic stance and defines rationality in terms of thoughts, feelings and actions that aid the individual in the pursuit of valued goals and purposes. Also, as described in the preceding section, RET clearly acknowledges that cognition (or thinking), emotion and behaviour interact and cannot be treated as distinct and separate entities. Hence, RET holds the non-rationalist position that intellectual processes do not represent the sole vehicle to either psychological health or disturbance.

Nevertheless, RET is noted within the fields of counselling and psychotherapy for the special place it accords cognition in human psychological processes. It especially emphasises the role played by evaluative cognitions (or beliefs, in RET parlance) in producing either psychological health or disturbance, and embodies the constructivistic view that human beings create (and can modify) the beliefs to which they subscribe. In fact, one of rational-emotive theory's unique contributions to the field of counselling lies in the distinction it makes between rational beliefs (evaluative cognitions that help people to achieve their basic goals and purposes) and irrational beliefs (evaluative cognitions that prevent people from achieving these goals). We will elaborate upon this distinction in the following chapter; however, we would like the reader to keep in mind throughout the book that although rational-emotive counselling does accord a special place to cognition in human functioning, it agrees with the interactionist position reviewed above and will employ cognitive, behavioural and emotive techniques in the service of helping clients to achieve beneficial therapeutic change.

Chapter 2
Cognition and Action in Rational–Emotive Theory

Overview

In this chapter we consider in detail the different types of cognitions that are relevant to counselling, namely: beliefs, inferences, decisions, self-instructions, and problem-solving cognitions. We point out that while rational–emotive theory emphasises that these cognitions interact and overlap, it also accords a central role to *beliefs* in psychological functioning. We also note that cognitions may occur in the form of words and images. Finally, we consider the role of action in rational–emotive theory. In this respect, we note the purposive nature of actions, introduce the concepts of 'action tendencies' and 'response options' and comment on the issue of behavioural competence.

Although rational–emotive theory has become most well known for its contribution to our understanding of one type of cognition (i.e. beliefs), RET counsellors also focus on other types of cognitions in the course of their practical work with clients. In the following section we distinguish among these different cognitions and although for purposes of clarity we consider them separately, we wish to stress that in reality they interact and overlap.

Types of Cognition

Beliefs

One of rational–emotive theory's unique contributions to the field of counselling lies in its distinction between rational beliefs and irrational beliefs.

Rational beliefs

In rational–emotive theory, rational beliefs are *evaluative cognitions* of personal significance which are preferential (i.e. non-absolute) in nature. They are expressed in the form of desires, preferences, wishes, wants and 'likes' (and they can, of course, also take a negative form, e.g. 'I don't want X to occur').

Positive (non-absolute) *evaluative conclusions* result when individuals either get what they want or don't get what they don't want (e.g. 'It is *good* that . . .'). Similarly, negative (non-absolute) evaluative conclusions result when individuals either don't get what they want or do get what they don't want (e.g. 'It is *bad* that . . .').

Positive emotions of pleasure and satisfaction are experienced when individuals get what they want, whereas positive feelings of relief tend to occur when individuals don't get what they don't want. Likewise, negative emotions of displeasure and dissatisfaction (e.g. sadness, concern, regret, annoyance and disappointment) are experienced when people either don't get what they want, or do get what they don't want. These positive and negative emotions (the intensity of which is closely related to the strength of the individual's preference or desire) are regarded in rational–emotive theory as appropriate responses to negative events, and are unlikely to interfere significantly with a person's pursuit of established or new goals and purposes. This is one good reason why the term 'rational' in rational–emotive counselling should not be equated with the term 'unemotional'.

Rational beliefs also tend to be logically and empirically consistent. These two qualities can perhaps be best illustrated by examining an example of a rational belief: 'It is good to have an intimate, loving relationship with another person; therefore I *want* to have such a relationship.' This belief can be considered logically consistent, as it is quite reasonable to desire something regarded as being positive in nature. It is empirically consistent (i.e. verifiable and in congruence with consensual reality), as most human beings would agree that an intimate, loving relationship is 'good' in the sense that it can add an important dimension of pleasure to a person's life.

To summarise, rational beliefs are considered 'rational' in four respects: (1) they are non-absolute (or relative) in nature, (2) they tend not to impede attainment of a person's basic goals and purposes, (3) they are logical and (4) they are consistent with reality.

Irrational beliefs

Absolute (or dogmatic) *evaluative cognitions* of personal significance are termed irrational beliefs within rational–emotive theory. Such beliefs are expressed in the form of 'musts', 'shoulds', 'have to's', 'ought to's', 'got to's', etc. (and they can, of course, also occur in the form of 'must not's', 'should not's', etc.).

Positive (absolute) *evaluative conclusions* result when individuals get what they believe they *must* have, or don't get what they believe they *must not* get (e.g. 'It is absolutely wonderful that . . .'). Negative (absolute) *evaluative conclusions* result when individuals either don't get what they believe they *must* have, or do get what they believe they *must not* get (e.g. 'It is absolutely terrible that . . .').

Rational–emotive theory holds that positively toned emotions of mania are experienced when individuals either get what they believe they *must* have or don't get what they believe they *must not* get. Negative emotions such as depression, anxiety, guilt, anger, etc. are experienced when individuals either don't get what they believe they *must* have, or do get what they believe they *must not* get. These negative emotions are regarded in RET as inappropriate responses to negative events, and will tend to significantly interfere with a person's ability to make a constructive adjustment when their existing goals cannot be achieved.

Unlike rational beliefs, irrational beliefs tend to be illogical and are not consistent with reality. By way of illustration, consider the following irrational belief: 'Because I believe it is desirable to have an intimate, loving relationship with another person, I *must* have such a relationship'. This belief is illogical, as one does not *have to* achieve that which is deemed desirable. It is inconsistent with reality because if it were true that an individual *must* have an intimate, loving relationship, then that person would have to have such a relationship regardless of what she happened to believe. Also, with regard to the issue of empirical consistency, it would be difficult to find evidence to support the contention that an intimate, loving relationship with a partner is an absolute necessity for an adult human being.

Thus, irrational beliefs are 'irrational' in four respects: (1) they are absolute (or dogmatic) in nature, (2) they tend to impede goal attainment, (3) they are illogical, and (4) they are not consistent with reality.

Rational–emotive theory makes four additional important points about beliefs:

1. People often *escalate* their rational beliefs into irrational beliefs. For example, a person may begin by believing: 'I want very much to do well in my examination' and then escalate this non-absolute belief into an absolute one thus: 'Since I want to get a good mark in my examination, therefore I absolutely have to do so'. It is important to note that this escalation process often occurs implicitly, and in counselling individuals it is helpful to check whether escalation has occurred whenever clients report rational beliefs. When clients stick rigorously to their rational beliefs (i.e. do not escalate their non-absolute beliefs into irrational beliefs) statements like '. . . but I don't have to', '. . . but there is no reason why I must' etc. are present, again often implicitly e.g. 'I want very much to do well in my examination, (but I don't *have to* do so)'.

2. Rational beliefs seem to underlie rational or functional actions (which facilitate the attainment of one's basic goals and purposes), whereas irrational beliefs tend to underpin irrational or dysfunctional actions

such as withdrawal, procrastination, alcoholism and substance abuse
(which impede goal achievement) (Ellis, 1982a).
3. Beliefs (both rational and irrational) can be either general or specific.
   Taking the example of irrational beliefs: 'I must succeed at all important
   tasks' is an example of a general irrational belief, while: 'I must succeed
   at this particular task' is an example of a specific one. As Wessler and
   Wessler (1980) note, a specific belief may represent a special case of a
   general belief.
4. As one of us has noted elsewhere (Dryden, 1986), it is important to
   distinguish between a word and its meaning. This principle should be
   borne in mind when considering beliefs in rational–emotive counselling.
   For example, take the word 'should'. The word 'should' *can* represent
   the presence of an irrational belief (e.g. 'You should not cheat me' - this
   really means here 'You *absolutely* should not cheat me'). However, the
   word 'should' has other meanings in the English language. For example,
   in a previous sentence, while referring to the important distinction
   between words and meanings, we wrote: 'This principle should be
   borne in mind when considering beliefs in RET counselling'. We hope as
   readers of this book, you can see that we are not dogmatically insisting
   that you bear this point in mind; rather we are advising or recom-
   mending you to do so. Thus, not all 'shoulds', 'musts', etc. indicate the
   presence of irrational beliefs.

Inferences

Inferences (or interpretations) are cognitions that go beyond the information that is immediately available to a person. In order to fully understand
what inferences are it is first necessary to introduce another type of
cognition called a *description* (Wessler and Wessler, 1980).

Descriptions are cognitions that report the nature of any stimulus a
person is aware of. They do not add anything that cannot be directly
observed. For example, imagine that a man is standing facing a window with
his hands in his pockets so that you can only see his back. If you were asked
to describe his behaviour you might say: 'He is standing facing the window
with his hands in his pockets'. This constitutes a description because you
have not gone beyond the information that is immediately available to you.
However, were you to say: 'He is looking out of the window', then that
would not be a description in that you would be going beyond the data at
hand; since his eyes may in fact be closed. You would be making an
inference about what you observe.

So, inferences go beyond the data at hand. They are, in fact, hypotheses
(or hunches) about the nature of reality. Since inferences are best viewed as
hypotheses they need to be tested against the available data. This point is
important since clients often make the error of confusing their 'hypotheses'

with 'facts'. Inferences, of course, can be accurate as well as inaccurate, e.g. in the above example the man *may* have been looking out of the window. Sometimes it is impossible to test the validity of one's inferences. Again, take the example where the man is facing the window with his eyes closed. Imagine that you have made the inference that he is looking out of the window. In order to test the validity of your inference you would need to determine whether, in fact, he has his eyes open. Thus, you would have to approach him and look at his eyes. Just before you look at his eyes, however, they may be open but he decides to close them just before you look at them. Thus your previous inference would have been correct, but in the process of testing it, the situation changes and it *seems* as if your inference has been invalidated.

While making inferences people are influenced by interpersonal and physical contexts. Thus, it is reasonable to expect that when a person has his hands in his pockets and is facing a window, then he is looking out of the window. Psychologists often say that a person's inference (e.g. 'You are looking out of the window') represents the 'best bet' that can be made given the context and the available information (compare Gregory, 1966). In RET counselling (as in other forms of cognitive–behavioural counselling, compare Dryden and Golden, 1986), we often find that clients make the 'worst bet' in forming hypotheses about themselves, other people, and the world, in that their inferences can be viewed as distorted (particularly in a negative direction).

Inferences are non-evaluative

Inferences are best seen as *non-evaluative* in nature in order to differentiate them from beliefs which are *evaluative* cognitions (as has been noted in the section on beliefs). This distinction can often appear blurred as some inferences seem to have an evaluative component. For example, during a counselling session a female client predicted that other people would laugh at her during a class presentation. Her inference, 'Other people will laugh at me', seems to imply a negative evaluation. However, we do not know just from her stated inference whether her evaluation is an absolute negative one ('It would be terrible if they laugh at me'); a non-absolute negative one ('It would be unfortunate if . . .'); an absolute positive one ('It would be absolutely marvellous if . . .'); a non-absolute positive one ('It would be good if . . .'); or a neutral one (I don't care if . . .'). Thus inferences do not tell us what a person's beliefs (or evaluative cognitions) might be. As we shall see later in the book the best way of identifying a person's evaluations is to examine carefully whether his/her emotions are inappropriate/self-defeating i.e. irrational (e.g. depression, anxiety or guilt etc.) or appropriate/self-promoting i.e. rational (e.g. sadness, concern or regret). Thus, inferences, no matter how distorted, are rarely reliable guides to a person's emotions because they do not contain *explicit* reference to evaluative cognitions. Thus in rational–emotive theory: *emotions are based largely on evaluative thinking rather than on inferential thinking*.

Inferences can be grouped into various categories and we will briefly review those that are most relevant to counselling.

Causal attributions

This category of inferences represents attempts to account for the 'causes' of one's own or another's emotions and actions. Causal attributions can be internal to the 'author' of the experience ('He didn't turn up on time because he didn't care enough'; 'I cry easily because I'm too sensitive'); external to the 'author' of the experience ('He didn't turn up on time because he was delayed by the traffic'; 'I cry easily because my parents didn't love me as a child'), or a combination of internal and external factors ('He didn't turn up on time because someone called on him at the last moment and he was too unassertive to excuse himself'; 'I cry easily because my family members play on my oversensitivity').

One of the initial major tasks of rational–emotive counsellors is to help clients shift from making causal attributions about emotional and behavioural disturbance which are *exclusively* external in nature (e.g. 'I'm depressed because my lover has left me') to making causal attributions which are *largely* (but not exclusively) internal in nature (e.g. 'I'm depressed about my lover leaving me because that event has encouraged me to conclude that I am worthless'). It should be noted from the previous sentence that RET counsellors guard against encouraging clients from making causal attributions, which are exclusively internal in nature, about psychological disturbance. They do so because, according to RET theory, external events do *contribute* to (but do not '*cause*') such disturbance.

Predictions

Predictions vary along the important dimension of probability of occurrence. In general, high-probability events tend to have greater influence on people's responses than low-probability events. However, some clients will not, for example, take steps towards a valued goal if there exists the slightest chance that their efforts may prove unsuccessful. This is a very good sign that they are making dire evaluations (irrational beliefs) about the slight chance that they may fail ('It would be terrible if I were to fail').

In counselling, clients' predictions typically relate to others' responses to self (e.g. 'If I ask that woman to dance, then she will reject me'); changes in the physical environment (e.g. 'If I don't check one last time that I have turned off the oven, then it will explode during the night') or to one's own future reactions (e.g. 'If I go into that crowded supermarket, then I will faint'). Although most clients' predictions refer to events that would be evaluated negatively, some positively evaluated predictions feature in clients' problems (e.g. the compulsive gambler who predicts that he will win a fortune this time if he bets a week's wages on the favourite in the 3.30 race at Ascot).

Motives

Frequently, people try to infer why they and others act as they do, and discussions concerning these motives often occur in the counselling process. For example, in a recent counselling session, a young depressed student who regarded herself as unlovable inferred that the reason why a fellow student was being nice to her was that the other person wanted to borrow her notes. Testing such hypotheses, particularly those that relate to the motives of others, is fraught with difficulties. When it was suggested to the client that she could check this by asking the student concerned she replied: 'She would only deny wanting to borrow my notes and she would be lying'.

Rational–emotive theory makes these additional important points about inferences:

1. As has been noted about beliefs, inferences can be either general or specific. Wessler and Wessler (1980) have argued that general inferences (e.g. 'All women will eventually leave me') tend to be more enduring than specific inferences ('Sarah will eventually leave me'). The latter may be specific examples of the former.
2. Clients may have particular inferential styles (i.e. consistent and recurring ways of forming inferences). Thus, some clients may consistently make causal attributions which are internal in nature. This may be particularly so with regard to their own behaviour. Thus, one particular client viewed 'intelligence' as accounting for much of the variance in people's behaviour. He consistently minimised the impact of environmental factors on behaviour. Clients who display an internal attributional style tend to use a small number of 'filters' in viewing the world. Clients often reveal the following typical filters through which they tend to view the world: 'caring', 'sanity', 'strength', 'intelligence', etc.
3. Inferences are often 'chained' together (Moore, 1983). The following represents a typical example of an inference chain that a client may reveal in counselling: 'If I speak up in class then I will say something stupid – If that happens then everybody will laugh at me – If that happens then I will blush severely – If I blush then people will play on that in the future – If they do that it will prove that they think I'm stupid'. As we shall see in Chapter 6, it is frequently helpful in counselling individuals to find the most relevant inference in the chain, i.e. the one which the client evaluates. This is often, but not always, the last reported inference in the chain.

Decisions

Wessler and Hankin-Wessler (1986) have stressed that decisions (or decisional cognitions) play an important role in the perpetuation of psychological disturbance and in determining whether or not people make changes in their lives. People can decide whether to inspect their distorted inferences and irrational beliefs and choose whether or not to change them. People can also decide to tolerate or avoid their own painful emotions and decide to change their behaviour or to continue to act in a dysfunctional manner. A very common form of decision that is often expressed by clients is 'I can't . . .'. It is important to realise that this statement may provide clues that the person is making negative inferences and holding irrational beliefs about events and his or her response options. In rational–emotive counselling it is often important to deal with these cognitions before tackling decisions.

It is helpful to distinguish between short- and long-term goals when discussing clients' decisions. A common focus in rational–emotive counselling is to encourage clients to tolerate uncomfortable emotions while they pursue their valued goals. Although a client may, for example, desire the long-term goal of gaining increasing social confidence, he or she may also have the short-term goal of avoiding discomfort. In order to gain the benefit of the former, the person has to *decide* to tolerate the latter. In our experience as rational–emotive counsellors, it is not only important to help clients to challenge and change their negative inferences and irrational beliefs about the experience of discomfort, but also to help them to see the reasons why deciding to tolerate discomfort is so important in the change process.

Finally, as Greenwald (1973) has shown, it is important for clients to realise that the process of making decisions to change is not a singular event. Decisions to change cognitions or behaviours have often frequently to be reaffirmed if clients are to derive lasting benefits from counselling.

Self-instructions

One of the assumptions of rational–emotive counselling is that people have both an experiencing and an observing part of themselves. Thus, people 'detach' their 'observing self' from their 'experiencing self' when identifying and deciding whether or not to change the cognitions that underpin psychological disturbance. The 'observing self' can also give instructions to the 'experiencing self'. These are known as *self-instructions*. Here the work of Meichenbaum (1977, 1985) is particularly helpful. Meichenbaum has shown that people can help themselves by instructing themselves to tolerate and to cope with certain negative emotions, to act in productive ways, and to provide themselves with praise for doing well.

Coping with negative emotions

Imagine a person who is scared of having a panic attack. A counsellor might encourage this person to use the following self-instructions to cope with her anxious feelings: 'When anxiety comes, just pause; keep focusing on the present; label my anxiety on a 0–10 scale and watch it change; don't try to eliminate anxiety totally, just keep it manageable; take slow controlled breaths', etc.

Facilitating productive action

For a client who gets overwhelmed when confronted with many tasks, the counsellor might suggest the following self-instructions: 'Look at what I have to do; get my tasks into order of priority; focus on one thing at a time.'

Self-rewarding

When clients have succeeded in coping with their negative emotions and/or acting in a productive manner, they can instruct themselves in the following ways that are deemed to be self-rewarding: 'I handled my feelings pretty well; I did well that time, that's good; I'm really making progress on this'. When clients fail to cope with their negative emotions and/or act productively, they often get discouraged. To counteract this tendency counsellors need to help them to develop constructive self-instructions concerning their 'failures'. For example, they can use the following: 'OK I had a panic attack. Look for what went wrong; I didn't manage it this time. Look for what can be learned from this experience.'

Clients can also use self-instructions to direct themselves to identify and challenge their distorted inferences and irrational beliefs. For example, a person might say 'OK I'm anxious; look for and challenge my demands; seek out and correct my negative thoughts'.

Problem-solving cognitions

The ability to solve problems related to psychological disturbance has been broken down into several cognitively based skills (compare Platt, Prout and Metzger, 1986). People who do bring a problem-solving 'set' to their difficulties appear to use specific cognitions that are usually implicit or covert in nature. Very often clients lack these cognitions and have to be taught to use them during counselling. The following cognitively based skills are often associated with effective personal and interpersonal problem solving.

Problem defining

Clients often fail to solve personal and interpersonal problems because of the very way they define them (e.g. 'My anxiety proves that I'm a nervous type and nothing can be done about it'). Helping clients to overcome problems involves encouraging them to redefine problems in a way that encourages problem solving (e.g. 'My anxiety is based on irrational beliefs that can be changed'). Redefining also involves the skill of *alternative thinking*, the capacity to generate and apply alternatives to personal and interpersonal problems (e.g. 'What other ways are there to view the situation?')

Consequential thinking

This involves the capacity to consider the consequences of one's actions. Impulsive clients, for example, often do not consider what impact their actions might have on themselves and other people and can be trained to use outcome-oriented cognitions to good effect (e.g. 'What is likely to happen if I do this?')

Means-ends thinking

While clients are developing alternative solutions to problems, they often need to consider the sequencing of planned remedial steps leading to their goals (e.g. 'What steps do I have to take before I can do 'X?', 'What should I preferably do first?'). In addition, clients often need to anticipate obstacles and plan to overcome them if they are to achieve their ends (e.g. 'If 'Y' happens, what can I do to overcome it?')

Perspective taking

This involves the ability to stand back and look at a situation from someone else's point of view, and the ability to put oneself into the position of others. This latter ability is particularly helpful when a client would judge others less harshly than she considers others would judge her. Clients often fail to solve their problems because they only judge themselves, other people and situations from one fixed, and often distorted, perspective. Teaching clients perspective taking involves encouraging them to employ cognitions like: 'What would other people think if they were in my position?'; 'If other people did what I've just done would I judge them as I think they are judging me?'.

Cognitive interactionism and the centrality of beliefs

Although the types of cognitions reviewed in this chapter have been discussed separately, in reality they overlap and interact with one another. However, rational-emotive theory places beliefs (or evaluative cognitions) at the heart of this process of interacting cognitions. Thus, according to RET theory, people's beliefs have a greater influencing effect on their other cognitions (i.e. inferences, decisions, self-instructions and problem-solving thinking), than these cognitions have on their beliefs.

One of us (W.D.) has conducted a series of experiments which provide empirical support for the hypothesis that beliefs can influence the form that inferences will take (Dryden, Ferguson and Clark, 1989; Dryden, Ferguson and Hylton, 1989; Dryden, Ferguson and McTeague, 1989). In one of these studies (which is essentially similar to the other two with respect to design and outcome), subjects were divided into two groups. Subjects in group 1 (the 'irrational belief' group) were asked to imagine that they truly believed: 'I absolutely must not see a spider and it would be really terrible if I did'. Subjects in group 2 (the 'rational belief' group) were asked to imagine that they believed: 'I prefer not to see a spider and it would be bad if I did, but not the end of the world'. Both groups were then asked to rate (while adhering to their assigned belief) the likelihood of there being a spider in the room; the size of the spider; the likelihood of their seeing the spider; the distance between themselves and the spider; the likelihood of the spider moving towards them; and the number of spiders in the room (i.e. inferences concerning probability, size, movement and number). The results of this experiment were as follows: relative to subjects in the 'rational belief' group (group 2), subjects holding an irrational belief (group 1) predicted a greater likelihood of there being a spider in the room; estimated a larger size of spider; thought it more likely that they would see the spider; predicted less distance between themselves and the spider; predicted it to be more likely that the spider would be moving towards them; and tended to predict larger numbers of spiders in the room. Thus, within the context of this role-playing task, the differing beliefs assigned to the two groups of subjects did appear to colour the sort of inferences that were made.

In an unpublished follow-up to the above study, two additional groups of subjects were provided with the inferences formerly made by the 'rational belief' group and the 'irrational belief' group, respectively. Both of these new groups were then asked to judge whether they held rational or irrational beliefs, assuming that they had just made their particular set of inferences about spiders. The results of this second experiment were far less clear-cut, suggesting that inferences, as such, are not reliable guides to the kinds of beliefs people hold about stimuli (in this case, spiders).

Words and images

RET counsellors share the view of other cognitive psychotherapists that cognitions can take the form of either words or images. However, given the central role accorded to beliefs in determining emotions in rational–emotive theory, it is not the words and images themselves which have direct impact on emotions, but the evaluative meaning implicit in them. For example, one of us (W.D.) used to be very anxious when travelling on the

London underground system at a time when he had mental images where he threw himself in front of a train. His anxiety could not be attributed to the images, because he still occasionally has these images, but without anxiety. Rather, the anxiety was largely determined by an irrational belief about the image ('It is terrible to have such images that I really should not have'). His present feelings are those of discomfort rather than anxiety whenever he has the image because he now rationally believes 'I don't like having this image, but there is no reason why I must not have it'. In addition, as discussed in the previous section, his beliefs also coloured his inferences, i.e. when his belief about the image was irrational he estimated that the likelihood that he would actually throw himself in front of a train was much greater than when his belief about the image was rational.

The Role of Action in Rational–Emotive Theory

Rational-emotive theory holds that people have the greatest chance of fulfilling themselves when they actively pursue their basic goals and purposes. Happiness is maximised when people actively absorb themselves in vocational and avocational pursuits, and when they engage in appropriate recreational activity (Ellis, 1979a). Conversely, when people are inactive they tend to sabotage their chances of happiness. Thus, action plays an important role in rational-emotive theory.

Actions and beliefs

As has already been noted, people's actions are largely (but not exclusively) determined by their beliefs about themselves, others, and present and future situations. Productive (or rational) actions tend to stem from rational beliefs while unproductive (or irrational) actions tend to stem from irrational beliefs.

Actions can be purposive

RET counsellors tend to agree with their Adlerian colleagues that actions can be purposive, i.e. they seek to achieve something, such as the cessation of an emotional state (anxiety) or a response from the physical and interpersonal environment. An example of the latter might be a man who acts in a withdrawn and sulking manner when his wife refuses to have sex with him. Although he probably does hold the irrational belief 'It's terrible when I don't get what I want. Poor me!', his behaviour can also be seen as purposive in that his action is designed, albeit implicitly, to elicit a response from his wife - in this case remorse, and later, sex. It is important to note in this context that other people respond to our actions and behavioural expressions of emotion, rather than to the emotions themselves.

Action tendencies and response options

When people experience emotions they also have a tendency to act in a certain number of ways, depending upon the emotion that is experienced. Action tendencies are purposive; if actualised, they serve to help the person achieve a particular goal. In the emotional disorders such goals tend to be productive in the short term, but unproductive in the long term. Action tendencies can be seen as *general* categories of behaviour rather than as *specific* responses (withdrawal rather than walking out of church).

As an illustration consider a person who is experiencing anxiety and has a pronounced tendency to withdraw from a threat. This action tendency, if actualised, tends to help the person to avoid discomfort, but it is unproductive in the long term as it tends to discourage the person from dealing constructively with the threat. Whether or not people actually respond according to an action tendency depends largely upon what alternative ways of responding exist, and the inferences and evaluations the person makes of these response options (response options are *specific* ways of responding that are available to the person in a given situation).

Imagine a woman who is anxious about going to church. Given her anxiety, she chooses from among her response options to sit near the exit so that she can leave easily if she gets anxious (action tendency = to withdraw). If she were to sit in the middle of a row near the front of the church, far from the exit, and become anxious in these circumstances, she might not choose the response option of leaving the church even though she still has the tendency to withdraw. This is because she infers that, were she to do so, other people might notice her and consider her to be 'strange', a prospect which she would evaluate in an absolute and negative manner (irrational belief = 'It would be terrible if other churchgoers were to think that I am strange'). Given that she has now excluded leaving the church as a viable response option, she is now left to experience her anxiety with no constructive ways of dealing with it. She is now caught in a dilemma since she believes both that 'It is terrible to be anxious in church', and 'It would be terrible to be noticed and considered strange'. It is little wonder that this woman did have a panic attack at her own wedding.

Among a person's response options are specific responses which serve to actualise given action tendencies and specific responses which run counter to given action tendencies. An important feature of rational–emotive counselling is encouraging clients to act against their habitual self-defeating action tendencies – a strategy which aims to help them to tolerate discomfort and thence begin to cope better with the problematic situation.

Behavioural competence

Rational–emotive theory recognises that people execute behaviours at varying levels of skill and RET counsellors try, when appropriate, to help their clients to become more skilful at executing acts that already exist in their behavioural repertoire, and to acquire behavioural responses that are absent from their repertoire (e.g. relaxation skills and assertive skills).

In addition, RET counsellors pay attention to the inferences and evaluations clients make about their level of competence. For example, at the inferential level, people can either underestimate or overestimate their level of skill, or give an improved level of skill a particular interpretative meaning (e.g. 'If I become more assertive then I will lose my sensitivity towards people'). At the evaluative level people may rate *themselves* for having a certain level of skill (e.g. 'I'm not very socially skilled; that proves I'm no good' = irrational belief), or evaluate the effort that it may take to become more skilful ('It will take a lot of practice to learn more productive study skills; I wish it were easier but that doesn't mean that I can't tolerate the effort' = rational belief).

In conclusion, while it can be seen from this section that rational-emotive theory accords action an important role in human functioning, it can also be seen that cognitions are deemed to play an influential part even in the realm of human action. However, the emphasis throughout this book will be on changing beliefs.

Chapter 3
Psychological Disturbance and Health

Overview

In this chapter we consider psychological disturbance and health from a rational-emotive perspective. After outlining the rational-emotive view on the nature of psychological disturbance and health, we focus on how humans acquire and perpetuate their own psychological disturbance. We conclude the chapter by considering the rational-emotive theory of therapeutic change.

The Nature of Psychological Disturbance and Health

Psychological disturbance

Irrational beliefs and their derivatives

Rational–emotive theory posits that at the heart of psychological disturbance lies the tendency of humans to make devout, absolutist evaluations (i.e. irrational beliefs) of the inferred in their lives. As has been shown, these evaluations are couched in the form of dogmatic 'musts', 'shoulds', 'have to's', 'got to's', and 'oughts'. These absolutist cognitions represent a philosophy of religiosity which, according to rational–emotive theory, is the central feature of human emotional and behavioural disturbance (compare Ellis, 1983a). As has been shown, these beliefs are deemed to be irrational in that they usually (but not invariably) impede and obstruct people in the pursuit of their basic goals and purposes. Absolute musts do not invariably lead to psychological disturbance because it is possible for a person to devoutly believe 'I must succeed at all important projects', have confidence that he or she will be successful in these respects, and actually succeed in them, and thereby not experience psychological disturbance. However, the person remains vulnerable because there is always the possibility that he or she may fail in the future. So although on probabilistic grounds RET theory argues that an absolutist philosophy will frequently lead to psychological disturbance it does not claim that this is absolutely so. Thus, even with respect to its view of the nature of human disturbance rational–emotive theory adopts an anti-absolutist position.

Rational–emotive theory goes on to posit that if humans adhere to an absolutist and devout philosophy they will strongly tend to make a number of core irrational conclusions which are deemed to be derivatives of their 'musts'. These major derivatives are viewed as irrational because they too tend to sabotage a person's basic goals and purposes.

The first major derivative is known as *awfulising*. This occurs when an inferred event is rated as being more than 100 per cent bad – a truly exaggerated and magical conclusion which stems from the belief: 'This must not be as bad as it is'.

The second major derivative is known as *I-can't-stand-it-itis*. This means believing that one cannot experience virtually any happiness at all, under any conditions, if an event which 'must' not happen actually occurs, or threatens to occur.

The third major derivative, known as *damnation*, represents a tendency for people to rate themselves and other people as 'subhuman' or 'undeserving' if they or other people do something that they 'must' not do, or fail to do something which they 'must' do. 'Damnation' can also be applied to the world or life conditions which are rated as being 'rotten' for failing to give the person what he or she 'must' have.

While RET holds that 'awfulising', 'I-can't-stand-it-itis' and 'damnation' are secondary irrational processes, in that they stem from the philosophy of 'musts', these processes can sometimes be primary (Ellis, 1984a). Indeed, Wessler (1984) has argued that they are more likely to be primary and that 'musts' are derived from them. However, the philosophy of 'musts', on the one hand, and those of 'awfulising', 'I-can't-stand-it-itis' on the other, are, in all probability, interdependent processes and often seem to be different sides of the same 'cognitive coin'.

Other forms of distorted thinking stemming from irrational beliefs

Rational–emotive theory notes that humans also make numerous kinds of illogicalities when they are disturbed (Ellis, 1985b). In this respect it agrees with cognitive therapists (Beck, Rush, Shaw and Emery, 1979; Burns, 1980) that such cognitive distortions are a feature of psychological disturbance. However, rational–emotive theory holds that such distortions almost always stem from the 'musts', although this hypothesis has yet to be empirically tested. Some of the most frequent distortions are:

1. *All-or-none thinking*: 'If I fail at any important task, as I *must* not, I'm a *total* failure and *completely* unlovable!'.
2. *Jumping to conclusions and negative non-sequiturs*: 'Since they have

seen me dismally fail, as I *should* not have done, they will view me as an incompetent worm'.

3. *Fortune telling*: 'Because they are laughing at me for failing, they know that I *should* have succeeded, and they will despise me forever'.

4. *Focusing on the negative*: 'Because I *can't stand* things going wrong, as they *must* not, I can't see any good that is happening in my life'.

5. *Disqualifying the positive*: 'When they compliment me on the good things I have done, they are only being kind to me and forgetting the foolish things that I *should* not have done'.

6. *Allness and neverness*: 'Because conditions of living *ought* to be good and actually are so bad and so intolerable, they'll *always* be this way and I'll never have any happiness'.

7. *Minimisation*: 'My good shots in this game were lucky and unimportant. But my bad shots, which I *should* never have made, were as bad as could be and were totally unforgivable'.

8. *Emotional reasoning*: 'Because I have performed so poorly, as I *should* not have done, I feel like a total idiot, and my strong feeling proves that I *am* no damned good!'

9. *Labelling and overgeneralisation*: 'Because I *must* not fail at important work and have done so, I am a complete loser and failure!'.

10. *Personalising*: 'Since I am acting far worse than I *should* act and they are laughing, I am sure they are only laughing at me; and that is *awful!*'.

11. *Phoneyism*: 'When I don't do as well as I *ought* to do and they still praise and accept me, I am a real phoney and will soon fall on my face and show them how despicable I am!'.

12. *Perfectionism*: 'I realise that I did fairly well, but I *should* have done perfectly well on a task like this, and am therefore really an incompetent!'.

Although RET counsellors at times discover all the illogicalities just listed – and a number of others that are less frequently found with clients – they particularly focus on the unconditional shoulds, oughts and musts that seem to constitute the philosophic core of irrational beliefs that lead to emotional disturbance. For they hold that if they do not get to and help clients surrender these core beliefs, the clients will most probably keep holding them and create new irrational derivatives from them.

RET counsellors also particularly look for 'awfulising', for 'I-can't-stand-it-itis', and for 'damnation'; and they show clients how these almost invariably stem from their 'musts' and can be surrendered if they give up their absolutist demands on themselves, on other people, and on the universe. At the same time, rational–emotive counsellors usually encourage their clients to have strong and persistent desires, wishes, and preferences, and to avoid feelings of detachment, withdrawal and lack of involvement.

More importantly, RET holds that unrealistic and illogical beliefs do not in themselves create emotional disturbance. Why? Because it is quite possible for people to unrealistically believe, 'Because I frequently fail, I always do' and it is possible for them also to believe illogically, 'Because I have frequently failed, I always will'. But they can, in both these instances, rationally conclude, 'Too bad. Even though I always fail, there is no reason why I must succeed. I would prefer to but I never have to do well. So I'll manage to be as happy as I can be even with my constant failure'. They would then rarely be emotionally disturbed.

To reiterate, the essence of human emotional disturbance, according to rational–emotive theory, consists of the absolutist *musts* and *must nots* that people think *about* their failure, *about* their rejections, *about* their poor treatment by others, and *about* life's frustrations and losses. Rational–emotive counselling therefore differs from other forms of cognitive-behavioural counselling such as those inspired by Beck (1976), Bandura (1969, 1977), Goldfried and Davison (1976), Janis (1983), Lazarus (1981), Mahoney (1977), Maultsby (1984), and Meichenbaum (1977), in that it particularly stresses therapists looking for clients' dogmatic, unconditional *musts*, differentiating them from their preferences, and teaching them how to surrender the former and retain the latter (Ellis, 1984a).

Psychological health

If the philosophy of religiosity is at the core of much psychological disturbance then what philosophy is characteristic of psychological health? Rational–emotive theory argues that a philosophy of relativism or 'desiring' is a central feature of psychologically healthy humans. This philosophy acknowledges that humans have a large variety of desires, wishes, wants, preferences, etc., but if they refuse to escalate these non-absolute values into grandiose dogmas and demands they will not become psychologically disturbed. They will, however, experience appropriate negative emotions (e.g. sadness, regret, disappointment, annoyance) whenever their desires are not fulfilled. These emotions are considered to have constructive motivational properties in that they both help people to remove obstacles to goal attainment and aid them to make constructive adjustments when their desires cannot be met. This point will be developed further in Chapter 4.

Three major derivatives of the philosophy of desiring are postulated by rational–emotive theory. They are deemed to be rational in that they tend to help people reach their goals, or formulate new goals if their old ones cannot be realised.

The first major derivative is known as *rating* or *evaluating badness*. Here, if people do not get what they want they acknowledge that this is bad. However, because they do not believe 'I have to get what I want' they contain their evaluation along a 0–100 per cent continuum of 'badness' and do not therefore rate this situation as 'awful' – a magical rating which is placed on a nonsensical 101 per cent – ∞ (infinity) continuum. In general, when people adhere to the desiring philosophy, the stronger the desire the greater their rating of badness will be when they do not get what they want.

The second major derivative is known as *tolerance* and is the rational alternative to 'I-can't-stand-it-itis'. Here the person acknowledges that an undesirable event has happened (or may happen); believes that the event should occur empirically if it does (i.e. does not demand that what exists must not exist); rates the event along the badness continuum; attempts to change the undesired event, or accepts the 'grim' reality if it cannot be modified; and actively pursues other goals even though the situation cannot be altered.

The third major derivative known as *acceptance* is the rational alternative to 'damnation'. Here the person and others are accepted as fallible human beings who do not have to act other than they do and as too complex and fluid to be given any legitimate or global rating. In addition, life conditions are accepted as they exist. People who have the philosophy of acceptance fully acknowledge that the world is highly complex and exists according to laws which are often outside their personal control. It is important to emphasise here that acceptance does not imply resignation. A rational philosophy of acceptance means that the person acknowledges that whatever exists empirically should exist, but does not have to exist in any absolute sense forever. This prompts the person to make active attempts to change reality. The person who is resigned to a situation usually does not attempt to modify it.

Criteria of psychological health

Rational–emotive theory puts forward 13 criteria of psychological health (Ellis and Bernard, 1985):

1. *Self-interest:* as has already been noted, emotionally healthy people tend to be primarily interested in themselves and to put their own interests at least a little above the interests of others. They sacrifice themselves to some degree for those for whom they care – but not overwhelmingly or completely.

2. *Social interest:* social interest is usually rational and self-helping because most people choose to live and enjoy themselves in a social group or community; and if they do not act morally, protect the rights of others, and abet social survival, it is unlikely that they will create the kind of a world in which they themselves can live comfortably and happily.

3. *Self-direction:* healthy people tend to assume responsibility for their own lives while simultaneously preferring to cooperate with others.

They do not need or demand considerable support or succour from others.

4. *High frustration tolerance*: rational individuals give both themselves and others the right to be wrong. Even when they intensely dislike their own and others' behaviour, they refrain from damning themselves or others, as persons, for unacceptable or obnoxious behaviour. People who are not plagued with debilitating emotional distress tend to go along with St Francis and Reinhold Niebuhr by changing obnoxious conditions they can change, accepting those they cannot, and having the wisdom to know the difference between the two.

5. *Flexibility*: healthy and mature individuals tend to be flexible in their thinking, open to change, and unbigoted and pluralistic in their view of other people. They do not make rigid, invariant rules for themselves and others.

6. *Acceptance of uncertainty*: healthy men and women tend to acknowledge and accept the idea that we seem to live in a world of probability and chance, where absolute certainties do not, and probably never will, exist. They realise that it is often fascinating and exciting, and definitely not horrible, to live in this kind of probabilistic and uncertain world. They enjoy a good degree of order but do not demand to know exactly what the future will bring, or what will happen to them.

7. *Commitment to creative pursuits*: most people tend to be healthier and happier when they are vitally absorbed in something outside themselves and preferably have at least one powerful creative interest, as well as some major human involvement, that they consider so important that they structure a good part of their daily existence around it.

8. *Scientific thinking*: non-disturbed individuals tend to be more objective, rational and scientific than more disturbed ones. They are able to feel deeply and act concertedly, but they tend to regulate their emotions and actions by reflecting on them and evaluating their consequences in terms of the extent to which they lead to the attainment of short- and long-term goals.

9. *Self-acceptance*: healthy people are usually glad to be alive and accept themselves just because they are alive and have some capacity to enjoy themselves. They refuse to measure their intrinsic worth by their extrinsic achievements, or by what others think of them. They frankly choose to accept themselves unconditionally; and they try to completely avoid rating their totality or their being. They attempt to enjoy rather than to prove themselves.

10. *Risk taking*: emotionally healthy people tend to take a fair amount of risk and to try to do what they want to do, even when there is a good chance that they may fail. They tend to be adventurous, but not foolhardy.

11. *Long-range hedonism*: as was noted earlier, well adjusted people tend to seek both the pleasures of the moment and those of the future, and do not often court future pain for present gain. They are hedonistic, that is, happiness-seeking and pain-avoiding, but they assume that they will probably live for quite a few years and that they had therefore better think of both today and tomorrow, and not become obsessed with immediate gratification.

12. *Non-Utopianism*: healthy people accept the fact that Utopias are probably unachievable and that they are never likely to get everything they want or avoid all pain. They refuse to strive unrealistically for total joy, happiness, or perfection, or for lack of anxiety, depression, self-downing and hostility.

13. *Self-responsibility for own emotional disturbance*: healthy individuals tend to accept a great deal of responsibility for their own disturbance, rather than defensively blaming others or social conditions for their self-defeating thoughts, feelings and behaviours.

Acquisition and Perpetuation of Psychological Disturbance

Acquisition of psychological disturbance

Rational-emotive theory does not put foward an elaborate view concerning the acquisition of psychological disturbance. This partly follows from the rational-emotive hypothesis that humans have a distinct *biological* tendency to think and act irrationally (Ellis, 1976), but it also reflects the viewpoint that theories of acquisition do not necessarily suggest therapeutic interventions. Although rational-emotive theory holds that humans' tendencies towards irrational thinking are biologically rooted, it also acknowledges that environmental variables do contribute to psychological disturbance and thus encourage people to make their biologically based demands (Ellis, 1976). Ellis (1984b) said 'parents and culture usually teach children *which* superstitions, taboos and prejudices to abide by, but they do not originate their basic tendency to superstitiousness, ritualism and bigotry' (p. 209).

Rational-emotive theory also posits that humans vary in their disturbability. Some people emerge relatively unscathed psychologically from being raised by uncaring or overprotective parents, while others emerge emotionally damaged from more 'healthy' childrearing regimes (Werner and Smith, 1982). In this respect, rational-emotive theory claims that 'individuals with serious aberrations are more innately predisposed to have rigid and crooked thinking than those with less aberrations, and that consequently they are likely to make less advances' (Ellis, 1984b, p. 223).

Here Ellis is talking about severity of emotional and behavioural disorders. Thus, the rational–emotive theory of acquisition can be summed up in the view that as humans we are not made disturbed simply by our experiences; rather we bring our ability to disturb ourselves to our experiences.

Perpetuation of psychological disturbance

Although rational–emotive theory does not posit an elaborate view to explain the acquisition of psychological disturbance, it does deal more extensively with how such disturbance is perpetuated.

The three RET insights

First, people tend to maintain their psychological problems by their own 'naïve' theories concerning the nature of these problems and to what they can be attributed. They lack what RET calls *RET insight no. 1:* that psychological disturbance is primarily determined by the absolutist irrational beliefs that people hold about negative life events. Rather they consider that their disturbances are 'caused' by these situations. Since people make incorrect hypotheses about the major determinants of their problems, they consequently attempt to change the events rather than their irrational beliefs. Secondly, people may have RET insight no. 1 but lack *RET insight no. 2:* that people remain disturbed by reindoctrinating themselves *in the present* with their irrational beliefs. Although they may see that their problems are determined by their beliefs, they may distract themselves and thus perpetuate their problems by searching for the historical antecedents of these beliefs, instead of directing themselves to change them as currently held. Thirdly, people may have RET insights nos 1 or 2 but still sustain their disturbance because they lack *RET insight no. 3:* only if people diligently work and practise in the present as well as in the future to think, feel and act against their irrational beliefs are they likely to change them, and make themselves significantly less disturbed. People who have all three insights clearly see that they had better persistently and strongly challenge their beliefs cognitively, emotively and behaviourally to break the perpetuation of disturbance cycle. Merely acknowledging that a belief is irrational is usually insufficient to effect change (Ellis, 1979c).

The philosophy of low frustration tolerance (LFT)

Rational-emotive theory contends that the major reason why people perpetuate their psychological problems is because they adhere to a philosophy of low frustration tolerance (LFT) (Ellis, 1979b, 1980a). Such people believe that they must be comfortable, and thus do not work to effect change because such work inevitably involves experiencing discomfort. They are short-range hedonists in that they are motivated to avoid short-term discomfort even though accepting and working against their temporary uncomfortable feelings would probably help them to reach their long-range goals. Such people evaluate cognitive and behavioural therapeutic tasks as 'too painful', and even more painful than the psychological disturbance to which they have achieved some measure of habituation. They prefer to remain with their 'comfortable' discomfort rather than face the 'change-related' discomfort which they believe they must not experience. Maultsby (1975) has argued that people often back away from change because they are afraid that they will not feel right about it. He calls this the 'neurotic fear of feeling a phoney' and actively shows clients that these feelings of 'unnaturalness' are in fact the natural concomitants of relearning. Another prevalent form of LFT is 'anxiety about anxiety'. Here, individuals believe that they must not be anxious, and thus do not expose themselves to anxiety-provoking situations because they might become anxious if they did so – an experience they would evaluate as 'awful'. As such, they perpetuate their problems and restrict their lives to avoid experiencing anxiety.

Disturbances about disturbances

'Anxiety about anxiety' constitutes an example of the clinical fact that people often make themselves disturbed about their disturbances. Having created secondary (and sometimes tertiary) disturbances about their original disturbance, they become preoccupied with these 'problems about problems' and thus find it difficult to get back to solving the original problem. Humans are often very inventive in this respect. They can make themselves depressed about their depression, guilty about being angry, as well as anxious about their anxiety, and so on. Consequently, people often need to tackle their disturbances about their disturbances before they can successfully solve their original problems (Ellis, 1979b, 1980a).

Defences

Rational–emotive theory endorses the Freudian view of human defensiveness in explaining how people perpetuate their psychological problems (Freud, 1937). Thus, people maintain their problems by employing various defence mechanisms (e.g. rationalisation, avoidance) which are designed to help deny the existence of these problems, or to minimise their severity. The rational–emotive view is that these defences are used to ward off self-damnation tendencies and that, under such circumstances, if these people were to honestly take responsibility for their problems, they would severely denigrate themselves for having them. In addition, these defence mechanisms are also employed to ward off discomfort anxiety; again, if such people admitted their problems they would rate them as 'too hard to bear' or 'too difficult to overcome'.

Payoffs

Rational–emotive theory notes that people sometimes experience a form of perceived payoff for their psychological problems other than avoidance of discomfort (Ellis, 1979a). The existence of these payoffs serves to perpetuate the problems. Thus, a woman who claims to want to overcome her procrastination may avoid tackling the problem because she is afraid that should she become successful she might then be criticised by others as being 'too masculine', a situation she would evaluate as 'awful'. Her procrastination serves to protect her, she believes, from this 'terrible' state of affairs. It is important to note that rational–emotive theory considers that people are affected by payoffs because they make inferences and evaluations about the consequences, or likely consequences of their behaviour. They are not influenced directly by these consequences.

Self-fulfilling prophecies

Finally, the well documented 'self-fulfilling prophecy' phenomenon helps to explain why people perpetuate their psychological problems (Jones, 1977; Wachtel, 1977). Here, people act according to their evaluations and consequent predictions, and thus often elicit from themselves or from others responses which they then interpret in a manner which confirms their initial hypotheses. Thus, a socially anxious man may believe that other people would not want to get to know 'a worthless individual such as I truly am'. He then attends a social function and acts as if he were worthless, avoiding eye contact and keeping away from others. Unsurprisingly, such social behaviour does not invite approaches from others – a lack of response which he interprets and evaluates thus: 'You see, I was right. Other people don't want to know me. I really am no good'.

   In conclusion, rational–emotive theory holds that people 'naturally tend to perpetuate their problems and have a strong innate tendency to cling to self-defeating, habitual patterns and thereby resist basic change. Helping clients change then poses quite a challenge for RET practitioners' (Dryden, 1984a, p. 244).

The Rational–Emotive Theory of Therapeutic Change

The rational–emotive view of the person is basically an optimistic one. Although it posits that humans have a distinct biological tendency to think irrationally, it also holds that they have the capacity to choose to work towards changing this irrational thinking and its self-defeating effects.

   There are various levels of change. Rational–emotive theory holds that the most profound and long-lasting changes that humans can effect are ones that involve philosophic restructuring of irrational beliefs. Change at this level can be specific or general. Specific philosophical change means that individuals change their irrational absolutist demands (musts, shoulds) about given situations to rational relative preferences. General philosophical change involves people adopting a non-devout attitude towards life events in general.

To effect a philosophical change at either the specific or general level, people had better:

1. Realise that to a large degree, they create their own psychological disturbances and that although environmental conditions can contribute to their problems, they are in general of secondary consideration in the change process.
2. Fully recognise that they do have the ability to significantly change these disturbances.
3. Understand that emotional and behavioural disturbances stem largely from irrational, absolutist dogmatic beliefs.
4. Detect their irrational beliefs and discriminate them from their rational alternatives.
5. Dispute these irrational beliefs using the logico-empirical methods of science.
6. Work towards the internalisation of their new rational beliefs by employing cognitive, emotive and behavioural methods of change.
7. Continue this process of challenging irrational beliefs and using multimodal methods of change for the rest of their lives.

When people effect a philosophical change by modifying their irrational beliefs to rational beliefs, they often are able to correct spontaneously their distorted inferences of reality (overgeneralisations, faulty attributions, etc.). However, they often had better challenge these distorted inferences more directly, as Ellis has always emphasised (e.g. Ellis, 1962), and as Beck (Beck et al., 1979) has also stressed.

Although rational–emotive theory argues that irrational beliefs are the breeding ground for the development and maintenance of inferential distortions, it is possible for people to effect inferentially based changes without making a profound philosophical change. Thus, they may regard their inferences as hunches about reality rather than facts, may generate alternative hypotheses and may seek evidence and/or carry out experiments which test out each hypothesis. They may then accept the hypothesis which represents the 'best bet' of those available (Gregory, 1966).

Consider a man who thinks that his co-workers view him as a fool. To test this hypothesis he might first specify their negative reactions to him. These constitute the data from which he quickly draws the conclusion: 'They think I'm a fool.' He might then realise that what he has interpreted to be negative responses to him might not be negative. If they seem to be negative, he might then carry out an experiment to test out the meaning he attributes to their responses. Thus, he might enlist the help of a colleague whom he trusts to carry out a 'secret ballot' of others' opinions of him. Or, he could test his hunch more explicitly by directly asking them for their view of him. As a result of these strategies this person may conclude that his co-workers find some of his actions foolish, rather than considering him to be a complete fool. His mood may lift because his inference of the situation has changed, but he may still believe: 'If others think I'm a fool that would be awful and prove that I really am worthless'. Thus, he has made an inferential change, but not a philosophical one. If this person were to attempt to make a philosophical change he would first assume that his inference was true, then address himself to his beliefs about this inference and hence challenge these if they were discovered to be irrational. Thus he might conclude, 'Even if I act foolishly that makes me a person with foolish behaviour, not a foolish person. And even if they deem me a total idiot, this is simply their view with which I can choose to disagree'. Rational–emotive counsellors hypothesise that people are more likely to make a profound philosophical change if they first assume that their inferences are true and then challenge their irrational beliefs, rather than if they first correct their inferential distortions and then challenge their underlying irrational beliefs. However, this hypothesis awaits full empirical enquiry.

People can also make direct changes in their situation. Thus, in the example quoted above, the man could leave his job or distract himself from the reactions of his colleagues by taking on extra work and devoting himself to this. Or he might carry out relaxation exercises whenever he comes in contact with his co-workers and thus distract himself once again from their perceived reactions. Additionally, the man might have a word with his supervisor, who might then instruct the other workers to change their behaviour towards the man.

When this model is used to consider behavioural change, it is apparent that a person can change his or her behaviour to effect inferential and/or philosophical change. Thus, again using the above example, a man whose co-workers view him as a fool might change his own behaviour towards them and thus elicit a different set of responses from them, which would lead him to reinterpret his previous inference (behaviour change to effect inferential change). However, if it could be determined that they did indeed consider him to be a fool then the man could actively seek them out and show himself that he could stand the situation and that just because they think him a fool does not make him one, i.e. he learns to accept himself in the face of their views while exposing himself to their negative reactions (behaviour change to effect philosophical change).

Although rational–emotive counsellors prefer to help their clients make profound philosophical changes in their beliefs, they do not dogmatically insist that their clients make such changes. If it becomes apparent that clients are not able at any given time to change their irrational beliefs, then RET counsellors would endeavour to help them either to change the situation directly by avoiding the troublesome situation, or by behaving differently, or to change their distorted inferences about the situation. This book focuses on rational-emotive methods of changing beliefs rather than inferences. For methods devoted to changing inferences, we recommend that the reader consult Beck et al. (1979) and Beck and Emery (1985).

In the next chapter, we build upon these theoretical underpinnings and consider a cognitively based analysis of the most common forms of psychological disturbance for which clients seek counselling.

Chapter 4
Understanding Clients' Problems

Overview

In this chapter, we present a cognitively based analysis of: (a) the major emotional and behavioural problems for which people seek counselling help and (b) their rational alternatives. We deal with anxiety and concern, shame/embarrassment and regret, depression and sadness, guilt and remorse, anger and annoyance, hurt and disappointment, morbid and non-morbid jealousy, and problems of self-discipline. We conclude the chapter by considering briefly a number of additional issues, namely: a mixture of emotions; 'false' emotions; and strength versus rationality of emotions.

It is important for the reader to understand at the outset of this chapter that rational-emotive theory uses 'feeling' words in a precise way; a major purpose of this chapter is to show how RET defines such feelings by clarifying their cognitive correlates. Since clients often use the same words in different ways from their rational-emotive counsellors (e.g. what a client means by anxiety may be different from its meaning in rational-emotive theory), the latter seek to adopt a shared meaning framework with their clients concerning emotions. This often involves teaching clients the rational-emotive language of emotions, but can also involve using the clients' own feeling language in a way that helps them to differentiate between the rational and irrational versions of these emotions (e.g. rational anxiety versus irrational anxiety).

Anxiety

Inferences

Typically, in anxiety people make inferences that there exists a threat to their personal domain, by which is meant those objects - tangible and intangible - in which they have an involvement (Beck, 1976). The threat refers generally to a future event, or to future implications of a current event.

Beliefs

RET theory states that anxiety results when a person believes: 'This threat must not occur and it would be terrible if it did' (irrational belief).

Action tendencies and response options

When people are anxious, their major action tendencies are to avoid or to withdraw from the inferred threat in order to obtain short-term relief from anxiety. As will be shown, they are more likely to avoid or withdraw from the threat when they cannot respond constructively to it. In addition to keeping away from, or physically withdrawing from a threat, people often engage in various forms of behaviour which serve the purpose of obtaining short-term relief from anxiety, but which also have long-term destructive effects on their growth.

Thus clients who present with anxiety often also report problems of self-discipline, e.g. procrastination, alcohol and drug abuse, etc. (specific responses which actualise the action tendency to avoid or to withdraw). Another action tendency associated with anxiety can be described as attempting to 'ward off' the threat. This may, for example, involve the use of obsessive and/or compulsive patterns of behaviour and thought. Such tactics serve to perpetuate anxiety and the dysfunctional cognitions upon which the anxiety is based. Seeking reassurance is another response that some individuals tend to make when they are anxious. Here they look to other people for guarantees that threats to their personal domain will not happen. When reassurance is given, there is short-term relief from anxiety, but once again, the dysfunctional cognitions that underpin the anxious experience are perpetuated. Finally, some people who experience anxiety have an action tendency which encourages them to expose themselves to *more* dangerous instances of the threat. This is known as 'counterphobic behaviour'.

Typically in anxiety, the person considers that she could not deal with the threat if it occurred. She may judge that there are no viable responses that she can make in the situation; she does not have the sufficient competence to execute such responses; or the responses which she could make would not nullify the threat. Because the person judges that she cannot deal effectively with the threat, she tends to assume that she will be over-whelmed by it.

Other issues

Ellis (1979b, 1980a) has distinguished between two types of anxiety. One occurs when the person has irrational beliefs about threats to her self worth (ego anxiety), and the other occurs when she has such beliefs about threats to her level of personal comfort (discomfort anxiety). These two types of anxiety often interact, leading to the spiralling effect of mounting anxiety or panic. A feature of this spiralling effect is that the person tends to experience very unpleasant bodily sensations which are, as recent research has found, exacerbated by a process called 'overbreathing' (an increase in the rate and depth of respiratory ventilation which occurs particularly when the individual is under stress; Clark, Salkovskis and Chalkley, 1985). Thus, while helping people to overcome anxiety, rational–emotive counsellors not only have to help them to change their inferences and beliefs about the threat, but also may usefully help those vulnerable to 'overbreathing' to utilise effective controlled breathing techniques when they experience anxiety.

Concern: The rational alternative to anxiety

In rational–emotive theory, concern is the rational alternative to anxiety. In concern, a person again makes an inference that there exists a threat to her personal domain, but her belief about this is rational: 'I don't want this threat to occur, but there is no reason why it must not happen. If it occurs, it is undesirable but not terrible'.

When a person is concerned but not anxious about an inferred threat to her personal domain, she tends to consider that she can deal with the threat, i.e. she can execute successfully assertive and/or coping options from her response repertoire. She is thus able to actualise her action tendency to confront and deal successfully with the threat, and not avoid or withdraw from it, as in anxiety.

Shame and Embarrassment

Inferences

In shame, a person tends to infer that (1) she has revealed a personal weakness (or acted stupidly) in public, and (2) others will notice this display and will evaluate her negatively. In embarrassment, the same types of inferences are made as in shame, with the exception that the personal weakness is regarded by the person as less serious than in shame (e.g. spilling coffee versus stammering).

Beliefs

Both shame and embarrassment tend to result when the person agrees with the negative evaluations that she infers others have made of her, e.g. 'They're right, I am worthless for revealing my weakness'. Such conclusions tend to stem from such irrational beliefs as: 'I must not reveal my weaknesses in public', and 'I must not be disapproved by others'. Thus self-devaluation is a core cognitive process in both shame and embarrassment.

Action tendencies and response options

When a person is feeling ashamed or embarrassed, her major action tendency is to remove herself from the 'social spotlight', or the gaze of others, e.g. through avoiding eye contact or through physical withdrawal from the social situation. When the person remains in the situation she feels awkward ('I don't know what to do with myself') yet still feels as if she wants to withdraw ('I want the ground to open up and swallow me'). Remaining in the situation, the person may paradoxically display further signs that may draw attention to herself, e.g. through blushing or becoming agitated.

However, as Duck (1986) has shown, other people may come to the person's rescue, particularly when her social 'gaffe' is not too serious, e.g. by disclosing that similar incidents have happened to them, or by reassuring the person that no harm has been done. Yet, when the person is in a self-devaluing frame of mind and considers that others are unsympathetic to her, she may not be able to use such cues to restore the social equilibrium, and may indeed draw further attention to herself by failing to take advantage of such help.

Regret: the rational alternative to shame/embarrassment

In rational-emotive theory, regret is the rational alternative to shame and embarrassment. In regret, a person again makes an inference that she has revealed a personal weakness or acted stupidly in public and that others will notice this and may evaluate her negatively, but her belief about this is rational: 'I don't like the fact that I've acted in this way and the fact that others may think badly of me, but there's no reason why I must not have committed this shameful or embarrassing act, and there's no reason why people must not think badly of me. It's a pity that this has happened, but not terrible, and I choose to accept myself as a fallible human being for acting in this way'.

When a person experiences regret, but not shame or embarrassment, about revealing a personal weakness in public, she tends to consider that she can choose to focus on the humour implicit in the event, if it exists, or to apologise without desperation for inconveniencing others, if this is relevant. She is also able to utilise the attempts of others to help her to restore the social equilibrium. She is thus able to actualise her action tendency to continue to participate actively in social interaction.

Depression

Inferences

According to the rational-emotive model, depression tends to occur when a person makes inferences that she has experienced a significant loss to her personal domain (Beck, 1976). The loss might be the death of a significant other, the loss of a love relationship, the loss of a limb, the loss of personal functioning, or the loss associated with failure to achieve a valued goal.

Beliefs

However, while inferences of loss tend to be present when the person is psychologically depressed, according to rational–emotive theory, they do not by themselves account for the person's depression. Rather, the person has to hold irrational beliefs about the loss, e.g. when a man believes: 'I absolutely should not have experienced this loss' he then tends to conclude that the loss 'is terrible and unbearable', and the loss means either that 'I am no good' or that 'the world and other people are no good for allowing the loss to occur'. Such irrational beliefs tend to underpin the fact that depressed persons are often hopeless about the future.

Action tendencies and response options

When a person is depressed, her major action tendency is to withdraw from experiences that were previously reinforcing to her, or from other people who were previously valued. The person tends to withdraw 'into herself' and to become immobilised. Another behavioural pattern that often accompanies less severe psychological depression is related to problems of self-discipline. Thus, for example, a person may start drinking when depressed, or may get involved in other self-defeating activities in order to escape from the pain of depression, e.g. promiscuous sexual relationships and drug taking.

Typically in depression, the person considers that she is unable to execute appropriate responses to the loss ('helplessness'), or that nothing she could do will improve the situation ('hopelessness').

Other issues

As in anxiety, depression can be related to losses in self worth (ego depression) or losses in personal comfort (discomfort depression). Again, both types of depression often interact and people can experience ego depression about their discomfort depression and vice versa (Teasdale, 1985).

Hauck (1971) has discussed two types of depression that are prominently featured in rational–emotive theory (his third type will be discussed in the section on 'hurt'). First, Hauck argues, as shown above, that depression can occur because the person has a negative view of self. Thus, a client may become depressed because she concludes: 'I am unworthy (or less worthy) because I did not achieve a valued goal as I should have done'. This is depression based on self-devaluation or ego depression. Secondly, depression may be related to 'other pity' which, in our opinion, occurs less frequently in clinical practice than ego depression. Here the person focuses on the misfortunes or losses of others and believes: 'Such misfortunes or losses should not have occurred. It is terrible that the world allows such things to happen'.

Sadness: the rational alternative to depression

In rational–emotive theory, sadness is the rational alternative to depression. In sadness, the person again makes an inference that she has experienced a significant loss to her personal domain, but her belief about this is rational: 'I didn't want this loss to occur, but there is no reason why it should not have happened. It is bad that it has occurred but not terrible'. In this respect healthy grief is seen in rational–emotive theory as profound sadness.

When a person is sad but not depressed about a loss to her personal domain, she tends to consider that she can engage in constructive actions from her response repertoire. She is able to actualise her action tendency to express her feelings about her loss and to talk about it with significant others and not withdraw into herself, as in depression.

Guilt

Inferences

Typically, in guilt a person infers that she has broken her personal code of moral values either by doing something that she considers to be 'bad' (the 'sin' of commission), or not doing something she considers to be 'good' (the 'sin' of omission).

Beliefs

Rational–emotive theory states that guilt results when a person believes: 'I absolutely should not have done what I did, or should have done what I did not. I am a damnable individual for doing so, or not doing so, and should be punished'.

Action tendencies and response options

When a person is feeling guilty, her major action tendencies involve: (1) 'undoing' – this process which aims to 'right the wrong' is often unproductive e.g. attempting to repair 'broken relationships' by desperately begging forgiveness from others (often accompanied by statements of self-loathing); (2) self-punishment, where the person may harm herself in a physical way, or involve herself in activities that may lead her into harm because she believes that she deserves punishment; (3) attempting to anaesthetise herself from the pain of guilt, usually in a self-defeating manner by taking drugs or alcohol; or (4) avoiding responsibility, by making defensive excuses whereby the person claims that she did not do wrong, or blames others for her actions.

Typically in guilt, since the person is in a self-condemnatory frame of mind, she is likely to choose options from her response repertoire which tend to make it more likely that she will 'sin' in future. For example, a common pattern in eating disorders involves the person resolving to diet, establishing a strict dieting regime, breaking this regime, condemning herself, and eating to take away the pain of guilt.

If the person experiencing guilt considers that she has wronged another, she is likely to make unrealistic promises to the other to the effect that 'I will never do that again', without attempting to understand the factors which led her to act that way. She thus finds it difficult to learn from her errors, and thus tends not to be able to keep such promises. Thus, people who experience guilt are often so preoccupied with 'purging' their badness, or with self-punishment, that they tend not to look for explanations for their behaviour other than those that involve internal attributions of badness.

Remorse: the rational alternative to guilt

In rational–emotive theory, remorse or sorrow is the rational alternative to guilt. In remorse, a person again infers that she has violated her personal code of moral values, but her belief about this is rational: 'I don't like what I did, or didn't do, but there's no reason why I must not have done it. I'm a fallible human being who did the wrong thing and therefore not damnable'.

When a person feels remorse, but not guilt, about breaking her personal code of moral values, she tends to take responsibility for her actions without damning her 'self' and tries to understand why she acted or failed to act as she did. If others are involved the person may choose to communicate to them the reasons for her actions, and apologise without desperation to them for 'causing' them pain. She is thus able to repair 'broken' relationships in a rational manner, i.e. while accepting self and others, and to make reparation where appropriate.

Other issues

It is important to distinguish between 'feeling' guilt (i.e. condemning self for acting badly) and acknowledging that one is guilty of doing something wrong – better termed 'accepting responsibility for one's actions'. When a rational–emotive counsellor asks whether the client wishes to overcome her feelings of guilt, the client often thinks that she is being asked to consider that she hasn't broken her moral code rather than to consider the option of accepting herself as a fallible human being for transgressing this code (the latter strategy represents the counsellor's actual intent).

As noted above, clients often consider that having guilty feelings will prevent them from breaking their moral code in the future. However, often the reverse is true. Since guilt involves the belief 'I am bad', a self-fulfilling prophecy often comes into play since a person who considers herself 'bad' will tend to act 'badly' in the future.

Anger

The term anger has several meanings in the counselling literature. Rational–emotive theory differentiates damning anger, which tends to be an irrational emotion, from non-damning anger, which tends to be a rational emotion. Here I will use the term anger to refer to damning anger, and annoyance to refer to its non-damning counterpart.

Inferences

There appear to be three major inference patterns in anger. First, a person may make an inference that a frustrating circumstance exists which serves to block her from achieving goals which she deems important in her personal domain. As Wessler and Wessler (1980) note: 'The source of frustration can be external or internal, so anger can be directed at other people, the world in general or oneself' (p. 98).

Secondly, a person may make an inference that another person, an institution, e.g. a company, a tax office or university, or the person herself has transgressed a personal rule deemed important in her personal domain. When the transgressor of the rule is oneself, the rule in anger tends to be non-moral, in contrast to guilt when the rule is in the moral domain. Whilst Wessler and Wessler (1980) observe that transgression of personal rules represents a major source of inferred frustration, we prefer to see the rule-transgression inference pattern as separate from inference patterns associated with frustration, since it occurs frequently in counselling practice.

Thirdly, in a certain type of anger that we call 'self-defence' anger, a person makes an inference that the actions of another person, or the responses of an institution, threaten her 'self-esteem' (see 'other issues' below).

Beliefs

Rational–emotive theory states that, while inferences of frustration, rule transgression or threat to self-esteem tend to be present when the person is angry, they do not, by themselves, account for anger; rather, the person tends to hold irrational beliefs about these inferences, e.g. 'You must not act in this way and you are damnable for doing so'. It is important to stress then that damning another person, an institution or oneself is an important cognitive dynamic in anger.

Action tendencies and response options

When a person is feeling angry, her major action tendency is to attack either physically or verbally the relevant source of the frustration, rule-breaking or threat to self-esteem in some way. This attack often has a retaliatory intent. If this attack cannot be mounted directly, as strict social rules often restrict the expression of aggression, the person may tend to displace her attack onto another person, usually of lower status or less powerful than the original source, an animal ('kicking the cat') or an object. Another major action tendency associated with anger is withdrawal, as when a person 'storms' out of a meeting.

Typically in anger, a person tends to choose options from her response repertoire that are characterised by retaliation. The person seeks to get even in some way by choosing, for example, to respond to another person's criticism with damning criticism of that other person in return. When the person's anger is passive–aggressive, this retaliation is expressed indirectly and without the recipient necessarily knowing where the attack has come from, for example, sending anonymous poison-pen letters, since the person tends also to be anxious of attacking the other directly.

While the person who is angry could theoretically choose to engage in productive responses from her response repertoire, e.g. honest non-damning communication, the fact that she is in a 'damning' frame of mind makes this unlikely. This explains why rational–emotive counsellors seek to help clients to work to overcome their anger before helping them to communicate constructively with others (Dryden, 1985a).

Other issues

It is often difficult to help people to overcome their anger because anger tends to have positive short-term results. Thus anger often helps people to 'feel' powerful and it may, in certain circumstances, help them to get what they want from others, at least initially. However, anger also tends to have negative long-term consequences for the person. Thus anger tends to encourage the deterioration and disintegration of relationships and tends to lead to high blood pressure and other cardiovascular disorders (Chesney and Rosenman, 1985).

As noted earlier, anger can form an entry point or a 'gateway' to the experience of other emotions such as anxiety or hurt. For example, a client may be angry with her husband for forgetting her birthday, not just because the other person has broken a personal rule and should be punished (although there is that element to the experience), but because she infers that her husband has acted in an uncaring manner. In this example, hurt underpins the experience of anger, i.e. the woman believes that it is terrible to be treated in a way she did not deserve. Another example of anger as a 'gateway' emotion occurred when W.D. once became angry when a friend enquired about the progress of a writing project. He responded with anger not because he believed that his friend should not have made this enquiry, but because the friend should not have reminded him of his sense of personal inadequacy due to the fact that the project was not going well (threat to his self-esteem). If he was more accepting of himself on that occasion when being reminded of his poor performance, he would still have been annoyed since he would not have liked being reminded of his inadequacy, but he would not have been angry.

Annoyance: the rational alternative to anger

In rational–emotive theory, annoyance is the rational alternative to anger. In annoyance, a person again makes an inference that concerns frustration, rule-breaking or threat to self-esteem, but her beliefs about these are rational, e.g. 'I don't like your behaviour and I prefer you didn't act in this way. But there's no reason why you must not act in this bad manner. You are not damnable but a fallible human being who, in my opinion, is acting badly'. Thus acceptance of the other or oneself as 'fallible' is an important cognitive dynamic in annoyance.

When a person is annoyed but not angry, she tends to actualise her tendency to remain in the situation and deal with it constructively by choosing responses from her repertoire that may include assertion and requesting (but not demanding!) behavioural change from others. As in remorse, the person who is annoyed at her own behaviour tends to take responsibility for her own actions, tries to understand her reasons for breaking her own, non-moral rule, and takes corrective action in the future.

Hurt

Inferences

Typically in hurt, a person infers that a significant other has acted towards her in an 'unfair' manner. The other might have ignored the person or disregarded her desires, acted in a non-caring way towards the person, or betrayed the person in some way. Another important inference pattern in hurt which often accompanies the inferences referred to above, involves the person considering that she is undeserving of such treatment.

Beliefs

Rational–emotive theory states that hurt results when a person believes 'The other person absolutely should not have treated me in this unfair manner'. Typical conclusions that follow from this irrational premise can be threefold: (1) It's terrible to be treated in this way, particularly as I do not deserve it. Poor me! The world is a rotten place for allowing this to happen'.

This can be referred to as 'self-pitying hurt'; (2) 'I'm no good for being treated this way'. This can be referred to as 'depressed hurt'; and (3) 'You are no good for treating me in this way'. This can be referred to as 'angry hurt'. Often in hurt, the person has a blend of these three irrational beliefs.

When deservingness is an issue for the person, when she is hurt she tends to believe 'I must get what I deserve' or 'I must not get what I do not deserve'.

Action tendencies and response options

When a person is feeling hurt, her major action tendencies involve withdrawing and closing communication channels with the person who has 'hurt' her (colloquially referred to as 'sulking'), and criticising the other person normally without disclosing what she feels hurt about. Both often serve the purpose of getting even with the other. Other action tendencies in 'depressed hurt' and 'angry hurt' are similar to those associated with depression and anger.

Typically in hurt, the person, as noted above, often chooses to withdraw from the other who has 'hurt' her. She may also choose responses which are intended to encourage the other person to feel guilty, e.g. 'If you really cared about me you would know what you did to hurt me'. Underlying this notion is the person's magical belief that the other person should be able to read one's mind, or know the meaning underlying one's distress. When the person is hurt in a depressed or angry way, she tends to choose response options similar to those selected in depression and anger.

Disappointment: the rational alternative to hurt

In rational–emotive theory, disappointment is the rational alternative to hurt. In disappointment, a person again infers that another has acted unfairly towards her, but her belief about this is rational: 'I prefer to be treated fairly (or not to be treated unfairly), but there's no reason why I must be treated in the way that I prefer (even though I may 'deserve' it). I do not have to get what I deserve'. Typical conclusions that follow from this rational premise are: 'It's bad (but not terrible) to be treated in this way'; 'Being treated in this way does not affect my worth. I'm a fallible human being no matter how I am treated' – here the person's disappointment is tinged with sadness; and 'I don't like your behaviour but you are a fallible human being for acting unfairly. You are not damnable' – here the person's disappointment is tinged with annoyance.

When a person feels disappointment but not hurt about being treated unfairly, she tends to choose options from her response repertoire which actualise her action tendency to influence the other person to act in a 'fairer' manner. She communicates her feelings clearly, directly and assertively to the other person.

Morbid Jealousy

In this section, we will focus on romantic jealousy, since clients are most likely to seek counselling help for this type of jealousy.

Inferences

In morbid jealousy, a person can make a number of inferences including: (1) that the loss of her partner to another is imminent or has occurred; (2) that she does not have the exclusive love or attention of her partner; (3) that she is not the most important aspect of her partner's life; and (4) that her partner is acting in a way that violates her property rights (when she views her partner as her 'property'). These inferences are often linked to inferred threats to the jealous person's self-esteem.

While many people are jealous of their partner's actual or imagined sexual involvement with another person, others allow their partner to have sex with other people and only get jealous when their partner becomes emotionally involved with another person. This suggests that people differ in their jealousy 'rules' (Duck, 1986).

Beliefs

While one or more of the above inferences tend to occur when the person experiences morbid jealousy, they again do not, by themselves, account for the person's destructive jealous feelings. Rather the person has to hold irrational beliefs about these inferences, e.g. when a woman believes 'My husband must only be interested in me. If he shows interest in another woman that would be awful'. She may then conclude either: 'His interest in someone else proves that I am worthless' – (morbid jealousy tinged with depression) or 'He is no good (and/or the other woman is no good) for doing this to me' – (morbid jealousy tinged with anger).

Action tendencies and response options

When a person feels morbid jealousy, her action tendencies include monitoring the actions and feelings of her partner, e.g. constantly asking her partner for assurances that she is loved, or phoning her partner at work to check on his movements; searching for evidence that her partner is involved with someone else, e.g. checking his car for signs of sexual activity or accusing her partner of engaging in extramarital affairs; attempting to place restrictions on the movements of her partner, e.g. not allowing her partner to talk to other women at social gatherings; and retaliating, e.g. becoming sexually involved with another person to 'get even' with her partner for his actual or presumed infidelity, or angrily condemning her partner for his 'infidelity'.

As shown above, people who experience morbid jealousy often act in self- and relationship-defeating ways. Because they are anxious about losing their relationship and are yet convinced that this loss is imminent, they often hasten the end of the relationship by their constant checking, accusatory and prescriptive behaviour towards their partner, thus displaying the self-fulfilling prophecy effect commonly found in cases of morbid jealousy.

Non-morbid jealousy: the rational alternative to morbid jealousy

In non-morbid jealousy, the person may again make similar inferences as in morbid jealousy, but her beliefs about these are rational, e.g. 'I want my husband to be only interested in me, but there's no reason why I must have his exclusive interest. If he shows interest in another woman it would be bad, but not awful'. She may then conclude either 'I am still a fallible human being even if he shows an interest in someone else'; or 'He (and/or the other woman) is a fallible human being who is acting against my interests'. Ellis (1985c) has argued that non-morbid jealousy encourages a person to act and express herself in a loving manner towards her partner rather than taking him for granted; to do something effective to try and win her partner back if that is what she wants; to express her distress assertively and without anger and to ask her partner to set limits on his outside involvements; and to reorganise her life constructively without her partner if he leaves her, or if she decides to terminate the relationship given that it no longer meets her deepest desires.

While there is no research on the subject, rational–emotive theory would predict that the person who experiences non-morbid jealousy is less likely to consider that her partner has outside romantic interests in the absence of such evidence than the person who experiences morbid jealousy.

Problems of Self-discipline

Clients sometimes seek counselling for help with problems of self-discipline such as procrastination, eating disorders and addictions to, say, alcohol or drugs. Also such problems may also be involved in other emotional disorders – for instance, alcoholism is often a feature of aggression.

According to the framework presented in this book, problems of self-discipline are seen here in terms of the conversion of action tendencies into fixed patterns of response which have become habitual. It is important to note that self-discipline problems involve a complex interaction of ego disturbance, discomfort disturbance and responses chosen to actualise action tendencies, the main purpose of which is often to gain relief from immediate feelings of distress. One example will suffice.

People with drink problems often originally have ego anxiety, e.g. 'I must do well and I'm worthless if I don't'. They then experience discomfort anxiety about such ego anxiety, e.g. 'I can't stand being so anxious' and thence drink to rid themselves of their anxiety. In the next part of the chain they may have irrational beliefs about their drinking and/or about the results of their drinking – since alcohol often disrupts performance, e.g. 'I'm no good for doing so poorly' or 'I must not drink this much'. They then make themselves anxious about this ego anxiety and once again drink to rid themselves of these anxious feelings. It should be apparent then that such people set up and maintain a vicious circle of disturbance, while often simultaneously and paradoxically denying that they have a problem. This process of denial probably accounts for the reluctance often shown by such individuals to seek help for their problems.

Wessler and Wessler (1980) have argued that problems of self-discipline serve three major functions:

1. A *relief function*, whereby the person either abuses alcohol, food or drugs, or procrastinates to gain relief from immediate emotional disturbance, or to prevent such distress occurring.
2. A *self-protective function*, whereby the person uses her self-defeating behaviour as a protection against possible self-condemnation, e.g. the woman who overeats to make herself unattractive to men, thus attributing any rejection to her weight rather than to her inherent worthlessness.
3. A *'spurious' self-enhancement function*, whereby a person engages in self-defeating behaviour in order to obtain something positive that she believes she needs, e.g. the man who gambles compulsively in order to finance his entry into an elite social group to which he aspires, and which he thinks he must join.

To this list we can add a fourth function, what we call a *'positive feeling function'*, whereby the person engages in self-defeating behaviour, such as alcohol, drugs etc., in order to get quick intense positive feelings, or a state of relaxation, rather than to avoid negative feelings such as anxiety.

It is apparent, then, that people with problems of self-discipline adhere to a philosophy of low frustration tolerance (LFT) in that they believe they must get what they want, or must not get what they do not want, quickly and easily. Thus a major feature of rational–emotive counselling with such individuals is to help them to raise their level of frustration tolerance.

Additional Issues

We conclude this chapter by considering briefly some additional issues in understanding clients' problems.

A mixture of emotions

Although we have considered emotional problems separately, it is not uncommon in counselling practice for clients to describe a mixture of emotions. For example, some clients report feeling simultaneously depressed and guilty. In practice it is often helpful to separate these emotions and deal with them one at a time. Also, clients sometimes report experiencing 'blended' emotions as in 'hurt anger' or 'jealous anger'. Since, as has been shown, there are various types of anger, it is helpful to determine the nature of the emotional blend for assessment purposes, particularly when clients only refer to 'feeling angry', since the cognitions that underpin 'hurt anger' are somewhat different from those underlying 'jealous anger'.

'False' emotions

It is important to bear in mind that clients may report emotions that they do not, in fact, experience, or emotions that are less important to their actual problems than other feelings that they do not disclose. Clients who report emotions that they do not experience sometimes do so because they think that they are supposed to have these emotions (DiGiuseppe, 1984). Clients who report emotions peripheral to their real concerns do so for similar reasons and, in addition, may feel ashamed about their real emotions, e.g. clients who report feeling depressed rather than their true feelings of anger.

As Snyder and Smith (1982) have shown, some clients use emotions for impression management purposes. For example, some clients present with 'false' feelings of depression based on self-devaluation in order to elicit pity from other people or to ward off attack from other people. In the latter instance, such clients are often anxious about being criticised and ward off criticism by seeming to put themselves down before they are put down by others (most people will not criticise those who are already criticising themselves; indeed others are likely to boost the ego of those who are actively condemning themselves). It is difficult for counsellors to identify clients' 'false' emotions, at least initially. However, they should be alert to their existence, particularly when 'something does not seem to ring true' about clients' accounts of their emotional experiences.

Strength versus rationality of negative emotions

Some counsellors who misinterpret rational–emotive theory consider that strong negative emotions are reliable signs that these emotions are irrational. This is not necessarily the case. Thus one can experience mild anger (irrational emotion) and strong annoyance (rational emotion). Strong rational emotions occur when the person does not get what she strongly prefers, or gets what she strongly prefers not to get. Weak irrational emotions occur when the person demands weakly that she gets what she wants, or that she does not get what she does not want.

The clue to whether an emotion is rational or irrational is whether or not the person demands that her desires are met. Thus, counsellors who try to help clients to reduce the strength of their rational emotions make the unfortunate mistake of encouraging them to deny the strength of their desires.

Having covered the main features of rational-emotive *theory*, we now proceed to discuss the *practice* of rational-emotive counselling with individuals in Part II.

Part II
Practice

Chapter 5
Counselling Individuals: Rationale and Key Elements

Overview

In this chapter, we begin by outlining the indications and contraindications for individual counselling. We then present an overview of the key elements involved in the practice of rational-emotive counselling. Here we discuss counselling goals, aspects of the counselling relationship, the manner in which RET affects counsellors' choice of interventions, and the personal qualities of effective rational-emotive counsellors.

Considerations

Counselling and psychotherapy can be carried out in the context of individual, couples, family and group sessions. Although counsellors and therapists have all of these modalities from which to choose, research evidence suggests that most spend their working time engaged in individual treatment. Prochaska and Norcross (1983), for example, carried out a survey of the practices of 410 psychologists belonging to Division 29 (Psychotherapy) of the American Psychological Association (APA). In addition, they have reported on a similar survey (Norcross and Prochaska, 1982) of a representative sample of psychologists who are members of APA Division 12 (Clinical Psychology). Both of these surveys revealed that members of both Divisions spent most of their therapy time practising individual therapy (65.3 per cent Division 29 members; 63.5 per cent Division 12 members). Likewise, a recent survey of 993 British psychologists belonging to the Clinical Division of the British Psychological Society (BPS) indicated that those who practised individual therapy (99 per cent of the sample) allotted 74 per cent of their treatment time to that format (Norcross, Dryden and Brust, 1992). Although there are no available data on the distribution of working time of therapists and counsellors of different theoretical orientations, there is little reason to believe that a different pattern would be found among rational-emotive counsellors.

One of us has argued (Dryden, 1984b) that there are various sources of influence that impinge upon the counsellor and client as they seek to determine in which modality to work. First, counsellors are influenced by the settings in which they work. Such settings may impose practical limitations on the practice of counselling in modalities other than individual counselling. Alternatively, different settings may have different norms of practice which favour one particular modality over others. Counsellors who work in private practice usually find that the exigencies of this mode of work mean that individual counselling constitutes the major part of their workload. Secondly, counsellors are influenced by the ways in which they account for their clients' disturbances. Since the rational–emotive model of disturbance emphasises the role played by the individual's belief system upon his or her psychological problems, this may influence practitioners to work more frequently in the modality of individual counselling than in other modalities. Thirdly, clients' preferences are very salient here and these often exert a considerable influence on the choice of therapeutic modality.

In this regard, Ellis (in Dryden, 1984b, p. 15) has argued 'I am usually able to go along with the basic desire of any clients who want individual, marital, family or group psychotherapy. It is only in relatively few cases that I talk them into taking a form of therapy they are at first loath to try'. Information is needed concerning the impact of clients' precounselling modality preferences on the working practices of RET counsellors. Given that we do not have any data concerning how RET counsellors distribute their working time among the various counselling modalities, what factors determine such decisions, and who is largely responsible for making these decisions, much of our thinking on the issue of when and when not to undertake individual counselling is determined by clinical experience. Based upon this experience, we present the following lists of indications and contra-indications for individual counselling.

Indications for individual counselling

1. Individual rational–emotive counselling, by its nature, provides clients with a situation of complete confidentiality. It is indicated therefore when it is important for clients to be able to disclose themselves in privacy without fear that others may use such information to their detriment. Some clients are particularly anxious concerning how others, for example in a group counselling context, would react to their disclosures, and such anxiety precludes their productive participation in that modality. Similarly, clients who otherwise would not disclose 'secret' material are best suited to individual rational–emotive counselling. As in other situations, transfer to other modalities may be indicated later when such clients are more able and/or willing to disclose themselves to others.

2. Individual counselling, by its dyadic nature, provides an opportunity for a closer relationship to develop between counsellor and client than may exist when other clients are present. This factor may be particularly important for some clients who have not developed close relationships with significant people in their lives and for whom group counselling, for example, may prove initially too threatening.

3. Individual rational-emotive counselling can be conducted to best match the client's pace of learning. Thus, it is particularly suited for clients who, due to their present state of mind, or speed of learning, require their counsellor's full undivided attention. This is especially important for clients who are quite confused and who would only be distracted by the complexity of interactions that can take place in other therapeutic modalities.

4. Likewise, clients who feel hopeless and suicidal may benefit more from individual sessions in which they have the counsellor's full attention, as such sessions can allow the counsellor to more readily focus interventions upon helping the client to emerge from the suicidal crisis. It is noted, however, that counsellors have a responsibility to protect the welfare of suicidal clients who appear to be at risk of doing harm to themselves. In some circumstances this responsibility may preclude individual outpatient counselling, as when it appears advisable to recommend psychiatric hospitalisation.

5. Individual counselling is particularly indicated when clients' major problems involve their relationship with themselves rather than their relationship with other people.

6. Individual counselling may be indicated for clients who wish to differentiate themselves from others, for example, those who have decided to leave a relationship and wish to deal with individual problems that this may involve. Here, however, some conjoint sessions with the partner may also be helpful, particularly in matters of conciliation (Gurman and Kniskern, 1978).

7. It can be helpful for counsellors to vary their therapeutic style with clients in order to minimise the risk of perpetuating the client's problems by providing an inappropriate interactive style. Individual rational-emotive counselling provides counsellors with an opportunity to vary their interactive styles with clients free from the concern that such variation may adversely affect other clients present.

8. Individual counselling is particularly indicated for clients who have profound difficulties sharing therapeutic time with other clients.

9. Individual counselling may also be indicated for negative reasons. Thus, clients may be seen in individual counselling who may not benefit from working in other modalities. Therefore, clients who may monopolise a counselling group, be too withdrawn within it to benefit from the experience, or who are thought too vulnerable to benefit from

family counselling, are often seen individually in rational–emotive counselling.

Contraindications for individual counselling

1. Individual counselling is contraindicated for clients who are likely to
   become overly dependent on the counsellor, particularly when such
   dependency becomes so intense as to lead to client deterioration. Such
   clients may be more appropriately helped in group counselling where
   such intense dependency is less likely to develop due to the fact that the
   counsellor has to relate to several other people.
2. Individual rational–emotive counselling, which does not in general advocate close interpersonal relationships between counsellors and clients,
   can still be a close interpersonal encounter for the client and as such is
   less likely to be indicated for clients who may find such a degree of
   intimacy or the prospect of such intimacy unduly threatening.
3. Individual counselling may be contraindicated for clients who find this
   modality too comfortable. Based on the idea that personal change is
   often best facilitated in situations where there is an optimal level of
   arousal, individual counselling may not provide enough challenge for
   such clients. Ravid (1969) found that it may be unproductive to offer
   individual therapy to clients who have had much previous individual
   therapy, but still require further therapeutic help.
4. Individual counselling may not be appropriate for clients for whom
   other modalities are deemed to be more therapeutic. For example,
   clients who are particularly shy, retiring and afraid to take risks are more
   likely to benefit from group counselling (if they can be induced to join)
   than from the less risky situation of individual counselling. Secondly,
   partners who can productively use the conjoint situation of couples
   counselling often benefit more from this modality than from working in
   individual rational–emotive counselling. This is particularly true when
   they have largely overcome their disturbed feelings about their unproductive relationship and are dealing with issues devoted to enhance-
   ment of relationship satisfaction, a situation which particularly warrants
   their joint participation.

Other issues

Once counsellors and clients have decided to work in a particular modality
it is important to stress that this decision is not irrevocable. Clients may
move from modality to modality and thus individual counselling, in this
context, can be best viewed as part of a comprehensive treatment strategy.
This can occur for both positive and negative reasons. Productive movement to and from individual counselling occurs when clients have made
therapeutic gains in one modality, but may benefit further from being

transferred to a different one. Negative movement in and out of individual counselling occurs when the clients do not improve in a given therapeutic modality.

Although we have provided some indications and contraindications for the practice of individual counselling, we conclude by stressing that the state of the art concerning this issue is far from being well developed and would advise RET counsellors thus: work with clients in the modality which seems to be most productive for them but regard such decisions as tentative and to a large degree experimental. Perhaps the best way of determining whether a client will benefit or not from individual counselling is in fact to work with them in that modality and to monitor their response to it.

We will next consider key elements involved in the practice of rational-emotive counselling.

Key Elements in the Practice of Rational–Emotive Counselling

As described in Part I, RET presents a clear and coherent theory as to the manner in which human beings acquire and perpetuate their own psychological disturbance. Although this theory does not dictate rigid and absolutistic 'rules' for the implementation of rational–emotive counselling, it does suggest particular emphases and guidelines which may contribute to more effective practice. The sections that follow will outline the goals of rational–emotive counselling, important features of the relationship between counsellor and client, issues pertaining to therapeutic style, and the relationship between RET theory and counsellors' decisions concerning choice of therapeutic interventions. The chapter concludes with consideration of some of the personal qualities that may characterise effective rational–emotive counsellors.

The goals of rational–emotive counselling

Rational–emotive counsellors seek to help their clients minimise the frequency with which they experience emotional disturbance and engage in self-defeating patterns of behaviour. As RET theory holds that irrational beliefs are a major determinant of such psychological problems, counsellors set themselves the task of teaching clients how to detect and dispute the irrational beliefs to which they subscribe. Clients are further assisted to replace their irrational beliefs with more rational ones, which can help them to work more effectively toward their valued goals. This, in turn, may contribute to their experiencing more happiness and satisfaction in life.

Typically, clients first enter counselling because they are seeking relief from 'symptoms' which are distressing in a more or less immediate sense. Thus, a depressed client may seek relief from the emotional pain that her depression entails, while an obese client may seek relief from the distress associated with overeating and being unattractively overweight. Rational–emotive counsellors will attempt to help clients to overcome the emotional and behavioural disturbances which are of most immediate relevance to them, using the techniques and interventions which RET provides. It is noted, however, that rational–emotive counsellors maintain a therapeutic goal with more far-reaching implications than mere symptom relief: they are interested in helping their clients to attain a beneficial and enduring modification in their basic personal philosophies. Such profound philosophic change means that clients become less prone to placing rigid irrational demands upon themselves, other people, and circumstances as they exist in the world, with the result that they are able to greatly reduce their general tendencies to make themselves disturbed. When clients work at effecting the type of profound philosophic change which RET advocates, they are better able to approach the 13 criteria for psychological health which were presented in Chapter 3 (see pp. 32–34).

Rational–emotive counsellors recognise, however, that not all clients will be interested in expending the amount of time and effort which is very often required for attaining a profound philosophic change. They may be quite satisfied when they experience improvement in a circumscribed problem area, and may wish to terminate treatment at that point. Thus, while rational–emotive counsellors may encourage their clients to work at attaining a broad philosophic restructuring, they are flexible in terms of adjusting their goals to meet their clients' goals.

It is also noted that RET counsellors demonstrate flexibility when dealing with clients who are unable or unwilling to work at identifying and disputing the irrational beliefs that negatively affect specific areas of their functioning. Here, counsellors will modify their therapeutic goals and may choose to use strategies and techniques which, although less likely to result in philosophic change, may still offer some degree of relief from distressing symptoms. Hence, they may help certain clients to make changes in their inferences, modify the negative events in their lives, or directly work at changing their behaviour in some fashion, so that they experience self-defeating consequences less often. It is recognised, however, that these clients may well remain vulnerable to significant future upsets because they have not addressed the ideological core of their psychological problems.

The counselling relationship

RET not only recommends that counsellors be flexible in their choice of therapeutic goals and strategies; it also encourages them to exercise flexibility with regard to the parameters of the counselling relationship. Thus, rational–emotive counsellors are able to consider such variables as their own personality characteristics, their clients' personality characteristics, and clients' preferences concerning counsellor behaviour in making decisions as to the therapeutic conditions and styles most likely to facilitate effective counselling for given individuals. Nevertheless, RET counsellors tend to favour particular types of conditions and styles, as RET theory suggests that these will generally prove to be therapeutically beneficial for clients.

Therapeutic conditions

As noted in Chapter 3, RET posits that self-acceptance is one of the hallmarks of the psychologically healthy individual. While rational–emotive counsellors will often attempt to directly teach clients how to become more self-accepting, they will also employ less direct interventions to help clients approach this aspect of psychological health. Hence, throughout the course of treatment – regardless of how poorly clients might behave – counsellors strive to provide them with unconditional acceptance. By doing so they hope to encourage clients to accept *themselves* as fallible human beings who engage in both good and bad acts, but who are never *essentially* bad or good. Counsellors will, however, comment on aspects of a client's behaviour which appear to be self-defeating or negatively affect other individuals, including the counsellor (Ellis, 1973). Such feedback is given in order to assist clients in modifying patterns of behaviour that tend to garner negative consequences, and is provided in an atmosphere that encourages clients to critically examine and rate their acts while refraining from globally rating their 'self'.

RET counsellors strive to be as open as therapeutically feasible, and do not hesitate to give highly personal information about themselves should their clients ask for it, except when they judge that clients would use such information either against themselves or the counsellor (Dryden, 1991). In addition, rational–emotive counsellors generally do not engage in self-disclosure on a gratuitous basis; they attempt to employ it for therapeutic purposes. Thus, a counsellor may disclose to a client that she once had a problem similar to the one that the client is working on, and then describe the manner in which she used RET to overcome it. This intervention can serve several useful purposes:

1. It provides clients with a model of how they can work at overcoming their own problems.
2. It can increase the counsellor's credibility as an expert problem-solver.
3. It conveys to clients that their counsellor is not ashamed of having had personal problems, and that they need not feel ashamed of themselves.

This last function may be particularly important, as it highlights the fact that counsellor self-disclosure may serve as a vehicle for modelling self-acceptance to clients. Clients who are able to accept themselves with their psychological disturbance may well experience greater success in using RET to counter it.

Ellis (1977a, 1987) has noted that human beings may tend to make themselves more vulnerable to emotional disturbance when they take themselves and their problems, other people, and the world too seriously. As such, RET counsellors will often strive to inject various sorts of humorous interventions into their sessions with clients. Usually, this humour is directed at helping clients to see the absurd and illogical aspects of their irrational beliefs. Humour is never used, however, to poke fun at clients themselves, and rational-emotive counsellors take steps to make certain that clients do not perceive its use in this way. In addition, it is noted that RET opposes therapists unethically indulging themselves (by overusing or otherwise misusing any type of intervention) in order to enjoy counselling sessions at their clients' expense (Ellis, 1983b).

Rational-emotive counsellors are advised to remain alert to the likelihood that counsellors and clients may ascribe widely different meanings to the same words and phrases within counselling (Dryden, 1986). RET theory, for example, defines various 'feeling words' (such as anxiety, concern, depression and sadness) in very specific ways (see Chapter 4). Clients new to RET, however, will be unfamiliar with these definitions, hence they may often describe their affective experiences in an idiosyncratic fashion. It is desirable for RET counsellors to make inquiries which serve to clarify the manner in which clients use words to describe their feelings, and to teach clients RET's definitions of the various rational and irrational emotions. In a similar vein, counsellors can check with clients to be sure that the latter are correctly grasping the many other terms and concepts typically presented during a course of rational-emotive counselling. Treatment will generally proceed more smoothly (and a particular source of client resistance can be avoided) when counsellor and client are 'speaking the same language'.

RET counsellors show their clients a special kind of empathy. They not only offer them affective empathy (i.e. communicating that they understand how their clients feel), but also offer them philosophical empathy, i.e. showing them that they understand the philosophies that underlie these feelings.

Thus, with certain modifications, they agree with Rogers' (1957) views concerning counsellor empathy, genuineness and unconditional positive regard. However, rational-emotive counsellors are very wary of showing the vast majority of their clients undue warmth. Rational-emotive theory holds that if rational-emotive counsellors get really close to their clients and given them considerable warmth, attention, caring and support, as well as unconditional acceptance, then these counsellors run two major risks (Ellis, 1977c, 1982b). The first is that counsellors may unwittingly reinforce their clients' dire needs for love and approval - two irrational ideas which are at the core of much human disturbance. When this happens clients appear to improve because their counsellors are indeed giving them what they believe they must have. They begin to 'feel better' but do not necessarily 'get better' (Ellis, 1972). Their 'improvement' is illusory because their irrational philosophies are being reinforced. Since they seem to improve, their counsellors have restricted opportunities to identify these ideas, show them how they relate to their problems and help them challenge and change them. Consequently, while such clients are helped by their counsellors, they are not shown how they can help themselves, and are thus vulnerable to future upset.

The second major risk concerns the fact that counsellors may unwittingly reinforce their clients' philosophy of low frustration tolerance (LFT) – a major form of discomfort disturbance. Clients with LFT problems 'almost always try to seek interminable help from others instead of coping with life's difficulties themselves. Any kind of therapy that does not specifically persuade them to stop their puerile whining, and to accept responsibility for their own happiness, tends to confirm their belief that others *must* help them. Close relationship therapy is frequently the worst offender in this respect and thereby does considerable harm' (Ellis, 1977c, p. 15).

However, since rational–emotive theory is relative in nature and is against the formulation of absolute, dogmatic therapeutic rules, it does recognise that under certain conditions (e.g. where a client is extremely depressed, accompanied by powerful suicidal ideation), distinct counsellor warmth may be positively indicated for a restricted period of time (Ellis, 1985d).

Therapeutic style

RET can accurately be viewed as a psychoeducational approach to counselling. Ellis, in fact, has sometimes conceptualised the role of the effective RET counsellor as that of an authoritative (but not authoritarian) and encouraging teacher who strives to teach his or her clients how to be their own counsellor once formal counselling sessions have ended (Ellis, 1979c, 1984b). Given this view of the counsellor's role, and given the fact that it is often quite difficult for clients to relinquish their strongly held irrational beliefs, it is not surprising that Ellis (1979d) recommends that counsellors adopt an active–directive stance with most clients, and a particularly forceful version of that style with some very disturbed and resistant clients.

Not all rational–emotive counsellors, however, concur with this view. Garcia (1977) and Young (1977), for instance, recommend a more passive, gentle approach under specific or most conditions with clients. Eschenroeder (1979, p. 5) notes that it is important to ask in rational–emotive counselling 'which therapeutic style is most effective with which kind of client?'. In the same vein, recent proponents of eclectic forms of counselling argue that counsellors would be wise to vary their style of therapeutic interaction to meet the special requirements of individual clients (Lazarus,

1981; Beutler, 1983). While this is a scantily researched area in rational-emotive counselling, it may be best for RET counsellors to avoid an overly friendly, emotionally charged style of interaction with 'hysterical' clients; an overly intellectual style with 'obsessive-compulsive' clients; an overly directive style with clients whose sense of autonomy is easily threatened (Beutler, 1983); and an overly active style with clients who easily retreat into passivity. This line of reasoning fits well with the notion of flexibility which rational-emotive counsellors advocate as a desirable therapeutic quality. Varying one's therapeutic style in rational-emotive counselling does not mean departing from the theoretical principles on which the content of this approach to counselling is based. As Eschenroeder (1979, p. 3) points out, in rational-emotive counselling 'there is no one-to-one relationship between theory and practice'.

Finally, the nature of the relationship between counsellor and client often changes during the course of rational-emotive counselling, particularly with respect to the activity of the counsellor. At the outset the client usually does not have much insight into rational concepts and as such the counsellor usually is quite active in helping the client to understand these concepts. Once the client has understood the concepts and has begun to put them into practice the counsellor is usually less active and strives to remind the client of what she already knows whilst encouraging her to work continually to translate this knowledge into practice. At this later stage, the counsellor is usually less active than at the beginning of the counselling process.

Relationship between theory and choice of techniques

Since RET theory ascribes a place of central importance to irrational beliefs in producing and maintaining psychological disturbance, it logically follows that rational-emotive counsellors devote much of their therapeutic attention to helping clients surrender their upset-provoking shoulds, musts and ought tos. Their choice of strategies and techniques for accomplishing this end, however, is guided by a number of important rational-emotive principles.

Role of force and energy in therapeutic change

Rational-emotive theory posits that the human tendency to think irrationally has a biological basis. This perspective can assist RET counsellors in being mindful of the ease with which their clients create irrational beliefs, as well as the tenacity with which they often cling to them; it also suggests that counsellors may have to employ considerable force and energy within sessions in order to accomplish effective disputing. Ellis (1979d) advocates the use of force and energy as a therapeutic tool for effecting cognitive restructuring, and engages in a number of verbal behaviours in his own sessions with clients that can be considered characteristic of the manner in which he translates these terms into actual clinical practice. These behaviours include his (judicious) use of profanity, his repetition of rational messages, his persistence in disputing particular irrational beliefs that his clients hold, and his directive and confrontational stance (Yankura and Dryden, 1990). Over the course of treatment counsellors can communicate to clients the rationale and means for using force and energy to dispute their irrational beliefs, such that they become more effective at conducting disputation on an independent basis.

Multimodal emphasis

As noted in Chapter 1, RET theory adheres to the principle of psychological interactionism in so far as it acknowledges that cognition, emotion and behaviour are overlapping and interacting processes. As these three dimensions of human functioning influence each other to a significant degree, it makes sense for rational–emotive counsellors to utilise as many channels of intervention as practical in the service of helping clients to modify their self-defeating belief systems. Thus, they will not restrict themselves to using only cognitive disputing (as RET's critics sometimes inaccurately charge), and will employ a variety of cognitive, emotive–evocative, imaginal and behavioural techniques in order to approach the above goal. In this sense they agree with Lazarus' (1981) multimodal approach to therapy, which holds that the effectiveness of treatment can be significantly increased by attacking problem areas on a number of therapeutic fronts. In addition, RET counsellors are generally not averse to referring clients for medication when it appears that psychopharmacological intervention will increase their capacity to benefit from the counselling process.

Selective eclecticism

With its multimodal emphasis, RET encourages counsellors to utilise a wide range of therapeutic techniques and strategies, including some which have been originated within other, divergent schools of therapy. Rational–emotive counsellors do not subscribe to the theories of psychological disturbance which underpin these alternative approaches to therapy, however, and borrow techniques from them in order to assist clients in the process of identifying, challenging and replacing their irrational beliefs.

RET theory provides counsellors with guidelines that they can use when choosing therapeutic interventions. As pointed out in the earlier discussion of counsellor warmth, RET de-emphasises the use of interventions that may unintentionally serve to reinforce clients' irrational ideologies. Catharsis and abreaction techniques can also be considered to fall into this category, as they may actually help clients to practise and subscribe ever more strongly to their anger-producing philosophies (Ellis, 1982c).

In addition, rational–emotive counsellors will generally avoid using techniques that might serve to sidetrack clients from focusing their efforts on modifying their irrational belief system. Relaxation techniques, for instance, may help clients to attain some degree of relief from their emotional upsets; if clients utilise them to the point of excluding direct cognitive change methods, however, they may never address their self-defeating personal philosophies. In such an instance they will probably derive limited benefits from counselling, as their disturbance-producing irrational beliefs remain largely unchallenged. RET counsellors, then, attempt to practice a theoretically consistent approach to eclecticism (Dryden, 1987).

Utilisation of homework assignments

Counsellors and clients typically meet for a single 1-hour session per week. If this single hour comprises all of the time devoted to achieving therapeutic goals, counselling will probably proceed in a very gradual fashion. In order to increase the efficiency and effectiveness of treatment, counsellors from a number of different therapeutic schools (particularly those practising behavioural and cognitive–behavioural approaches) will encourage their clients to undertake extra-therapy activities between sessions.

Such activities, usually referred to as homework assignments, are viewed as particularly important within RET. Given the difficulty that human beings typically experience as they attempt to adopt more rational personal philosophies, RET theory holds that it is desirable for counselling clients to commit themselves to considerable work and practice in the service of this end. When clients in counselling devote effort to identifying and disputing their irrational beliefs on an independent basis, they will probably fare better (in terms of avoiding or dealing with new upsets) after their counselling has ended. Ellis (1983d) and Persons, Burns and Perloff (1988), in fact, have reported empirical data which suggest that clients who undertake homework assignments within cognitively oriented approaches to treatment achieve better outcomes than those who do not. Thus, rational–emotive counsellors place considerable value on homework assignments due to their recognition that irrational beliefs are difficult to modify, and that it is desirable for clients to become able to function independently without interminable assistance from a mental health professional.

In order to increase the probability that homework assignments will be enacted between sessions, RET counsellors attempt to convey a rationale for carrying them out and will work collaboratively with clients to negotiate their design. At the earlier stages of treatment, counsellors will generally take a more active and directive role with respect to promoting and designing homework assignments; as counselling proceeds, however, this responsibility is ideally transferred to the client. Throughout treatment, counsellors will assist clients in conducting troubleshooting when difficulty is experienced in implementing particular homework assignments.

Personal qualities of effective rational–emotive counsellors

Unfortunately, no research studies have been carried out to determine the personal qualities of effective rational–emotive counsellors. Rational-emotive theory, however, does put forward several hypotheses concerning this topic (Ellis, 1978), but it is important to regard these as both tentative and awaiting empirical study.

1. Since rational-emotive counselling is fairly structured, its effective practitioners are usually comfortable with structure but flexible enough to work in a less structured manner when the situation arises.
2. Rational-emotive counsellors tend to be intellectually, cognitively or philosophically inclined and become attracted to this approach to counselling because the approach provides them with opportunities to fully express this tendency.
3. Since rational-emotive counselling is often conducted in a strong active-directive manner, its effective practitioners are usually comfortable operating in this mode. Neverthless, they have the flexibility to modify their interpersonal style with clients so that they provide the optimum conditions to facilitate client change.
4. Rational-emotive counselling emphasises that it is important for clients to put their counselling-derived insights into practice in their everyday lives. As a result, effective rational-emotive practitioners are usually comfortable with behavioural instruction and teaching, and with providing the active prompting that clients often require if they are to follow through on 'homework' assignments.
5. Effective rational-emotive counsellors tend to have little fear of failure themselves. Their personal worth is not invested in their clients' improvement. They do not need their clients' love and/or approval and are thus not afraid of taking calculated risks if therapeutic impasses occur. They tend to accept both themselves and their clients as fallible human beings and are therefore tolerant of their own mistakes and the irresponsible acts of their clients. They tend to have, or persistently work towards acquiring, a philosophy of high frustration tolerance, and do not get discouraged when clients improve at a slower rate than they desire.
6. Thus effective rational-emotive practitioners tend to score highly on most of the criteria of positive mental health outlined in Chapter 3, and serve as healthy role models for their clients.
7. Rational-emotive counselling strives to be scientific, empirical, anti-absolutist and undevout in its approach to helping people overcome the obstacles to their goals (Ellis, 1978). Thus its effective practitioners tend

to show similar traits and are definitely not mystical, anti-intellectual or magical in their beliefs.

8. Rational–emotive counselling advocates the use of techniques in a number of different modalities: cognitive, imagery, emotive, behavioural and interpersonal. Its effective practitioners are thus comfortable with a multi-modal approach to treatment and tend not to be people who like to stick rigidly to any one modality.

Finally, Ellis notes that some practitioners of rational–emotive counselling often modify its preferred practice according to their own natural personality characteristics (Ellis, 1978). Thus, for example, some helpers practise rational–emotive counselling in a slow-moving passive manner, do little disputing, and focus counselling on the relationship between them and their clients. Whether such modification of the preferred practice of rational–emotive counselling is effective is a question awaiting systematic empirical enquiry.

In the following three chapters we outline the practice of rational–emotive counselling according to the following sequence: induction and assessment – promoting intellectual insight – promoting emotional insight – termination. For the sake of clarity, we will assume in these chapters that the client is seeking counselling help for one major psychological problem. Then, in Chapter 9, we illustrate the application of RET to an actual client problem by presenting the rational–emotive counselling sequence.

Chapter 6
Beginning Rational–
Emotive Counselling

Overview

In this chapter, we deal with the beginnings of the rational–emotive counselling process. We have assumed that counsellors will, at some point during the beginning phase of rational–emotive counselling, assess clients' suitability for this type of counselling and have deemed it to be a suitable mode of helping for them (see *Introduction* for a discussion of this issue). First, we discuss how clients can be inducted into RET counselling. Then we cover the basic elements and sequence of rational–emotive assessment of clients' emotional and behavioural problems. We conclude the chapter by outlining some assessment methods that are particularly vivid in nature.

Inducting Clients into RET Counselling

When clients seek help from rational–emotive counsellors they vary concerning how much they already know about the type of therapeutic process they are likely to encounter. Some may approach the counsellor because they know he or she is a practitioner of RET, while others may know nothing about this method of counselling. In any event, many rational–emotive counsellors consider that it is beneficial to explore clients' expectations for counselling at the outset of the process. Duckro, Beal and George (1979) have argued that it is important to distinguish between preferences and anticipations when expectations are assessed. Clients' preferences for counselling concern what kind of experience they want, while anticipations concern what service they think they will receive. Clients who have realistic anticipations for the rational–emotive counselling process and have a preference for this process, in general require far less induction into rational–emotive counselling than clients who have unrealistic anticipations of the process and/or preferences for a different type of therapeutic experience.

Induction procedures, in general, involve showing clients that rational–emotive counselling is an active-directive structured approach which is orientated to discussion about clients' present and future problems, and which requires clients to play an active role in the change process. Induction can take a number of different forms. First, counsellors may develop and use a number of precounselling role induction procedures where a typical course of rational–emotive counselling is outlined and productive client behaviours are demonstrated (Macaskill and Macaskill, 1983). Secondly, counsellors may give a short lecture at the outset of counselling concerning the nature and process of rational–emotive counselling. Thirdly, counsellors may employ induction-related explanations in initial counselling sessions using client problem material to illustrate how these problems may be tackled and to outline the respective roles of client and counsellor in rational–emotive counselling.

Albert Ellis, in his therapeutic practice, tends not to initiate any special induction procedures before he focuses on one of his client's major psychological problems. He is prepared to correct any misconceptions about rational–emotive counselling when it becomes clear, through problem-focused dialogue, that his client holds these. His clientèle tend to be relatively psychologically sophisticated and thus may not require elaborate induction into rational–emotive counselling. Howard Young (1984a), on the other hand, found through his work with lower-class clients of Huntington, West Virginia, USA, that specific induction procedures facilitated later problem-focused counselling. His clientèle would often demand services outside the scope of rational–emotive counselling and he developed a specific sequence for teaching clients the ground rules of counselling to obviate misunderstanding and future disappointment.

Young's sequence was as follows:

1. *Use a biographical data sheet* on which clients can state (amongst other things) the problems that bring them to counselling. This provides counsellors with a good idea concerning what given clients view as appropriate problems for counselling intervention.
2. *Ask the client what he or she expects from counselling.* This direct approach sometimes reveals startling misconceptions. For example, some of Young's clients gave answers ranging from 'a prescription for nerve pills' to 'the removal of warts'. The replies which clients give to this question often provide clear indications concerning how much induction-orientated education they will require before assessment is initiated. While Young (1984a) does not distinguish between anticipation- and preference-based expectations, it is often helpful to assess both at this phase of induction.
3. *Offer an example.* When it was clear that the client did require education about the counselling process, Young would offer a concrete example, often derived from work with another client and usually tailored to what he believed his client's own problem might be. Young

(1984a, p. 41) provides the following as an illustration: 'Yesterday, a woman came in to see me because she felt depressed – as if life no longer mattered. It seems all her children are grown, her husband works all the time, and she no longer feels needed. I'm helping her figure out how to cope with the situation'.

4. *Advise the client that counselling is primarily a thinking endeavour.* Young found that teaching his lower-class clients that counselling could help them to 'look at problems in another light' helped to counteract their tendency to want to forget or ignore their problems. At this point, we find it helpful to add that thinking about things differently can often help one not only to feel differently but also to deal with life more constructively, i.e. we emphasise that rational–emotive counselling is not just about thinking, but also about feeling and acting.

5. *Use a client-understood analogy.* At this point, Young would offer an analogy with which his clients could identify to reinforce other explanations about what takes place in counselling. We often tell our clients that going to see a rational-emotive counsellor is like going to see a golf professional, as in the following dialogue:

Counsellor: Imagine that many years ago your uncle taught you how to play golf, but taught you badly. Also imagine that you practised diligently the wrong strokes and only realised later that this way of playing was not helping you to lower your scores. If you wanted to improve your game who would you consult?

Client: A golf coach.

Counsellor: What kind of help would you hope to get from him or her?

Client: Well I would hope he would be able to diagnose my errors, point them out to me and show me how to put these right.

Counsellor: Right. And after he had shown you the correct strokes would that be sufficient for you to improve?

Client: No.

Counsellor: What more would be needed?

Client: I'd have to practise to learn the correct strokes.

Counsellor: Right, in order for them to become second nature you would have to practise. Now coming to see me is like going to see that golf pro. My skills are in helping you to diagnose where you've been going wrong psychologically and how to put this right. But just like a golf pro I can't practise for you. Your major task is putting into practice in your daily life what you learn in counselling. Now that process won't go smoothly, just as it won't in golf, and I'll be on hand to help you through the problems of practising. In doing so you'll begin to learn how to diagnose and correct any future psychological problems you may have. But just like in golf where no one player consistently plays perfect golf, you won't become perfectly free from these problems but you'll be able to deal with them.

It should be stressed that analogies are best tailored to the clients' interests. In this respect, it is often helpful to ask questions on biographical data forms about clients' hobbies and interests so that such specially tailored explanatory analogies can be best grasped by the client.

6. *Help the client understand what counselling cannot provide.* Young used to tell his clients that it is unlikely that counselling will cure all their problems such that they can live happily ever after. He also pointed out that 'sometimes therapy makes it easier to bear the problem that cannot be solved. Sometimes I explain it in terms of therapy helping one choose the lesser of two evils and learning to live with the results. It is important that therapy be explained to lower-class clients in this way, as in many cases the solution to their problems involves choosing between negative alternatives' (Young, 1984a, p. 41)

Rational–emotive counsellors generally make the distinction between practical problems (e.g. poor housing, financial problems, etc.) and psychological problems (e.g. depression, anxiety, procrastination), and stress that rational–emotive counselling aims to help people with their psychological problems. While it may encourage people to take productive steps to improve their housing conditions and financial situation by helping them overcome their psychological problems about such practical problems, it cannot directly alleviate the latter.

Finally, when working with individuals it is helpful to stress that rational–emotive counselling cannot directly change other people who are not involved in the counselling process. However, it can help the client try to influence or persuade others to change, if that is deemed to be productive. For example, one client came for help with changing her boss, who was sexually harassing her. She was first helped to overcome her destructive anger towards him and then assisted in reviewing the relative merits of her behavioural options, most of which centred on influencing the boss to change. None of the options she tried worked in the desired manner and she decided to leave her job, very pleased with the help she received. The important point here is that early on in counselling she was helped to distinguish between what she could change (her behaviour) and what she could not change (his behaviour).

The principle here is that as rational–emotive counsellors working with individuals, you can only help clients change what is in their power to change – *their* thoughts, feelings and actions. If bad events remain unchanged in their lives, clients do have a choice concerning how to view these events. Under such conditions counsellors can help the client to be merely sorry and disappointed about such events (i.e. by thinking rationally about them and experiencing rational negative emotions) rather than miserable about them (by thinking irrationally about them and experiencing irrational negative emotions).

In conclusion, as a final point about induction, we have often found it helpful to encourage clients to commit themselves to a 'trial' of rational-emotive counselling of about five sessions so that they can learn first-hand whether or not this approach to counselling will be helpful to them. In our experience, clients who agree to this arrangement will often become engaged in the counselling process such that they continue in treatment beyond their five-session trial.

Assessment in Rational–Emotive Counselling

As has been mentioned, some RET counsellors like to have their clients fill in a form which provides basic biographical information as well as information concerning their presenting problems. In Figure 6.1 the biographical information form routinely employed by counsellors at the Institute for RET in New York is presented as a representative example of such forms.

In addition, counsellors at the Institute routinely ask clients to fill out a Personality Data Form (Figure 6.2) which provides the counsellor with information concerning the irrational beliefs which are likely to underpin the client's problems. However, the use of this form is designed to supplement rather than to replace a thorough assessment of the client's problems.

Most RET counsellors like to structure the therapeutic process at the outset in order to emphasise that therapy will be problem-focused. For example, such questions as, 'What are you bothered most about?' and 'What is your major problem at this time?' are employed to encourage clients to adopt a problem-solving focus. Indeed, Albert Ellis routinely reads aloud the information provided by the client on Item 23 of the biographical information form and asks him or her to start talking about what is most bothersome among this list of problems.

Before proceeding to the assessment stage of counselling the RET practitioner often seeks an agreement with the client concerning the first problem to tackle. When this has been achieved the therapist proceeds to help the client to understand his or her problems according to rational–emotive counselling's ABC framework, where 'A' stands for an activating event or inferences about the activating event; 'B' stands for beliefs about the actual or inferred event; and 'C' stands for the emotional and behavioural consequences of holding the belief at 'B'.

Assessment: basic elements

Because RET counselling is strongly cognitive, emotive and behavioural, it not only assesses clients' irrational beliefs, but also their irrational feelings and self-defeating behaviours. The usual rational–emotive assessment process almost always includes the following:

1. Clients are helped to acknowledge and describe their irrational negative feelings – anxiety, depression, damning anger and self-hatred, and these

Date _____   Name _____

    mo.   day   yr.   (last)   (first)   (middle)

Consultation Center

Institute for Rational-Emotive Therapy

45 East 65th Street • New York, N. Y. 10021

Biographical Information Form

Instructions To assist us in helping you, please fill out this form as frankly as you can. You will save much time and effort by giving us full information. You can be sure that, like everything you say at the Institute, the facts on this form will be held in the strictest confidence and that no outsider will be permitted to see your case record without your written permission. PLEASE TYPE OR PRINT YOUR ANSWERS.

1. Date of birth: _____ Age: _____   Sex: M_____   F_____

                  mo.   day   yr.

2. Address: _____

               street   city   state   zip

3. Home phone: _____ Business phone: _____

4. Permanent address **(if different from above)** _____

_____

5. Who referred you to the Institute? **(check one)**

    _____(1) self   _____(2) school or teacher   _____(3) psychologist or psychiatrist   _____(4) social agency   _____(5) hospital or clinic   _____(6) family doctor   _____(7) friend   _____(8) relative   _____(9) other (explain) _____

    Has this party been here?   _____Yes   _____No

6. Present marital status:

    _____(1) never married   _____(2) married now for first time   _____(3) married now for second (or more) time

    _____(4) separated   _____(5) divorced and not remarried   _____(6) widowed and not remarried

    Number of years married to present spouse .... Ages of male children .... Ages of female children ....

7. Years of formal education completed (circle number of years):

    1 2 3 4 5 6 7 8 9 10 11 12 13 14 15 16 17 18 19 20   more than 20

8. How religious are you? **(circle number on scale that best approximates your degree of religiosity):**

        very   average   atheist

        1 2 3 4 5 6 7 8 9

9. Mother's age: _____If deceased, how old were you when she died? _____

10. Father's age: _____If deceased, how old were you when he died? _____

11. If your mother and father separated, how old were you at the time? _____

12. If your mother and father divorced, how old were you at the time? _____

13. Total number of times mother divorced _____   Number of times father divorced _____

14. Number of living brothers _____   Number of living sisters _____

Figure 6.1 Biographical information form. (Reproduced with the permission of the Institute for Rational-Emotive Therapy. © Institute for RET, 1968.)

15. Ages of living brothers _____   Ages of living sisters _____

16. I was child number _____ in a family of _____ children.

17. Were you adopted?   _____Yes   _____No

18. What kind of treatment have you previously had for emotional problems?

    _____ hours of individual therapy, spread over _____ years, ending _____ years ago.

19. Hours of group therapy _____   Months of psychiatric hospitalization _____

20. Are you undergoing treatment anywhere else now? _____Yes   _____No

21. Number of times during past year you have taken antidepressants _____

22. Type of psychotherapy you have mainly had (briefly describe method of treatment—ex., dream analysis, free association,

    drugs, hypnosis, etc.) _____

    _____

23. Briefly list (PRINT) your present main complaints, symptoms, and problems:_____

    _____

    _____

    _____

24. Briefly list any additional past complaints, symptoms, and problems: _____

    _____

    _____

25. Under what conditions are your problems worse? _____

    _____

    _____

26. Under what conditions are they improved?_____

    _____

    _____

27. List the things you like to do most, the kinds of things and persons that give you pleasure:_____

    _____

    _____

28. List your main assets and good points: _____

    _____

    _____

Figure 6.1   (continued)

29. List your main bad points: _____

_____

_____

_____

30. List your main **social** difficulties: _____

_____

_____

31. List your main **love and sex** difficulties: _____

_____

_____

32. List your main **school or work** difficulties: _____

_____

_____

33. List your main life goals: _____

_____

_____

34. List the things about yourself you would most like to change: _____

_____

_____

35. List your chief physical ailments, diseases, complaints, or handicaps: _____

_____

_____

36. What occupation(s) have you mainly been trained for? _____

Present occupation _____ ____Full time ____Part time

37. Spouse's occupation _____ ____Full time ____Part time

38. Mother's occupation _____ Father's occupation _____

39. Mother's religion _____ Father's religion _____

40. If your mother and father did not raise you when you were young, who did? _____

Figure 6.1   (continued)

41. Briefly describe the type of person your mother (or stepmother or person who substituted for your mother) was when you were a child and how you got along with her: _____ _____

_____

_____

42. Briefly describe the type of person your father (or stepfather or father substitute) was when you were a child and how you got along with him: _____

_____

_____

43. If there were unusually disturbing features in your relationship to any of your brothers, briefly describe:_____

_____

_____

44. If there were unusually disturbing features in your relationship to any of your sisters, briefly describe: _____

_____

_____

45. Number of close male relatives who have been seriously emotionally disturbed: _____ Number that have been hospitalized for psychiatric treatment, or have attempted suicide: _____ Number of close female relatives who have been seriously emotionally disturbed: _____ Number that have been hospitalized for psychiatric treatment. or have attempted suicide: _____

46. Additional information that you think might be helpful

_____

_____

_____

_____

_____

_____

_____

_____

_____

_____

_____

Figure 6.1 (continued)

Consultation Center

Institute for Advanced Study in Rational Psychotherapy

45 East 65th Street   •   New York, N. Y. 10021

Personality Data Form — Part 2

Instructions: Read each of the following items and circle after each one the word STRONGLY, MODERATELY, or WEAKLY to indicate how much you believe in the statement described in the item. Thus, if you strongly believe that it is awful to make a mistake when other people are watching, circle the word STRONGLY in item 1; and if you weakly believe that it is intolerable to be disapproved by others, circle the word WEAKLY in item 2. DO NOT SKIP ANY ITEMS. Be as honest as you can possibly be.

Acceptance

1.	I believe that it is awful to make a mistake when other people are watching	STRONGLY	MODERATELY	WEAKLY
2.	I believe that it is intolerable to be disapproved of by others	STRONGLY	MODERATELY	WEAKLY
3.	I believe that it is awful for people to know certain undesirable things about one's family or one's background	STRONGLY	MODERATELY	WEAKLY
4.	I believe that it is shameful to be looked down upon by people for having less than they have	STRONGLY	MODERATELY	WEAKLY
5.	I believe that it is horrible to be the center of attention of others who may be highly critical	STRONGLY	MODERATELY	WEAKLY
6.	I believe it is terribly painful when one is criticized by a person one respects	STRONGLY	MODERATELY	WEAKLY
7.	I believe that it is awful to have people disapprove of the way one looks or dresses	STRONGLY	MODERATELY	WEAKLY
8.	I believe that it is very embarrassing if people discover what one really is like	STRONGLY	MODERATELY	WEAKLY
9.	I believe that it is awful to be alone	STRONGLY	MODERATELY	WEAKLY

Figure 6.2 Personality data form (Ellis, 1968). (Reproduced with the permission of the Institute for Rational-Emotive Therapy. © Institute for RET, 1968.)

10. I believe that it is horrible if one does not have the love or approval of certain special people who are important to one　　STRONGLY　MODERATELY　WEAKLY

11. I believe that one must have others on whom one can always depend for help　　STRONGLY　MODERATELY　WEAKLY

Frustration

12. I believe that it is intolerable to have things go along slowly and not be settled quickly　　STRONGLY　MODERATELY　WEAKLY

13. I believe that it's too hard to get down to work at things it often would be better for one to do　　STRONGLY　MODERATELY　WEAKLY

14. I believe that it is terrible that life is so full of inconveniences and frustrations　　STRONGLY　MODERATELY　WEAKLY

15. I believe that people who keep one waiting frequently are pretty worthless and deserve to be boycotted　　STRONGLY　MODERATELY　WEAKLY

16. I believe that it is terrible if one lacks desirable traits that other people possess　　STRONGLY　MODERATELY　WEAKLY

17. I believe that it is intolerable when other people do not do one's bidding or give one what one wants　　STRONGLY　MODERATELY　WEAKLY

18. I believe that some people are unbearably stupid or nasty and that one must get them to change　　STRONGLY　MODERATELY　WEAKLY

19. I believe that it is too hard for one to accept serious responsibility　　STRONGLY　MODERATELY　WEAKLY

20. I believe that it is dreadful that one cannot get what one wants without making a real effort to get it　　STRONGLY　MODERATELY　WEAKLY

21. I believe that things are too rough in this world and that therefore it is legitimate for one to feel sorry for oneself　　STRONGLY　MODERATELY　WEAKLY

22. I believe that it is too hard to persist at many of the things one starts, especially when the going gets rough　　STRONGLY　MODERATELY　WEAKLY

23. I believe it is terrible that life is so unexciting and boring　　STRONGLY　MODERATELY　WEAKLY

24. I believe it is awful for one to have to discipline oneself　　STRONGLY　MODERATELY　WEAKLY

Figure 6.2 (continued)

Injustice

25. I believe that people who do wrong things should suffer strong revenge for their acts   STRONGLY   MODERATELY   WEAKLY

26. I believe that wrong doers and immoral people should be severely condemned   STRONGLY   MODERATELY   WEAKLY

27. I believe that people who commit unjust acts are bastards and that they should be severely punished   STRONGLY   MODERATELY   WEAKLY

Achievement

28. I believe that it is horrible for one to perform poorly   STRONGLY   MODERATELY   WEAKLY

29. I believe that it is awful if one fails at important things   STRONGLY   MODERATELY   WEAKLY

30. I believe that it is terrible for one to make a mistake when one has to make important decisions   STRONGLY   MODERATELY   WEAKLY

31. I believe that it is terrifying for one to take risks or to try new things   STRONGLY   MODERATELY   WEAKLY

Worth

32. I believe that some of one's thoughts or actions are unforgivable   STRONGLY   MODERATELY   WEAKLY

33. I believe that if one keeps failing at things one is a pretty worthless person   STRONGLY   MODERATELY   WEAKLY

34. I believe that killing oneself is preferable to a miserable life of failure   STRONGLY   MODERATELY   WEAKLY

35. I believe that things are so ghastly that one cannot help feel like crying much of the time   STRONGLY   MODERATELY   WEAKLY

36. I believe that it is frightfully hard for one to stand up for oneself and not give in too easily to others   STRONGLY   MODERATELY   WEAKLY

37. I believe that when one has shown poor personality traits for a long time, it is hopeless for one to change   STRONGLY   MODERATELY   WEAKLY

38. I believe that if one does not usually see things clearly and act well on them, one is hopelessly stupid   STRONGLY   MODERATELY   WEAKLY

39. I believe that it is awful to have no good meaning or purpose in life   STRONGLY   MODERATELY   WEAKLY

Figure 6.2 (continued)

Control

40. I believe that one cannot enjoy himself today because of his poor early life — STRONGLY — MODERATELY — WEAKLY

41. I believe that if one kept failing at important things in the past, one must inevitably keep failing in the future — STRONGLY — MODERATELY — WEAKLY

42. I believe that once one's parents train one to act and feel in certain ways, there is little one can do to act or feel better — STRONGLY — MODERATELY — WEAKLY

43. I believe that strong emotions like anxiety and rage are caused by external conditions and events and that one has little or no control over them — STRONGLY — MODERATELY — WEAKLY

Certainty

44. I believe it would be terrible if there were no higher being or purpose on which to rely — STRONGLY — MODERATELY — WEAKLY

45. I believe that if one does not keep doing certain things over and over again something bad will happen if one stops — STRONGLY — MODERATELY — WEAKLY

46. I believe that things must be in good order for one to be comfortable — STRONGLY — MODERATELY — WEAKLY

Catastrophizing

47. I believe that it is awful if one's future is not guaranteed — STRONGLY — MODERATELY — WEAKLY

48. I believe that it is frightening that there are no guarantees that accidents and serious illnesses will not occur — STRONGLY — MODERATELY — WEAKLY

49. I believe that it is terrifying for one to go to new places or meet a new group of people — STRONGLY — MODERATELY — WEAKLY

50. I believe that it is ghastly for one to be faced with the possibility of dying — STRONGLY — MODERATELY — WEAKLY

Figure 6.2 (continued)

are clearly differentiated from their rational negative feelings – concern, sadness, annoyance (or non-damning anger) and disappointment. In doing so, RET counsellors frequently teach clients the rational–emotive language of emotions and help them to distinguish between rational and irrational negative emotions by helping them to identify and distinguish between rational and irrational beliefs.

2. Clients are helped to acknowledge and delineate their self-defeating behaviours (e.g. compulsions, addictions, phobias and procrastination) rather than to overemphasise idiosyncratic but non-deleterious behaviours (e.g. unusual devotion to socialising, sex, study or work).

3. They are asked to point out specific activating events in their lives that tend to occur just prior to their experienced disturbed feelings and behaviours.

4. Their rational beliefs that accompany their activating events, and that lead to constructive emotive and behavioural consequences, are assessed and discussed.

5. Their irrational beliefs that accompany their activating events and that lead to disturbed emotive and behavioural consequences are assessed and discussed.

6. Their irrational beliefs that involve absolutistic musts and grandiose demands on themselves, others, and the universe are particularly determined.

7. Their second-level irrational beliefs that tend to be derived from their absolutistic shoulds and musts – e.g. their 'awfulising', their 'I can't-stand-it-itis', and their 'damning' of themselves and others – are also revealed.

8. Their irrational beliefs that lead to their disturbance about their disturbance – e.g. their anxiety about their anxiety and their depression about being depressed – are particularly revealed and discussed.

As these specialised components of RET assessment are instituted, specific treatment plans are made, normally in close collaboration with clients, to work first on the most important and self-sabotaging emotional and behavioural symptoms that they present, and later on related and possibly less important symptoms. Rational–emotive counsellors, however, always try to maintain an exceptionally open-minded, sceptical and experimental attitude towards clients and their problems, so that what at first seems to be their crucial and most debilitating ideas, feelings and actions may later be seen in a different light and the emphasis may be changed to working on other equally or more pernicious irrationalities that might not be evident during the early sessions.

RET counsellors, in general, spend little time gathering background information on their clients, although they may ask them to fill out forms designed to assess which irrational ideas they spontaneously endorse at the outset of counselling (Figure 6.2). Rather, they are likely to ask clients for a description of their major problem(s). As clients describe their problems, RET counsellors intervene fairly early to break these down into their ABC components.

Assessment: basic sequence

In RET, A and C are normally assessed before B, and are usually assessed in the order that the client reports. When A is assessed, RET counsellors usually encourage clients to provide a representative concrete example of the events, actual or inferred, that they are disturbed about. Clients are encouraged to be as specific as they can about A and not to go into unnecessary detail about the event. Clients sometimes jump from event to event or give unnecessary historical material relating to the event at hand. When this happens the counsellor should preferably interrupt them tact-fully and bring them back to the original A, or the A which they now see as most relevant.

C refers to both the emotional and behavioural consequences of the rational and irrational beliefs that are operative at B. Careful assessment of emotional Cs is advocated in RET, since they serve as a major indicator of what type of evaluations are to be found at B. In this regard, it is important to reiterate that 'rational' negative emotions are different from 'irrational' negative emotions (as discussed in Chapter 4). To review: emotions such as sadness, regret, annoyance and concern are termed 'rational' in RET, in that they are deemed to stem from rational, preferential beliefs at B and encour-age people to attempt to change, for the better, obnoxious situations at A. The 'irrational' versions of the above emotional states are depression, guilt, anger and anxiety. These are deemed to stem from irrational, *must*urbatory beliefs at B, and tend to interfere with people's constructive attempts to change undesirable situations.

When emotional Cs are being assessed, it is important to bear in mind the following points. First, clients do not necessarily use affective terminology in the same way as RET counsellors do (as shown in Chapter 4). It is often helpful to inform them about the nature of the unique discriminations made between 'rational' and 'irrational' negative emotional states, so that coun-sellor and client can come to use a shared emotional 'language'.

Secondly, emotional Cs are often chained together. For example, anger is frequently chained to anxiety in that one can experience anger to cover up feelings of inadequacy. And one can feel depressed after a threat to one's self-esteem – the 'anxiety–depression' chain (Wessler, 1981).

Thirdly, rational-emotive counsellors are advised to realise that clients do not always want to change every 'irrational' negative emotion as defined by rational-emotive theory; i.e. they may not see a particular 'irrational' emotion such as anger as being truly self-defeating. Thus, a good deal of flexibility and clinical acumen is called for in the assessment of emotional Cs to be targeted for change.

Fourthly, clients sometimes find it difficult to admit to themselves and/or to their counsellors that they experience certain emotions. This may be due to their belief that they are not supposed to have such feelings and/or that they are worthless for having them. In other words, such clients have second-order problems about their original feelings. If counsellors suspect that this is the case, they can ask the clients how they would feel if they did experience the emotion in question, thus switching their assessment strategy to the second-order problem.

Fifthly, clients often become emotional in counselling sessions and when this happens, counsellors have a good opportunity to assess the beliefs that underpin these expressions of affect as they occur. Thus counsellors may ask clients a question such as the following: 'I see that you're feeling upset. What are you telling yourself *right now* to bring on that upset?'

Sixthly, as mentioned in Chapter 4, emotions can sometimes be blended rather than pure. Thus clients talk about feeling 'hurt anger' or a 'guilty depression'. In such cases counsellors can either treat the blended emotion (e.g. 'hurt anger') as C, or separate it into its component parts – hurt and anger – and deal with each accordingly.

Finally, as we also mentioned in Chapter 4, clients' 'emotional problems' at C can be 'false', i.e. not germane to their real problems. It is difficult to determine this immediately in the assessment process and counsellors are urged to keep this in mind as a possibility and to ask themselves whether such emotions may mask serious problems. For example, one particular client complained of feeling depressed about her marriage. Assessment proceeded in the normal way, but the client was not really involved in the process. She was then asked, 'If you didn't feel depressed what would you feel?' She was taken aback and got quite scared in the session. It transpired that what she called 'depression' was really a numbness that served to protect her from feelings of anxiety about coping on her own.

Although we have chosen to highlight the assessment of emotional Cs, similar points can be made about the assessment of behavioural Cs. As noted earlier, withdrawal, procrastination, alcoholism and substance abuse are generally regarded as dysfunctional behaviours and related to irrational beliefs at B (Ellis, 1982a). Counsellors can thus regard such behaviours as Cs in their own right and thence proceed to an assessment of irrational beliefs at B that underpin them. Another strategy that is often helpful is to remember that such behaviour can be purposive (see Chapter 2) and may serve to protect clients from an emotional experience (such as anxiety) or encourage clients to obtain an emotional experience (e.g. pleasant sensations associated with being 'stoned'). Taking the example of procrastination, which often serves to protect clients from an emotional experience: it is fruitful to view such behaviour as the actualisation of an action tendency (see Chapter 2). The client might be taught about action tendencies and the feelings that occasion them, and be asked to reflect on what possible feelings might have promoted such behaviour. Also, the client might be shown that such behaviour is only one of a number of response options available to her in the given situation that she describes. Enquiries might then be directed towards possible emotional Cs that might be experienced if a more productive response option were chosen. Thus the counsellor might say, 'If you decided to sit down to work on that essay rather than deciding to procrastinate, what might you have felt?'.

As a prelude to assessing B, some rational–emotive counsellors like to employ a procedure known as *inference chaining* (Moore, 1983; Dryden, 1991) in order to identify the particular aspect of A that serves to trigger clients' irrational beliefs, given that C is self-defeating. In conducting inference chaining, Moore (1983) advises that counsellors employ 'then what?' and 'why?' questions as a means of prompting clients to verbalise their inferences about problematic As. The following example illustrates how such questions were used to identify the specific inference that triggered a given client's irrational beliefs:

Client: So . . . I get very scared when I think about going to the supermarket.
Counsellor: What do you think you are scared of?
Client: I'm afraid I might start feeling faint while waiting in line to pay for my purchases. [Inference 1]
Counsellor: And if that happens, then what?
Client: Well . . . I'd panic!
Counsellor: Why?
Client: Because I might pass out. [Inference 2]
Counsellor: And if you did, then what?
Client: People would gather round me and think that I'm strange. [Inference 3]
Counsellor: And if they did?
Client: Oh, God! I just couldn't stand to have that happen!

In this example, 'then what?' questions are utilised to elicit further inferences in the chain. 'Why' questions are employed to prompt continued reporting of inferences when the client's reference to an emotional consequence ('. . . I'd panic!') threatens to derail the assessment process.

In our experience, clients sometimes appear to experience difficulty in responding to 'then what?' questions with further inferences. This potential difficulty can often be avoided or overcome by utilising assessment questions that are anchored to some variant of the client's target emotion (C):

Client: . . . I might pass out.
Counsellor: If you did, then what?
Client: Um . . . I'm not sure.
Counsellor: Well, what would be anxiety-provoking in your mind about that?
Client: Oh! People would gather round me and think that I'm strange.

It is noted that inference chaining may sometimes yield unexpected data of clinical importance, in terms of revealing additional Cs that were not clearly evident in a client's initial presentation of a problem. This type of outcome is illustrated below:

Counsellor: So, what was your major feeling here?
Client: I guess I was angry.
Counsellor: Angry about what? [The counsellor has obtained a particular C and is probing for A.]
Client: I was angry that my boyfriend didn't send me a birthday card. [Initial description of A]
Counsellor: And what was anger-provoking in your mind about that? [Probing to see if this is the most relevant aspect of A]
Client: Well . . . he promised me he would remember. He broke his promise! [Inference 1]
Counsellor: Okay – and what was anger-provoking about the fact that he broke his promise? [Probing for relevance of Inference 1]
Client: I felt that he didn't care enough about me. [Inference 2]
Counsellor: For the moment, let's assume that's true. What would be distressing about that? [Probing for relevance of Inference 2]
Client: He might leave me. [Inference 3]
Counsellor: And if he did, then what? [Probing for relevance of Inference 3]
Client: I'd be all alone [Inference 4]
Counsellor: And if you were alone? Then what? [Probing for relevance of Inference 4]
Client: Oh, that would be absolutely awful! I couldn't make it on my own!

In this example, the counsellor and client began the exchange with a focus upon the client's feeling of anger. Inference chaining, however, revealed an aspect of A ('I'd be all alone') likely to be related to some other emotional C (in this case, probably anxiety). The counsellor is thus presented with two potential foci in terms of treatment, and has to make a decision as to whether to deal with the client's feeling of anger toward her boyfriend, or her anxiety connected to the prospect of being alone. This decision can be facilitated by obtaining feedback from the client as to the inference that is most relevant in the chain:

Counsellor: Okay, let's back up a minute. What would be most distressing for you: the birthday card incident, the fact that your boyfriend doesn't care, being abandoned by your boyfriend, or being alone?
Client: Definitely being alone.

The above example also shows that, for the purposes of getting to B, the counsellor does not question the accuracy of the client's inferences, but treats them as if they are correct for the time being. In other dialogues clients may be encouraged to assume the worst about their inferences, so that again B can properly be assessed. Thus, with a client who is afraid to fly in an aeroplane because she assumes it might crash, the counsellor would not initially discuss with the client the relatively low probability of such an event ever occurring. Instead, the counsellor would encourage the client to assume (for the moment) that this event *will* occur. This leaves the way open for the client to express irrational beliefs about this eventuality or to express further inferences that might be more relevant to her anxiety. In one particular case, the client was scared not about flying but about surviving a crash as a paraplegic!

After the counsellor has assessed adequately the irrational C and the A, he can then begin to assess B. This is frequently done by asking such questions as: 'What were you telling yourself to make yourself angry?'; 'What did that experience mean to you?'; or even 'What *must* were you telling yourself about the possibility of failure?' The important point here is for counsellors to employ a variety of questions to elicit clients' irrational beliefs rather than repeating questions which have not yielded statements of irrational beliefs.

In Chapter 3, we mentioned that irrational beliefs occur in the form of a premise, e.g. 'I *must* pass my exam' and a derivative, e.g. 'I'm no good if I fail my exam'. The premise of irrational beliefs occurs in the form of absolute 'musts', 'shoulds', 'have-to's', etc., whereas irrational derivatives may represent examples of 'awfulising', 'I can't-stand-it-itis' or 'damnation'. When assessing irrational beliefs, we find it helpful, if possible, to assess both the premise and associated derivatives. While Ellis seems to prefer to target 'musts' as a priority for assessing irrational beliefs, he sometimes switches to an assessment of irrational derivatives when 'must assessment' is not productive.

When irrational beliefs are assessed clients are helped to see the link between these irrational beliefs and their 'irrational' affective and behavioural consequences at C. Some rational–emotive counsellors like to give a short lecture at this point on the role of the 'musts' in emotional disturbance, and how they can be distinguished from 'preferences'. Ellis, for example, often uses the following teaching dialogue:

Ellis: Imagine that you prefer to have a minimum of £11 in your pocket at all times and you discover you only have £10. How will you feel?

Client: Frustrated.

Ellis: Right. Or you'd feel concerned or sad, but you wouldn't kill yourself. Right?

Client: Right.

Ellis: OK. Now this time imagine that you absolutely *have to* have a minimum of £11 in your pocket at all times. You must have it, it is a necessity. You *must*, you *must*, you *must*, have a minimum of £11, and again you look and you find you only have £10. How will you feel?

Client: Very anxious.

Ellis: Right – or depressed. Right. Now remember it's the same £11 but a different belief. OK, now this time you still have that same belief. You *have to* have a minimum of £11 at all times, you *must*. It's absolutely *essential*. But this time you look in your pocket and find that you've got £12. How will you feel?

Client: Relieved, content.

Ellis: Right. But with that same belief - you *have to* have a minimum of £11 at all times – something will soon occur to you to scare you shitless. What do you think that would be?

Client: What if I lose £2?

Ellis: Right. What if I lose £2, what if I spend £2, what if I get robbed? That's right. Now the moral of this model – which applies to all humans, rich or poor, black or white, male or female, young or old, in the past or in the future, assuming that humans are still human – is: People make themselves miserable if they don't get what they think they must, but they are also panicked when they do – because of the must. For even if they have what they think they must, they could always lose it.

Client: So I have no chance to be happy when I don't have what I think I must – and little chance of remaining unanxious when I do have it?

Ellis: Right! Your *must*urbation will get you nowhere – except depressed or panicked!

We have stressed that an important goal of the assessment stage is to help clients distinguish between their primary problems (e.g. depression, anxiety, withdrawal, addiction) and their secondary problems, that is, their problems about their primary problems (e.g. depression about depression, anxiety about anxiety, shame about withdrawal, and guilt about addiction). Rational–emotive counsellors often assess secondary problems before primary problems because these often require prior therapeutic attention – since, for example, clients frequently find it difficult to focus on their original problem of anxiety when, for example, they are severely blaming themselves for being anxious. Secondary problems are assessed in the same manner as primary problems. If such second-order problems are identified it is important for the counsellor to help the client to understand why such problems are assessed and targeted for change *before* the client's primary problems. For example, a client may be shown that if she is guilty about her anger, she will be less successful at working on and overcoming her anger problem while she is guilty about it. However, there are occasions when clients will not accept this rationale despite the counsellor's explanations. A guiding rule under these conditions is for the counsellor to work at a level that the client will accept.

Three other points relevant to the assessment stage of RET bear mention. First, counsellors are advised to be alert to problems in *both* major areas of disturbance, i.e. ego and discomfort disturbance. In particular, ego and discomfort disturbance often interact and careful assessment is required to disentangle one from the other. Secondly, RET counsellors pay particular attention to other ways that humans perpetuate their psychological problems and attempt to assess these carefully in counselling. Thus, humans often seek to defend themselves from threats to their ego and sense of comfort. Counsellors are often aware that much dysfunctional behaviour is defensive and help their clients to identify the irrational beliefs that underlie such defensive dysfunctional behaviour. In addition, psychological problems are sometimes perpetuated because the person defines their consequences as payoffs. These payoffs also require careful assessment if productive therapeutic strategies are to be implemented. Finally, during the assessment process, counsellors are also concerned with correcting any misconceptions that clients may have about the therapeutic enterprise. As in induction procedures, counsellors endeavour to show their clients that RET counselling is a form of help that is problem-focused and educational in nature, and that counsellors will often adopt an active and directive approach. Counsellors also encourage clients to see that their initial task is to learn to focus on the cognitive determinants of their problems and, in particular, to learn to search for absolute musts and their derivatives when they are disturbed at C.

Vivid Assessment Methods

Effective rational–emotive counselling depends initially on the counsellor gaining a clear understanding of the client's problems in cognitive, emotional and behavioural terms, and the contexts in which the client's problems occur. To a great extent the counsellor is dependent on the client's verbal reports to help him gain such an understanding. It is in this area that many obstacles to progress may appear. Some clients have great difficulty identifying and/or accurately labelling their emotional experiences. Other clients are in touch with and able to report their emotions, but find it hard to relate these to activating events, either external or internal. Yet a further group of clients is easily able to report problematic activating events and emotional experiences, but has difficulty seeing how these may relate to mediating cognitions. Vivid methods, i.e. those that are rich, stimulating and arousing, can be used in a variety of ways to overcome such obstacles to a valid and reliable assessment of client problems.

Vividness in portraying activating events

With some clients traditional assessment procedures through verbal dialogue do not always yield the desired information. When this occurs, rational–emotive counsellors often use imagery. They ask clients to conjure up evocative images of activating events. Such evocative imagery often stimulates the client's memory concerning his or her emotional reactions, or indeed in some instances leads to the re-experiencing of these reactions in the session. While focusing on such images, the client can also begin to gain access to cognitive processes below the level of awareness that cannot be easily reached through verbal dialogue.

One particularly effective use of imagery in the assessment of client problems is that of bringing future events into the present. This is illustrated by the following exchange with a client who was terrified that her mother might die, which led her to be extremely unassertive with the mother.

Counsellor: So you feel you just can't speak up to her. Because if you did, what might happen?
Client: Well, she might have a fit.
Counsellor: And what might happen if she did?
Client: She might have a heart attack and die.
Counsellor: Well, we know that she is a fit woman, but let's go along with your fear for the moment. Okay?
Client: Okay.
Counsellor: What if she did die?
Client: I just can't think . . . I . . . I'm sorry.
Counsellor: That's okay. I know this is difficult, but I really think it would be helpful if we could get to the bottom of things. Okay? (Client nods). Look, Marjorie, I want you to imagine that your mother has just died this morning. Can you imagine that? (Client nods and begins to shake). What are you experiencing?
Client: When you said my mother was dead I began to feel all alone . . . like there was no-one to care for me . . . no-one I could turn to.
Counsellor: And if there is no-one who cares for you, no-one you can turn to?
Client: Oh God! I know I couldn't cope on my own.

Instructing clients to vividly imagine something that has been warded off often leads to anxiety itself. It is important to process this anxiety as it is sometimes related to the client's central problem. Issues like fear of loss of control, phrenophobia (fear of going mad) and extreme discomfort anxiety are often revealed when this anxiety is fully assessed. However, some clients do find it difficult to spontaneously imagine events and require counsellor assistance.

Although imagery is now routinely used in cognitive–behavioural counselling (e.g. Lazarus, 1984), there has been little written on how counsellors can stimulate clients' imagery processes. We have used a number of vivid methods to try and help clients utilise their potential for imagining events.

Vivid, connotative counsellor language

One effective way of helping clients to use their imagery-potential is for the counsellor to use rich, colourful and evocative language while aiding clients to set the scene. Unless the counsellor has gained prior diagnostic information, he or she is sometimes uncertain about which stimuli in the activating event are particularly related to the client's problem. Thus, it is best to give clients many alternatives. For example, with a socially anxious client one of us (W.D.) proceeded thus after attempting to get him to use his own potential for imagery without success:

Counsellor: So at the moment we are unclear about what you are anxious about. What I'd like to suggest is that we use your imagination to help us. I will help you set the scene based on what we have already discussed. However, since we have yet to discover detailed factors, some of the things I say might not

	be relevant. Will you bear with me and let me know when what I say touches a nerve in you?
Client:	Okay.
Counsellor:	Fine. Just close your eyes and imagine you are about to walk into the dance. You walk in and some of the guys there glance at you. You can see the smirks on their mocking faces and one of them blows you a kiss. (Here the counsellor is testing out a hypothesis based on previously gained information). You start to *seethe* inside and . . .
Client:	Okay, when you said I was starting to seethe, that struck a chord. I thought I can't let them get away with that, but if I let go I'll just go berserk. I started feeling anxious.
Counsellor:	And if you went berserk?
Client:	I couldn't show my face in there again.
Counsellor:	What would happen then?
Client:	I don't know I . . . It's funny – the way I see it I would never go out again.

Here, words like 'smirks', 'mocking', 'blows' and 'seethe' were deliberately used in an attempt to stimulate the client's imagination. It is also important for the counsellor to vary his or her tone so that this matches the language employed.

Photographs

We have at times asked clients to bring to interviews photographs of significant others or significant places. These are kept on hand to be used at relevant moments in the assessment process. We have found the use of photographs particularly helpful when the client is discussing an event in the past that is still bothering him or her. Thus, for example, one client who spoke without feeling about being rejected by his father who died 7 years previously, broke down in tears when asked to look at a picture of him and his father standing apart from one another. Feelings of hurt and anger, with their associated cognitions, were expressed, which enabled counsellor and client to move on to the disputing stage.

Other mementoes

In a similar vein, we have sometimes asked clients to bring in mementoes to counselling sessions. These may include pictures they have drawn, paintings that have meaning for them and poems either written by themselves or by other people. The important point is that these mementoes are to be related to issues that the client is working on in counselling. A roadblock to assessment was successfully overcome with one client when she was asked to bring in a memento that reminded her of her mother. She brought in a bottle of perfume that her mother was accustomed to wearing. When she was asked to smell the perfume at a point in counselling when the assessment process, through verbal dialogue, was again breaking down, the client was helped to identify feelings of jealousy toward her mother, which she experienced whenever her mother left her to go out socialising. Moreover, the client was ashamed of such feelings. This issue was centrally related to her presenting problem of depression.

Another client was depressed about losing her boyfriend. It proved difficult to help her to identify any related mediating cognitions through traditional assessment procedures. Several tentative guesses on the counsellor's part also failed to pinpoint relevant cognitive processes. She was then asked to bring to her next session anything that reminded her of her ex-boyfriend. She brought in a record of a popular song that had become known to them as 'our song'. When the song was played at an appropriate point in the interview, the client began to sob and expressed feelings of abandonment, hurt and fear for the future. Again a vivid method had unearthed important assessment material where traditional methods had failed.

It should be noted from the above examples that quite often such dramatic methods lead to the expression of strong affective reactions in the session. This is often an important part of the process because such affective reactions are gateways to the identification of maladaptive cognitive processes that are difficult to identify through more traditional methods of assessment.

The empty chair technique

Rational–emotive counselling embodies theoretically consistent eclecticism, whereby techniques are borrowed from other counselling approaches for purposes consistent with rational–emotive theory. Thus, we have sometimes used the empty chair technique, popularised by gestalt therapists. For example, traditional assessment methods did not reveal important clinical material with a client who suffered from tension headaches after visiting her mother. She was thus encouraged to imagine that her mother was sitting in an empty chair which was placed before her and then invited to disclose her feelings to her mother. An example follows:

Client:	I feel numb when I'm in your presence . . .
Counsellor:	Now sit in the empty chair and talk as your mother to yourself.
Client (as Mother):	You're such a child. You've got no backbone. Never have.
Counsellor:	Now reply to her from your chair.
Client:	Damn it. You're always criticising me. I hate you.

This technique demonstrates that the client felt angry with her mother. This discovery led to a discussion about her being scared to express negative feelings towards her mother in case her mother disowned her completely.

The 'Interpersonal nightmare technique'

This technique may be best used with clients who are able to identify only sketchily an anticipated 'dreaded' event involving other people, but are neither able to specify in any detail the nature of the event, nor how they would react if the event were to occur. First the client is given a homework assignment to imagine the 'dreaded' event. He or she is told to write a brief segment of a play about it, specifying the exact words that the protagonists would use. The client is encouraged to give full rein to imagination while focusing on what he or she fears might happen. One example will suffice. The following scenario was developed by a 55-year-old woman with alcohol problems who was terrified of making errors at the office where she worked as a typist.

Scene: Boss's office where he sits behind a very large desk. He has found out that one of the typists has inadvertently filed a letter wrongly and sends for her. She comes in and is made to stand in front of the boss.

Boss: Have you anything to say in this matter?

Typist (me):   Only that I apologise and will be more careful in the future.

Boss: What do you mean by saying you will be more careful in the future – what makes you think you have a future? (At this point he starts banging on the desk). I have never yet met anyone less competent or less suited to the job than you are. You mark my words, I will make life so uncomfortable for you that you will leave. When I took over this job I intended to have the people I wanted working for me and you are not on that list. I have already got rid of two typists, and I shall see that you are the third. Now get out of my office you stupid, blundering fool and remember I shall always be watching you and you will never know when I shall be behind you.

The scene was reviewed with the client, and she was asked to describe the tone in which she thought her boss would make these statements and to identify which words the boss would emphasise. Arrangements were then made for a local actor who was the same age as the boss to enact the scene realistically on cassette. In the next session the client was instructed to visualise the room in which the encounter might take place. She briefly described the room, paying particular attention to where her boss would be sitting and where she would be standing. She was then played the cassette, which evoked strong feelings of fear of being physically harmed and humiliated. Again important data had been collected which traditional assessment procedures had failed to uncover.

Rational–emotive problem solving

Knaus and Wessler (1976) have described a method which they call rational–emotive problem solving (REPS). This method involves the coun-sellor creating conditions in the counselling session that approximate those the client encounters in his or her everyday life and which give rise to emotional problems. Knaus and Wessler contend that this method may be used either in a planned or impromptu fashion, and is particularly valuable when clients experience difficulty in identifying emotional experiences and related cognitive processes through verbal dialogue with their counsellors. One of us (W.D.) employed this method with a male client who reported difficulty in acting assertively in his life, and claimed not to be able to identify the emotions and thoughts that inhibited the expression of assertive responses. During the session W.D. began to search around for his pouch of pipe tobacco. Finding it empty, he interrupted the client and asked him if he would drive to town and purchase his favourite tobacco, adding that if he hurried he could return for the last five minutes of the interview. He immediately got up, took the money and walked out of the office towards his car! W.D. rushed after him, brought him back into the office and his reactions to this simulated experience were processed.

It is clear that this technique must be used with therapeutic judgement and that its use may threaten or even destroy the therapeutic alliance between client and counsellor. However, since rational–emotive counsellors value risk-taking they are often prepared to use such techniques when more traditional and less risky methods have failed to bring about therapeutic improvement. It is further important, as Beck et al. (1979) have stressed, for the counsellor to ask the client for the latter's honest reactions to this procedure, to ascertain whether it may have future therapeutic value for the client. When a client indicates that he or she has found the rational–emotive problem-solving method unhelpful, the counsellor is advised to then explain the rationale for attempting such a procedure, and disclose that he or she intended no harm but was attempting to be helpful. Normally clients respect such disclosures and in fact the counsellor, in doing so, provides a useful model for the client: namely that it is possible to acknowledge errors non-defensively without damning oneself. However, with this method, it is apparent that counsellors cannot realistically disclose their rationale in advance of initiating the method, since this would detract from its potential therapeutic value.

Paradoxical counsellor actions

This method is often best used when clients, through their actions, communicate to the counsellor messages about themselves based on irrational beliefs. For example, W.D. once saw a female client who experienced a lot of rheumatic pain but had an attitude of low frustration tolerance toward it. Her behaviour in sessions indicated the attitude: 'I am a poor soul, feel sorry for me'. This prompted W.D. to adopt an overly sympathetic and diligent stance towards her. Thus, at the beginning of every session he treated her as if she could hardly walk and escorted her by arm to her chair and made frequent enquiries about her comfort. This eventually prompted her to make statements like: 'Don't treat me like a child', 'I can cope', 'It's not as bad as all that', etc. W.D. then helped her to identify some of her implicit irrational messages. Whenever she began to lapse back into her self-pitying attitude, W.D. began to behave in an overly solicitous manner again, which provided a timely reminder for her to attend to the behavioural components of her philosophy of low frustration tolerance, and then to the philosophy itself.

Using the counsellor–client relationship

Wessler (1984) has written that it is important for the rational–emotive counsellor to enquire about the nature of the client's reactions to him or her, that is, to examine some of the client's here-and-now beliefs. Little has been written about this approach in the rational–emotive literature, and thus relatively little is known about its potential as a framework for identifying irrational beliefs. Wessler (1984) also advocates that counsellors give clients frank feedback about the clients' impact on them and to explore whether clients have a similar impact on other people. Such generalisations must of course be made with caution, but such discussion is often a stimulus for clients to become more sensitive to their impact on other people and often leads them to ask other people about their interpersonal impact (Anchin and Kiesler, 1982).

The advantage of using the counsellor–client relationship in this way is that it provides both parties with an opportunity to process the client's beliefs in an immediate and often vivid fashion. For example, one particular client who complained of loneliness had the habit of putting his feet up on his counsellor's coffee table. The counsellor did not mention this at first, but later on, when he became irritated by the client's behaviour, he disclosed that he was annoyed by it and wondered if other people had similar reactions to him. The counsellor suggested that he get some feedback from other people. The client did so and reported that other people reported the same reactions as the counsellor. This led to a discussion concerning his implicit beliefs that underpinned such soundly aversive behaviour and the following irrational belief was identified: 'I must be able to do what I want in social affairs without being criticised'. This belief helped to explain why this client had no friends.

Dreams

Although Albert Ellis once wrote a regular column for Penthouse magazine, providing rational–emotive interpretations of readers' dreams, rational–emotive counsellors are not generally noted for using dream material. However, there is no good reason why dream material cannot be used in rational–emotive counselling as long as it does not predominate in the therapeutic process and the counsellor has a definite purpose in mind in using it.

Freeman (1981, pp. 228-229) has outlined a number of further guidelines for the use of dreams for assessment purposes:

1. The dream needs to be understood in thematic rather than symbolic terms.
2. The thematic content of the dream is idiosyncratic to the dreamer and must be viewed within the context of the dreamer's life.
3. The specific language and imagery are important to the meaning.
4. The affective responses to the dreams can be seen as similar to the dreamer's affective responses in waking situations.
5. The particular length of the dream is of less import than the content.
6. The dream is a product of and the responsibility of the dreamer.
7. Dreams can be used when the patient appears stuck in counselling.

W.D. inadvertently stumbled on the usefulness of dream material for assessment purposes when working with a 28-year-old depressed student who would frequently reiterate: 'I'm depressed and I don't know why'. W.D. had virtually exhausted all the assessment methods he knew, including those described in this chapter, to help her identify depressogenic thoughts in situations where she experienced depression, but without success. In a desperate last attempt, he asked her if she could remember any of her dreams, not expecting in the least that this line of inquiry would prove fruitful. To his surprise she said yes, she did have a recurring dream. In this dream she saw herself walking alone along a river bank, and when she peered into the river, she saw a reflection of herself as a very old woman. This image filled her with extreme sadness and depression. On further discussion she said that she believed that this dream meant that she had no prospect of finding any happiness in her life, either in love relationships or in her career, and that she was doomed to spend her years alone, ending up as a sad, pathetic old woman. This account of the dream and subsequent discussion of its meaning enabled W.D. to help her identify a number of irrational beliefs which provided the focus for subsequent cognitive restructuring.

Daydreams may also provide important material for assessment purposes. For some people, particular daydreams occur in response to and as compensation for a negative activating event. Thus, one client reported having the daydream of establishing a multinational corporation after failing to sell insurance to prospective customers. The use of such daydreams by clients may not necessarily be dysfunctional, but may impede them, as in the above example, from getting to the core of their problems. Often daydreams are an expression of our hopes and aspirations, and we have found it valuable to ask clients not only about the content of such material but also what would stop them from actualising their goals. Much important assessment material is gathered in this manner, in particular concerning ideas of low frustration tolerance.

In vivo counselling sessions

Sacco (1981) has outlined the value of conducting counselling sessions in real-life settings in which clients experience emotional difficulties. We have found moving outside the interview room to such settings particularly useful in gaining assessment material when traditional methods have failed to provide such data. For example, W.D. once saw a male student who complained of avoiding social situations. He did so in case others would see his hands tremble. Traditional assessment methods yielded no further useful data. To overcome this treatment impasse, W.D. suggested to him that they needed to collect more data and they eventually conducted a counselling session in a coffee shop, where he was asked to go and get two cups of coffee. He refused because he feared that his hands might tremble, but W.D. firmly persisted with his request. The client was able to identify a stream of negative cognitions on his way from the table to the service counter. He returned without the coffees but with valuable information, which was processed later in W.D.'s office. It is important for counsellors to explain their rationale for conducting in vivo sessions in advance in order to gain client cooperation. In addition, obtaining clients' reactions to these sessions is often helpful particularly if in vivo sessions are planned for use later in the therapeutic process.

Some cautions about the use of vivid methods in rational-emotive counselling

In this chapter we have introduced the concept of using vivid methods in rational-emotive counselling and will reintroduce the concept in the chapters on 'Promoting intellectual insight' and 'Promoting emotional rational insight'. However, we wish at this stage to outline some cautions about using such methods in rational-emotive counselling:

1. It is important for counsellors to determine the impact on clients of introducing vivid methods into the therapeutic process. Thus, using the guidelines of Beck, Rush, Shaw and Emery (1979) it is perhaps wise for the counsellor to ask the client at various points to give frank feedback concerning the methods and activities used. While the counsellor may not always agree not to use such techniques just because a client has a negative reaction to them, clients' negative reactions to particular procedures should be obtained and understood.

2. It is important in the use of vivid-dramatic techniques not to overload the client. One vivid and dramatic method carefully introduced into the counselling session at an appropriate time is much more likely to be effective than several dramatic methods employed indiscriminately in a session.

3. It is also important that rational-emotive counsellors be clear about the rationale for using vivid methods and not see their use as a goal in itself. The important thing to remember is that vivid methods are to be used as a vehicle for facilitating assessment and promoting client attitude

change, and not to make the therapeutic process more stimulating for the counsellor. It is also extremely important to ascertain what the client has learned from the vivid methods the counsellor has employed. The client will not magically come to the conclusion the counsellor wants him or her to. It is also important that counsellors do not promote 'false' change in their clients. Change is 'false' when the client feels better as a result of some of these vivid methods but does not get better. Ellis (1972) has written an important article on such a distinction. Thus, counsellors should invariably ask questions like: 'What have you learned from doing this vivid method?' and 'How can you strengthen this learning experience for yourself outside counselling?'.

4. Dramatic and vivid methods are not appropriate for all clients. They are particularly helpful for those clients who use intellectualisation as a defence and/or who use verbal dialogue to tie rational–emotive counsellors in knots. Although there are no data at the moment to support the following hypothesis, we would speculate that it is inadvisable to use dramatic and vivid methods with clients who have overly dramatic and hysterical personalities. It is perhaps more appropriate to assist such clients to reflect in a calm and undramatic manner on their experiences than to overstimulate an already highly stimulated personality.

With these words of caution, we leave the issue of assessment and consider the issue of promoting intellectual rational insight in the following chapter.

Chapter 7
Promoting Intellectual Rational Insight

Overview

In this chapter, we deal with issues concerning the promotion of intellectual rational insight. First, we distinguish between two forms of rational insight: intellectual and emotional. Then we cover standard and vivid methods of disputing irrational beliefs (premises and derivatives) which are designed to help clients achieve intellectual insight. We conclude the chapter by discussing various homework aids that clients can use to facilitate this process.

Rational Insight: Intellectual and Emotional

Once the client can see clearly and agree that her emotional or behavioural problem C is based on an irrational belief B and that in order to get over her problem at C she needs to change her irrational belief at B, then the therapeutic stage is set for the counsellor to help the client to change this belief. The counsellor tries to effect this change by disputing the client's belief, i.e. asking for evidence to support or refute it. The major goal of the disputing process at this stage of counselling is to help the client understand and acknowledge that there is no evidence that exists to support her irrational belief but that there *is* evidence to support its rational equivalent. When the client can acknowledge this – i.e. see that it is true – then it is assumed that she has achieved intellectual rational insight, which is defined here as 'weak and occasional conviction that an irrational belief is false and a rational belief is true'. Here the rational belief is lightly and occasionally held. Intellectual rational insight, in general, does not lead to significant emotional and behavioural change. In this chapter we describe rational-emotive techniques designed to help clients achieve intellectual rational insight.

Intellectual rational insight is distinguished from emotional rational insight, which is defined here as 'strong and frequent conviction that an irrational belief is false and a rational belief is true'. Here the rational belief is strongly and frequently held. Emotional rational insight does often lead to significant emotional and behavioural change. In the next chapter we consider rational-emotive techniques designed to help clients move from intellectual to emotional rational insight. At this point, it should be noted that intellectual rational insight very frequently precedes emotional rational insight. It is extremely rare for a client to relinquish an irrational belief and immediately believe in its rational alternative with such conviction that she will be able to act on it straight away.

Disputing Irrational Beliefs

When disputing irrational beliefs, rational-emotive counsellors often attempt to engage their clients in a Socratic dialogue. This involves asking clients questions about the validity of their irrational beliefs, helping them to see why their wrong answers are incorrect, and then asking again for evidence supporting the validity of the same irrational belief. This process is continued until the client can acknowledge that there exists no evidence in favour of the irrational belief, but that evidence does exist in favour of the rational belief. In other words, the process continues until the client achieves intellectual rational insight.

Debating and discriminating

Disputing involves two major activities: debating and discriminating (Phadke, 1982). Debating consists of the counsellor asking a variety of questions designed to help the client examine the validity of her irrational belief. Questions that are frequently employed include: 'Where is the evidence that . . .?'; 'Where is the law of the universe that . . .?'; 'Where is the proof that . . .?'; 'How does it follow that . . .?' Discriminating involves the counsellor helping the client to distinguish clearly between her rational belief (want, preference, desire, etc.) and her irrational belief (must, absolute should, have-to, etc.). These two activities are frequently used in concert as the counsellor strives to teach the client the differences between rational and irrational beliefs, and that there exists no evidence in favour of irrational beliefs. An example of this process follows:

Counsellor: So you can see that your anxiety is based on your belief that you must achieve, in the academic arena anyway, whatever you set your sights on?
Client: Yes.
Counsellor: So if you want to get over your anxiety what would it be advisable for you to change?
Client: That belief.
Counsellor: Right. So now I'm going to ask you some questions to help you assess the validity of that belief. Why *must* you achieve whatever you set your sights on? (Debating intervention).
Client: Because it's important to me to do so.

Counsellor: No, that's why it's desirable. Note that I didn't ask you the question why is it desirable for you to achieve your academic goals but why do you absolutely have to do so. Can you see the difference between your belief 'I want to achieve my academic goals' and your belief 'I must achieve my academic goals'? (Discriminating intervention).

Client: Not really.

Counsellor: Well, the belief 'I want to achieve my academic goals' is relative. It allows for the possibility that you won't achieve them. That belief, if fully stated, is really: 'I want to achieve my goals, but there is no law in the universe which states that I absolutely have to'. Whereas the belief 'I absolutely have to achieve my goals', is an absolute one. If that belief were true there would be no way for you to fail. That's the difference. Do you see that?

Client: Yes I do.

Counsellor: Fine, but I want to be sure that I've made myself clear. Can you put into your own words the differences between the two beliefs?

Client: Well, my belief 'I want to achieve my goals' is an expression of what's important to me, but doesn't mean that I necessarily will achieve them. The belief 'I must achieve my goals' means that no matter what I will achieve them.

Counsellor: That's right. Now let me ask you again. Where's the evidence that you *must* achieve what it's important for you to achieve? (Debating intervention).

Client: There isn't any.

Counsellor: That's it, and if you really work on convincing yourself that there is no evidence that you must achieve your goals, and stick rigorously with your rational belief that you really want to achieve them but don't have to, then you'll still be concerned about failing, but not anxious about it. And that concern will motivate you to try your best, whereas if you do as some of my clients do, jump to 'It doesn't matter if I pass or fail' then (a) you'll be lying to yourself because you really do care, and (b) you won't be motivated to try to do your best, since it won't matter to you.

Client: So desire is helpful and the *must* will lead to anxiety, which will interfere with me achieving my goals.

Counsellor: Yes, and indifference?

Client: That won't help me either.

Note from this exchange that when it is clear that a client does not understand the difference between his rational and irrational beliefs, the counsellor gives a brief explanation to clarify the difference between the two beliefs. Rational–emotive counsellors routinely employ Socratic disputing and didactic explanation where appropriate. In this exchange the counsellor does not persist in using a strategy (i.e. Socratic disputing) which does not appear to help the client. When the counsellor uses a didactic explanation to clarify a rational concept, note that his explanation is brief and concise and that he requests feedback from the client that the latter understands the difference between a rational belief and an irrational belief by asking the client to state his understanding of this point in his own words.

Note also that the counsellor helps the client to see the links between B and C. He stresses that the client's irrational belief leads to anxiety and that his rational belief will lead to concern – a rational emotion which is more likely to encourage the client to reach his goals than the irrational emotion of anxiety. This is an important point. When disputing clients' irrational beliefs it is often desirable to help them understand that rational alternatives to these irrational beliefs will lead to less debilitating negative emotions, and will often encourage clients to persist in goal-directed activities and to make a constructive adjustment when these goals can no longer be achieved. On this latter point it is likely that the client would feel depressed if he did not achieve his academic goals and clung to his irrational belief, whereas if he adhered to his rational belief in a rigorous manner he would only feel disappointed about his future. Disappointment would very likely promote his constructive adjustment to a situation where he could not achieve his goals, whereas depression would impede such adjustment.

The final point to note from this interchange is that the counsellor helps the client to discriminate between his rational belief based on desire and a belief based on indifference. Clients often consider that the only alternative to an irrational belief is one that is based on indifference, e.g. 'I don't care if I don't reach my academic goals'. Here the counsellor attempts to forewarn the client about this possibility, which the client appears to understand.

As has already been noted, an irrational belief has a premise and one or more derivatives. Disputing can therefore be targeted at the premise form of the irrational belief or at the derivative form or, of course, at both forms. We personally find it effective to dispute *both* the premise *and* the derivative forms of clients' irrational beliefs.

Disputing irrational premises

Disputing irrational premises involves challenging the validity of clients' irrational beliefs expressed in the form of 'musts', 'absolute shoulds', 'oughts', 'have-to's' etc. As above, the purpose of disputing 'musts' etc. is to show clients that there is no evidence in support of such absolute beliefs. Thus, if there was a law of the universe that stated, for example, that I must achieve my goals in life, I would have to achieve them *no matter what*. Thus absolute musts go against reality, and in this context it is often useful to help clients understand that when they believe in such dogmatic attitudes they are demanding that what exists absolutely *must not exist*. Indeed the *empirical* form of the word 'must' indicates that if I do not achieve my goals then conditions exist so that I must not achieve them, i.e. what does not exist must not exist.

Another helpful strategy in disputing absolute musts etc. is to help clients understand that the evidence that they provide in support of absolute musts constitutes, in reality, evidence in favour of their rational beliefs. For example, in a disputing sequence with a female client, the following items were listed as evidence in support of her irrational belief, 'I must be loved by my husband': (a) I would feel better if he did love me; (b) we would get on better if he loved me; and (c) his love means more to me than most other things in life. In response to the question 'Why do you want very much your husband's love?', she listed the same reasons. This helped her to see that she had not yet provided any support in favour of the irrational form of her belief.

When disputing clients' irrational beliefs expressed in the form of musts it is important to ascertain first that the must is indeed irrational, in the sense of being unconditional. As noted above not all musts are irrational and some musts are in fact conditional as in the phrase 'If I want to pass my examin-ation I must learn the material'. Here, passing the examination is conditional on learning the material. It is thus an error to dispute conditional musts.

The same point can be made when considering the word 'should', in that not all 'shoulds' are dogmatic and unconditional, and thus irrational in nature. In particular when disputing irrational beliefs expressed in the form of 'shoulds', it is important for the counsellor to help the client discriminate between 'preferably should' (rational belief) and 'absolutely should'. We recommend that when disputing irrational 'shoulds' the counsellor use the qualifier 'absolutely'. If the qualifier is not used the client may think that the counsellor is asking for evidence in support of the preferential form of the word 'should', and not the absolute form of the word. In such cases therapeutic impasses frequently ensue. As with other terms employed in rational–emotive counselling, it is important for the counsellor and client to share a commonly agreed meaning framework in the course of the thera-peutic work (Dryden, 1986).

Finally, it is important for the counsellor to discover which form of the irrational premise the client best understands as reflecting a statement of absolutism. Thus, with some clients, disputing 'have-to's' is more effective in this respect than disputing 'musts' etc., because for these clients the term 'have-to' best captures the meaning of absolutism and personal dogma.

Disputing irrational derivatives

As shown in Chapter 3, there are three major derivatives from irrational premises: 'awfulising', 'I-can't-stand-it-itis' and 'damning'.

Disputing 'awful'

In rational–emotive theory, the term 'awful', when it stems from an irrational belief, means '101 per cent bad' or 'worse than it absolutely must be'. In this sense it is not a synonym of the term 'very bad', although it is often judged to be so in everyday language. Thus, it is important for rational–emotive counsellors to help clients discriminate between such phrases as 'very bad' and the word 'awful'. When this is done clients are shown that whatever they evaluate as 'awful' could, in reality, be worse; and that the concept of 101 per cent badness is a magical one that does not exist except by definition. A good way of reinforcing this is to ask clients to rate what is evaluated as 'awful' on a 0–100 scale of badness, as in the following example:

Counsellor: So you're saying that being rejected by Harry is awful, right?
Client: Right.
Counsellor: So on a scale from 0 to 100 of badness, how bad would being rejected by Harry be?
Client: 100 per cent.
Counsellor: So if you are going to rate that as 100 per cent then how would you rate being rejected by Harry *and* losing a leg?
Client: (laughs). I hadn't thought of it like that. I guess that would be 100 per cent.
Counsellor: OK. Now where would you rate being rejected by Harry, losing a leg and having a very large rates bill that you couldn't pay?
Client: That would be 100 per cent too . . . Oh, now I see what you're getting at. Looking at it like that being rejected by Harry wouldn't be that bad.
Counsellor: Right, but it still would be very bad. Now can you see the differences between very bad and awful?
Client: Yes I see that now.
Counsellor: Right, awful doesn't really exist, unless we invent it because we can keep adding bad things to the list and if we do that when will we ever get to 100 per cent badness?
Client: Never, I guess, because things could always be worse.
Counsellor: That's exactly it. Now awful really stems from the belief 'It mustn't be as bad as it is'. Now granted that being rejected by Harry is bad why *must* that not be as bad as it is? . . .

Ellis (personal communication) has argued that the method whereby clients are encouraged to rate events as 'bad' rather than 'awful' should be used with caution. This is because a person could rate a situation as 40 per cent bad and still believe that it *must not* be as bad as it is and thus make herself disturbed. Thus, when using this method it is important *also* to dispute any remaining irrational premises, as in the example presented.

In addition, when clients are encouraged to rate events as bad rather than awful, counsellors should be careful to stress the distinction between these two terms (e.g. 'Right, so if you continue to show yourself that it was *bad* that it happened, *but not awful*, then you will get over your depression').

An interesting way of disputing 'awfulising' beliefs has been described by Young (1984a) in his work with lower-class clients in West Virginia.

> I usually accomplish this by using a sheet of paper on which I put two columns. One column I label 'Pain in the neck – HASSLE' and the other column I label 'End of the world – HORRORS'. Next I encourage the client to tell me exactly what is wrong in his problem. Then, after we list all the disadvantages and inconveniences involved, I will ask the client in which column the problem belongs – the hassle column or the horror column. Clients always see the point and admit that their problems belong in

the hassle column. I ask them how they would feel if they could see their problem as a hassle instead of a horror. Clients usually admit that they would feel much less upset. I then inform them that their job is constantly to tell themselves the truth – that the problem is a pain-in-the-neck, nothing more and nothing less. (Young, 1984a, p. 47)

Note in this example that Young does not overtly deal with the philosophical issue that nothing merits inclusion in the 'end of the world horror' or 'awful' column. Young probably did not do this because his clientele would not grasp this point. This raises another important principle in rational-emotive counselling: *Work at a level that your client can understand*. Our own preference in this regard is to assume that clients will be able to grasp the full meaning of rational concepts until evidence is obtained that suggests otherwise.

Disputing 'I-can't-stand-it-itis'

The purpose of disputing 'I-can't-stand-it-itis' beliefs is to help clients see that this term, when it stems from an irrational premise, means 'I will never experience happiness again' and is thus rarely true. Indeed we find it helpful to encourage clients to see that even when they believe and tell themselves 'I can't stand it' they are, in fact, 'standing it', albeit not very well. The discussion can then shift to helping clients explore ways of tolerating it better. Another way of demonstrating to clients that they can stand what they believe they can't is to ask them if there are circumstances under which they could stand 'it', as is shown in the following interchange:

Counsellor: So you're saying that you can't stand that feeling of jelly legs when you go out and that's why you don't go out. Is that right?

Client: Yes, that's right.

Counsellor: Now as we've seen, as long as you believe that you can't stand that feeling you won't go out. But let's see if that belief is true. Let's suppose that your sister has been kidnapped by terrorists and the only way the terrorists will release her is if you delivered the ransom money on your jelly legs, or else they would kill her. Now under these conditions, should we arrange for her funeral or would you go?

Client: I'd go and deliver the money.

Counsellor: But how could you if you couldn't stand having these feelings of jelly legs?

Client: Well, I'd do it even though I couldn't stand it.

Counsellor: But if you couldn't stand it you'd collapse in the attempt – that's what you've been saying about the feeling isn't it?

Client: Well, I wouldn't focus on it in that instance.

Counsellor: You mean you could stand it enough not to dwell on it?

Client: I suppose so.

Counsellor: Now if you'd go out on jelly legs to save your sister will you do it for the sake of your recovery, even though it's damned uncomfortable?

Client: I see your point.

Counsellor: Now as you do this, really work on convincing yourself that you can stand these uncomfortable feelings even though you'll never like them. And don't forget to remind yourself that you're choosing to stand them for a reason – your mental health!

Here, as elsewhere, rational–emotive counsellors can use the methods of general semantics to show clients that when they say 'I can't stand it' they really mean, as in the above example 'I haven't learned to stand it yet' and 'I am having great difficulty standing it at the moment, but that doesn't mean that I never will'.

Disputing 'damning' beliefs

When applied to people the process of damning implies that a person can be given a global rating, that this is negative and that the person is damnable, i.e. subhuman. The purpose of disputing damning beliefs, which again tend to be derivatives from irrational premises, is to show the client that a person is too complex to be given a single rating; a person's traits, behaviours or thoughts are part of the person, but never equal to the person; and the essence of the person is fallibility, being capable of good and bad, rather than goodness or badness. Below, we provide one example to demonstrate each principle in action. Although they each refer to irrational beliefs about the self, similar points apply to irrational beliefs the client may hold about others.

1. The 'self' is too complex

Counsellor: OK, so you say that you're worthless for cheating on your wife, is that right?

Client: Yes that's what I believe.

Counsellor: OK, but let's test that out. Are you saying that you are worthless, or what you've done is worthless?

Client: I'm saying that I'm worthless, not just what I did.

Counsellor: OK, but let's see if that is logical. You know when you say 'I'm worthless' you are giving you, your personhood or your essence, a single rating. Can you see that?

Client: Yes.

Counsellor: But let's see if you warrant that. You're 35. How many thoughts have you had from the day you were born till now?

Client: Countless, I guess.

Counsellor: Add to that all your actions and throw in all your traits for good measure. From that time till now how many aspects to you are there?

Client: Millions, I guess.

Counsellor: At least now when you say that Y-O-U ARE WORTHLESS you can see that you're implying that you are about as complex as a single cell amoeba, and that this cell is worthless. Now is that true from what we've just been discussing?

Client: No, of course it's not.

Counsellor: So do you, in all your complexity, merit a single rating?

Client: No, but I did do a pretty worthless thing and it was serious.

Counsellor:	Agreed, but what has greater validity, the belief, 'I'm worthless in all my essence' or the belief, 'I am too complex to be rated, but I did do something lousy which I regret'.
Client:	The second.
Counsellor:	Right and if you really worked on believing that would you still feel suicidal as you do now?
Client:	No I wouldn't. I see what you mean.

2. I equal what I do (think, feel)

This example is taken from Young's (1984a) work with a lower-class client who is convinced that you are what you do.

Counsellor:	Maybe I can show you a better way to think about yourself. (I pointed at her hand). Is that your hand?
Client:	(laughing) Yes!
Counsellor:	Is it important to you?
Client:	Yes.
Counsellor:	Tell me why. Suppose you didn't have that hand?
Client:	It would handicap me. There would be lots of things I couldn't do. It would be pretty bad for me.
Counsellor:	So your hand's important! Now let me ask you this: Is that hand part of you or is it you? Now really think for me. Does that important hand equal you? Could you describe yourself simply as a hand?
Client:	No.
Counsellor:	Why not? You gave the right answer. Now tell me why it is the right answer.
Client:	Because my hand is only part of me.
Counsellor:	Do you have any other part, such as your eyes, ears, nose, or big toe that is your whole self? Is there any part of your body, inside or out, that you could say is you?
Client:	No, I guess I'm made up of a lot of parts.

3. The essence of the self is fallibility

In order to make the point that the essence of a person is fallibility W.D. will sometimes draw three big circles on a sheet of paper and show this to the client. He says that these three circles represent three people: A, B and C. First he takes circle A and sticks as many small gold stars within the circle as he can. Next he sticks as many black dots as he can within circle B. Finally he sticks a mixture of gold stars and black dots in circle C. He explains to the client that the gold stars represent good deeds, thoughts, feelings and traits; and the black dots represent bad deeds, thoughts, feelings and traits.

He then asks his client what we generally call someone who only has the equivalent of gold stars; who only has the equivalent of black dots; and who has a mixture of the two. The client usually gives such replies as: perfect, a saint, an angel; bad, the devil, evil; and human, normal, ordinary, respectively. W.D. then asks the client two more questions: whether she really knows anyone like the people represented by circles A and B, to which the answer is almost always no; and which circle best represents her, to which the answer is invariably 'C'. In this manner clients can see that the essence of human beings is a mixture of good and bad (or fallibility) and that they also belong in the category: 'fallible human being'.

A final note on language. As with irrational premises clients use different words to damn themselves and others. For example, Young (1984b) has shown that clients can be 'bad me' thinkers, 'less me' thinkers or 'damn me' thinkers. As elsewhere, it is recommended that the counsellor use the client's language in disputing sequences unless there are sound reasons to do otherwise.

Dissonance-inducing interventions

According to cognitive dissonance theory (e.g. Festinger, 1957), when a person is confronted with information that conflicts with one of his importantly held beliefs, a state of cognitive dissonance, a form of psychological tension, is induced. In order to reduce dissonance that person *may* change his belief. We stress the word *may* in the above sentence because in order to reduce dissonance the person may change other features of the dissonant situation, e.g. he may cast doubt on the validity of the conflicting information or on the credibility of the source of the new information. Thus, although rational–emotive counsellors employ dissonance-inducing interventions to promote intellectual rational insight, they do so with caution.

One dissonance-inducing intervention that is commonly used in rational-emotive counselling attempts to show clients that they have already engaged in adaptive behaviour which is inconsistent with their maladaptive belief. Thus clients who believe that they are 'failures' are asked to provide evidence of their successes; those who believe that they are unlovable are asked for evidence that they have been loved. Since clients frequently append 'but that doesn't count' to their evidence we have often found it helpful to say something like: 'Of course I realise that any evidence that you give you will immediately dismiss in some way, but let's hear it anyway', before letting the client answer. We do this to reduce in advance the potency of their attempts to maintain their irrational belief by denying the importance of their evidence. The success of this type of dissonance-inducing intervention often depends on the wealth of evidence the client provides, and then it is important to keep asking for more and more evidence until a healthy portfolio of evidence which conflicts with the client's irrational belief has been assembled.

Another dissonance-inducing intervention concerns the counsellor demonstrating that the client's irrational belief is incongruent with one of the client's cherished ideas, as in the following example:

Counsellor: So you're furious with Bill because he upset your friend and you believe he absolutely should not have done that. Is that right?

Client: Yes, indeed.

Counsellor: I remember you said on your biographical form that one of your pet hates is totalitarianism. Have I remembered correctly?

Client: That's right, but what's that got to do with it?

Counsellor: I'm coming to that, bear with me for a moment. Why are you against state control?

Client: Because it restricts the individual's freedom.

Counsellor: His or her freedom to act?

Client: Yes.

Counsellor: So even if the individual acts really badly he or she, in your opinion, should preferably have that choice?

Client: Yes. Of course there have to be laws and consequences for the individual, but basically yes.

Counsellor: So I guess you're saying all people have the right to act badly except Bill, because aren't you demanding, in a totalitarian way, that he absolutely should not have acted badly towards your friend?

Client: (Laughs loudly) OK, Doc, you've got me. I give in.

Counsellor: Now what would a non-totalitarian attitude towards Bill sound like?

A final dissonance-inducing strategy that is often quite powerful concerns showing the client that her attitude towards herself conflicts with her attitude towards her best friend, e.g.:

Counsellor: So you say that you're a bad person for having those evil thoughts. Is that right?

Client: Yes.

Counsellor: Well let's test that out. Now we'll agree for the moment that those thoughts of stabbing your child are evil. But how are you evil for having evil thoughts?

Client: Well, it's obvious isn't it?

Counsellor: Is it? Aren't you saying that because part of you is evil that you are thoroughly evil?

Client: Yes.

Counsellor: Well, does that follow?

Client: Well . . .

Counsellor: Let's put it another way. Who's your best friend?

Client: Cathy.

Counsellor: Well, let's suppose that Cathy came to you and said: 'Sue, I'm evil because I've had thoughts of stabbing my child'. Would you say to her 'Get out of my sight you evil person?'

Client: No I wouldn't.

Counsellor: Would you think it?

Client: No.

Counsellor: Why not?

Client: Because she isn't evil.

Counsellor: Even though she's had evil thoughts?

Client: I see what you mean.

Counsellor: Now do you think there should be one rule for Cathy and a different one for you? Does that make sense?
Client: No, I guess not.
Counsellor: So why not work at applying your attitude towards Cathy to you?

Here, as elsewhere, rational–emotive counsellors should guard against clients giving themselves second-order problems as a consequence of the counsellors' interventions. Thus some clients may conclude from the last example 'Oh, I am treating my friend more compassionately than myself as I must not. That really proves how worthless I am'. Questions like: 'How do you feel about the fact that you seem to be harsher on yourself than you are on your best friend' should preferably be asked after the intervention to determine the existence of such second-order problems.

Goals and rational beliefs

As we have already noted, an important part of the disputing process involves helping clients to discriminate between irrational and rational beliefs. As these distinctions are clarified it is advisable for counsellors to encourage clients to see that rational beliefs are related to more functional rational emotions, which are still often negative in nature. For example, imagine that a client is anxious about performing well in her driving test, because she is demanding that she must pass the test. In the process of helping this client to dispute this belief, the counsellor will show her that her rational belief is 'I very much want to pass the test but I don't have to', and that if she subscribed only to this belief she would feel concerned, but not anxious, about driving well. However, if the client's goal is to be calm and not concerned about the prospect of failing the test, she will resist adopting the new rational beliefs. Thus, rational–emotive counsellors often discuss clients' emotional and behavioural goals during the process of disputing their irrational beliefs to ensure that their goals can be achieved by adopting rational beliefs. In the example we have provided, the counsellor would attempt to show the client that concern is a rational negative emotion, based on a rational belief that will motivate her to do well, whereas calmness, which can only be achieved by the client lying to herself by telling herself 'It doesn't matter if I do well or not', hardly provides her with the motivational base to do as well as she can. Thus while rational–emotive counsellors often elicit their clients' emotional and behavioural goals, they do not accept uncritically clients' stated goals and are particularly sceptical of the functionality of goals which signify attitudes of indifference.

The above example also highlights another feature of the disputing process; namely, that counsellors attempt to help clients to understand the logical consequences of holding rational and irrational beliefs. Here, the counsellor might say, 'As long as you believe that you must do well you will be anxious, and this anxiety may interfere with your driving performance. However, if you work at believing that while it is important to you to do well, you don't have to, you'll be concerned, and thus be in a better frame of mind to do well'. This part of the disputing process, which can be done Socratically as well as didactically, as above, is often referred to as 'pragmatic disputing' in that it draws the client's attention to the pragmatic consequences of holding rational and irrational beliefs.

Comprehensive cognitive disputing

Earlier, we noted that we prefer to target both the premise and the derivative forms of clients' irrational beliefs during the disputing process. In our experience, this thoroughgoing approach helps to increase the likelihood that clients will achieve the types of attitude change that contribute to psychological health.

In a recent paper, DiGiuseppe (1991) presents a model for conducting thoroughgoing disputing within rational–emotive counselling. He describes four categories of variables which he views as having particular relevance to the disputing process, and advocates manipulation of these variables within counselling sessions as a means for ensuring that disputing will be accomplished in a complete and comprehensive manner. These variables include: (1) the *type* of disputing argument utilised by the counsellor; (2) the particular *style* by which the counsellor presents the disputing argument to the client; (3) the *level of abstraction* of the irrational beliefs targeted for disputing; and (4) the particular irrational belief *processes* targeted for disputing.

With respect to the *type* of disputing argument the counsellor employs, the reader will recall that Chapter 2 described irrational beliefs as illogical and anti-empirical in nature, and as representing significant impediments to goal attainment. Hence irrational beliefs can be disputed with logical, empirical and pragmatic arguments. With reference to Kuhn's (1970) work on the factors which influence scientists to reject old theories (or paradigms) in favour of new, alternative ones, DiGiuseppe (1991) argues that clients will be more likely to surrender their irrational beliefs and replace them with more rational ones when the former are attacked with all three types of disputing arguments. He further emphasises that it is desirable for counsellors to help their clients to construct new 'theories' about themselves and the world by working with them to formulate new, alternative rational beliefs of relevance to their particular problem areas. This recommendation is based upon the hypothesis that clients may be prone to cling to their old irrational beliefs – despite technically correct efforts at disputing these beliefs – if an alternative rational philosophy is not made available to them.

With regard to the manner in which disputing arguments are presented to clients, DiGiuseppe (1991) describes four particular disputing styles: didactic, Socratic, humorous and metaphorical. To this list we would add an additional category: self-disclosing style. DiGiuseppe (1991) hypothesises that clients are influenced as much by the manner of presentation of disputing arguments as they are by the arguments themselves. As such, it appears advisable for counsellors to judiciously experiment with these various disputing styles in order to identify the ones that work best with particular clients.

DiGiuseppe (1991) identifies the level of abstraction of the irrational beliefs targeted for change as another variable germane to comprehensive cognitive disputing. Clients may subscribe to irrational beliefs in a very general form (e.g. 'I *must* have what I want when I want it') and in increasingly specific forms as well (e.g. 'My friends and family *must* give me what I want'; 'My wife *must* give me what I want'). Disputing that is directed only at the most abstract form of a given irrational belief may fail to help clients deal more effectively with *specific* problematic activating events (which may trigger more concrete, specific forms of the irrational belief), whereas disputing targeted only at a specific form of the irrational belief may be of limited usefulness because it fails to convey general principles that could help clients to deal with a wide variety of difficult situations. By moving up and down the 'ladder of abstraction', counsellors can help to increase the probability that clients will be able to generalise their application of RET from one problematic activating event to others.

We have presented a model in this text wherein irrational beliefs are viewed as being comprised of a premise and one or more derivatives. With respect to irrational belief processes, DiGiuseppe (1991) presents the premise form of an irrational belief as embodying the core process of demandingness, with awfulising, person-rating, and I-can't-stand-it-itis representing belief processes that tend to stem from this core process. Counsellors are advised not to assume that their disputing efforts aimed at one irrational belief process will generalise to other irrational belief processes that a particular client may endorse, and to work at identifying and disputing all irrational belief processes that may be relevant to the client's emotional problems.

We concur with DiGiuseppe's (1991) recommendations concerning comprehensive cognitive disputing, as it is likely that this approach currently represents the most efficient and effective means for helping clients to surrender their irrational beliefs in favour of more rational ones. In addition, by manipulating the variables relevant to the disputing process, counsellors can significantly refine their disputing skills. In Chapter 9, 'The rational–emotive counselling sequence', we present a model for rational–emotive counselling that integrates the various components of disputing with key elements of assessment, homework utilisation and the working-through process.

Vivid Disputing Methods

In this section, we outline various vivid methods of disputing clients' irrational beliefs which many rational-emotive counsellors have employed, with good results. As with the other vivid methods described in this book, these tend to be used after the more traditional disputing methods, outlined in the previous section, have proved unsuccessful. Vivid techniques do need to be employed selectively and we refer the reader to the previous chapter for cautions about the use of such methods in rational-emotive counselling.

Biographical information

Before initiating the vivid disputing process we often find it helpful to gather certain information about the client, such as his or her interests, hobbies and work situations. We have found this information often helps us adapt our interventions, using phrases that will be meaningful to our clients given their idiosyncratic life situations. Thus, if a client is passionately interested in boxing, a message utilising a boxing analogy may well have greater impact than a golfing analogy.

We also find it helpful to discover who our clients admire. We do this because later we may wish to ask clients how they think these admired individuals might solve similar problems. This may prompt clients to identify with a model to imitate. Lazarus (1984) has employed a similar method with children. For example, one of us (W.D.) asked a male client to imagine that his admired grandfather experienced public speaking anxiety and inquired how he would have overcome it. This helped him to identify a rational belief which he subsequently used to overcome his own public speaking anxiety problem. This approach is best used if the client can also acknowledge that the admired individual is fallible and thus prone to human irrationality. In addition it is important that the client sees the feasibility of imitating the model.

We find it invaluable to ask clients about their previous experience of attitude change. We try and discern the salient features of such change for possible replication in our in-session disputing strategies. For example, one anxious female client indicated that she had changed her mind about foxhunting after reading a number of personal accounts offering arguments against foxhunting. As part of a disputing plan, this client was directed to autobiographies of people who had overcome anxiety. Another client claimed she had in the past received help from speaking to people who had experienced problems similar to her own. Arrangements were made for this client to speak to some ex-clients who had experienced but overcome comparable problems.

We now propose to outline a number of ways in which rational-emotive counsellors can employ vivid disputing techniques. The importance of tailoring interventions to meet the specific, idiosyncratic requirements of clients should be borne in mind throughout.

In the previous chapter we outlined a number of ways of vividly portraying activating events to help clients identify their emotional reactions and the cognitive determinants of these reactions. We outlined various visual, auditory and olfactory methods. These same methods can be used as context material in the disputing process. For example, one client brought along a drawing of herself and her mother. She portrayed her mother as a very large, menacing figure and herself as a small figure crouching in fear in front of her mother. The client was asked to draw another picture where she and her mother were of the same height, standing face to face looking each other in the eye. When she brought in this drawing, an inquiry was made as to how her attitude toward her mother differed in the two pictures. This not only provided her with a demonstration that it was possible for her to evaluate her mother differently, but also led to a fruitful discussion in which some of the irrational beliefs inherent in her first drawing were disputed, while having her focus on the second.

Imagery methods

One very effective imagery method that can be used in the disputing of irrational beliefs is that of time projection (Lazarus, 1984). When a client makes grossly exaggerated negative evaluations of an event, she often stops thinking about it and therefore cannot see beyond its 'dreaded' implications. The purpose of time projection is to enable clients to see vividly that time and the world continue after the 'dreaded event' has occurred. Thus, for example, a Malaysian student whose tuition fees were paid for by his village concluded that it would be terrible if he failed his exams because he couldn't bear to face his fellow villagers. He was helped to imagine his return to his village while experiencing shame; time was gradually advanced forward via imagery. He began to see that it was likely that his fellow villagers would eventually come to adopt a compassionate viewpoint toward him, and even if they did not, he could always live happily in another part of the country, or in another part of the world.

The rational–emotive counsellor as raconteur

Rational-emotive counsellors often capitalise on the therapeutic value of relating various stories, parables, maxims and aphorisms to clients. Each one, of course, is designed to teach a rational concept. For example, Wessler and Wessler (1980, p. 126) relate the story of Nathan Leopold to illustrate the concepts of human complexity and the futility of evaluating oneself and others.

Nathan Leopold . . . along with Richard Loeb committed the 'Crime of the Century' in the 1920s by kidnapping and killing a young boy. Years later, Leopold was pardoned as a changed person, became a social worker, married, and spent much of the rest of his life doing good works. After telling or reminding the client of Leopold's story we ask, 'Now was Nathan Leopold a good man or a bad man?'. Again we get a variety of answers. The one we are looking for is 'He was neither. He was a man who did both good and bad things'. Leopold is an extreme case (which makes him a good example) and leads to a discussion of human fallibility.

The story of 'The Wise Rabbi' may also be used to good effect with some clients. This tale is particularly helpful for conveying the fatuous nature of an awfulising philosophy, as it humorously illustrates the concept that circumstances can almost always be worse than they actually are:

Many years ago a religious Jewish couple were having difficulties arising from living in a one-room apartment with two screaming children. They both believed that their situation was awful, and they were making themselves disturbed as a result. They decided to seek help from their local rabbi, a wise old man respected for his sage advice. On listening to the couple's story he advised them to invite both sets of parents to live with them, and instructed them to return in a month's time to report on progress. The couple were perplexed by this advice, but since they thought highly of the rabbi they carried out his advice to the letter.

One month later they returned to the rabbi even more distressed than before. 'We're getting to the end of our tether, rabbi. Things have gone from bad to worse. Both sets of parents are arguing and the children are screaming even louder than before.' The rabbi listened carefully, and then pronounced the following words: 'I want you to go home and collect up all your geese and chickens from the yard and have them live with you, your children, and your respective parents – and come and see me again in a month's time.'

If the couple were perplexed before, they were dumbfounded now. But again, being dutiful, they followed the rabbi's advice to the letter.

One month later they returned at their wits' end. 'We're at the breaking point, rabbi,' they said. 'The animals are creating pandemonium, our parents have almost come to blows, and the children's screams can be heard at the other end of town. We're desperate, rabbi. Please, please, PLEASE help us!'

The rabbi again listened patiently and then said, 'I want you to go home, put the geese and chickens back into the yard, send both sets of parents home, and come and see me in a month's time'.

One month later, the couple returned. This time they looked cheerful and happy. 'Things are so much better, rabbi. You have no idea. It's so peaceful. The kids are still screaming but that's bearable now. You've helped us so much, rabbi – thank you!'

Frequently, it is important that the counsellor modify the content of such stories to fit the client's idiosyncratic situation. Telling identical stories to two different clients may well have two different effects. One client may be deeply affected by the story, while for another the story may prove meaningless. It is important that rational–emotive counsellors become acquainted with a wide variety of these stories and be prepared to modify them from client to client without introducing unwarranted distortions. In addition, it is recommended that counsellors check with clients to ensure that the intended meaning of the story has been understood.

Active–visual methods

Active-visual methods combine therapist or client activity with a vivid visual presentation. Young (1984b) has outlined one such method, which he uses to help clients see the impossibility of assigning a global rating to themselves. He asks a client to describe some of his behaviours, attributes, talents, interests, etc. With every answer the client gives, Young writes the attribute on a white sticky label, and sticks the label on the client. This continues until the client is covered with white sticky labels and can begin to see the impossibility of assigning one global rating to such a complex being. Wessler and Wessler (1980) outline similar active-visual methods to communicate a similar point. For example, they ask their clients to assign a comprehensive rating to a basket of fruit on a desk. Clients are encouraged to actively explore the components of the fruit basket while attempting to assign a global rating to it. They soon come to realise that they can rate components of the basket but not its essence.

Visual models

We have designed a number of visual models each of which demonstrates a rational message. For example, one of us (W.D.) employs a model called the 'LFT Splash'. In the model a young man is seated at the top of a roller coaster with a young woman standing at the bottom. Clients are told that the young man does not move because he is telling himself that he can't stand the splash. Clients are asked to think what the young man would have to tell himself in order to reach the woman. This model is particularly useful in introducing to clients the idea of tolerating acute time-limited discomfort which, if tolerated, would help them achieve their goals.

In the earlier section of this chapter on disputing clients' 'damning' beliefs, a counsellor/client dialogue was presented in order to illustrate the manner in which clients can be taught the concept that the 'self' is too complex to warrant a single, global rating. This concept can also be presented to clients with a visual model which we term the 'Big I/Little i' diagram. Created by Arnold Lazarus (1977), this model was used to good effect by W.D. in his work with his client 'Sarah' whose counselling experience forms the basis for the book, *Daring To Be Myself: A Case-Study in Rational-Emotive Therapy* (Dryden and Yankura, 1992). The following excerpt from this book shows how the model was utilised within Sarah's sixth counselling session, during a discussion of her guilt feelings about the occasional angry outbursts she would direct toward her husband, Art:

Dr Dryden: You just went from 'I've done something unpleasant' to 'I'm not a very pleasant person'. Can you see the sort of jump that you're making?

Sarah: (in a small voice) No, not really.

Dr Dryden: Well – have I ever spoken with you about the difference between the 'Big I' and the 'Little i'?

Sarah: No.

Dr Dryden: Okay – let me just write this out for you. I'm writing a big block 'I' here, and I'm making lots and lots of little 'i's' inside it. Now, I'm going to circle one of the little 'i's'. Take a look at this: the big 'I' represents you in your wholeness, your totality – right? But as you can see, you're made up of lots and lots of little 'i's'. You have lots of behaviours, lots of thoughts, lots of feelings. Now, how many little 'i's' do you think you're made up of?

Sarah: I suppose thousands, if you put it like that.

Dr Dryden: That's right! Now, the one circled is what you've just said to Art, which wasn't very pleasant, right? How does that one unpleasant . . .

Sarah: It doesn't make me a *whole* nasty person!

Dr Dryden: That's right!

Sarah: Mm.

Dr Dryden: Now, if you were to regard what you said as unpleasant and undesirable, but didn't jump to '*I* am an unpleasant person', what sort of difference do you think that would make?

Sarah: There's a big difference between saying there's a *little* part of me that can be nasty and snappy, and saying that all of me is! The way you've put it now – and thinking about what you've said in the past – I'm not *always* like that. Far from it!

It is noteworthy that when Sarah was interviewed by J.Y. for the above-mentioned book approximately 8 years after the last of her sessions with W.D., she described the 'Big I/Little i' diagram as being one of the most memorable and helpful features of her counselling.

Flamboyant counsellor actions

A common disputing strategy that rational–emotive counsellors use in verbal dialogue when clients conclude they are stupid for acting stupidly, is to ask some variant of the question 'How are you a stupid person for acting stupidly?' Alternatively, instead of asking such questions, the counsellor could suddenly leap to the floor and start barking like a dog for about 30 seconds and then resume his or her seat, then ask the client to evaluate this action. Clients usually say that the action is stupid. The counsellor can then ask whether that stupid action makes him or her a stupid person. Such flamboyant actions often enable clients to more easily discriminate between global self-ratings and ratings of behaviours or attributes.

Counsellor self-disclosure

In Chapter 5, it was noted that rational–emotive counsellors strive to be as open as therapeutically feasible with their clients. Some clients find self-disclosure by the counsellor an extremely persuasive method; for others, however, it is contraindicated. One way of attempting to ascertain a client's possible reactions to counsellor self-disclosure is to include an appropriate item in a precounselling questionnaire. It may well be wise for counsellors to avoid using self-disclosure with clients who respond negatively to the item. In any case, the counsellor should ascertain the client's reaction to any self-disclosing statements that he or she might make. The research literature on this topic indicates that it is inadvisable for counsellors to disclose personal information about themselves too early in the therapeutic process (Dies, 1973).

When counsellors do disclose information about themselves it is our experience that the most effective forms of self-disclosure are those in which they portray themselves as coping rather than mastery models. Thus, for example, it is better for the counsellor to say to the client: 'I used to have a similar problem, but this is how I overcame it' rather than to say: 'I have never had this problem, because I believe . . .'. Occasionally, W.D. will tell clients with shame-based anxieties how he overcame his anxiety about stammering in public. He tells them that he used to believe: 'It would be terrible if I stammered in public and it would prove I was worthless if I did'. He then discloses how he changed his belief to 'I don't like stammering in public but if I do I do, too bad! I can accept myself with my stammer even if others put me down'. At the end of a session in which he has disclosed his experience in overcoming this personal problem, W.D. will generally ask the client how she felt about his disclosure, what she learned from it, and whether or not she would have preferred to have this information. The client's feedback is used to gauge the likely future benefit of additional self-disclosure with that client.

Rational humorous songs

Ellis (1977a) has written about the use of his now famous rational songs in counselling. For example, the counsellor can hand a client a song sheet and sing, preferably in an outrageous voice, a rational song that has been carefully selected to communicate the rational alternatives to the client's target irrational belief. Since Ellis tends to favour songs that were written many years ago, it may be more productive for the counsellor to rewrite the words to more up-to-date and popular songs for clients not familiar with some of the 'old favourites'.

The following is a rational humorous song written by W.D. to the tune of 'God save the Queen':

> God save my precious spleen
> Send me a life serene
> God save my spleen

Protect me from things odious
Give me a life melodious
And if things get too onerous
I'll whine, bawl and scream

Once clients can identify their own irrational belief in the lyrics, they can be then helped to rewrite the words of the song to reflect a rational philosophy.

Rational prescriptions

One of us (J.Y.) will occasionally make a great show of writing the client a 'rational prescription' at session's end, as illustrated in the following dialogue:

Counsellor: Okay – we spent a good part of today's session discussing how you *can stand* feeling anxious while you're out driving in your car, even though you don't *like* feeling that way. We've run out of time now so we'll have to stop, but before we do, I just want to give you a prescription that will help you as you try to apply this concept. (Scribbles on a small notepad, tears off the sheet with a flourish, and hands it to the client.)

Client: (reading sheet) It says, 'TOUGH SHIT!'

Counsellor: That's right – and if you apply a 'tough shit' philosophy when you begin feeling anxious – meaning, 'I don't like it but I can stand it' – you'll be better able to resist the urge to flee homeward when you're out driving!

Client: (laughs) A 'tough shit' philosophy! I like that – and I can think of about a hundred other situations that I can use it for! (Client folds the 'prescription' and places it in her bag.)

It is noted that a good number of clients have actually reported that they stowed their 'rational prescriptions' in a safe place (such as a wallet or handbag) for use at times when they experienced a significant emotional upset. It is possible that these little slips of paper serve to augment clients' independent efforts at disputing their irrational beliefs in their everyday lives, as they may prompt recall of the counsellor's 'rational voice'. Ideally, as counselling proceeds, clients make progress in internalising a rational philosophy so that such external props are no longer required.

Reduction to absurdity

Here the counsellor assumes temporarily that the client's irrational belief is true and carries it to its logical extreme, thus illuminating its absurdity. For example, Richard Wessler, once Director of Training at the Institute for RET in New York, related the following episode when he was working with a client who irrationally demanded a guarantee that bad things would not happen in his life. Wessler suddenly jumped up and hid under his desk, inviting his client to join him there. His puzzled client enquired why and was told by Wessler that this was the only way to guarantee that the ceiling would not fall on them. The client refused to join Wessler, having understood the point of his intervention. Note how Wessler, in this example, combined a reduction to absurdity intervention with a flamboyant counsellor action to illustrate an appropriate rational concept.

We urge readers to be creative and devise novel vivid disputing methods, which should preferably be tailored to help individual clients. It has been our experience that effective rational–emotive counsellors are creative in this respect and tend to avoid the slavish replication of vivid techniques devised by others.

Homework Aids in Promoting Intellectual Rational Insight

While we have focused thus far on counsellors' in-session interventions, which aim to promote clients' intellectual rational insight, an important part of this process is carried out by clients between sessions. These are frequently embodied in 'homework' assignments negotiated between client and counsellor.

Listening to audiotapes of sessions

It sometimes occurs that clients become confused during the disputing process in counselling sessions. This may happen, for example, when clients become emotionally distracted in the sessions, and/or counsellors work too quickly for the clients' level of understanding. In such cases clients can often facilitate their acquisition of rational concepts by reviewing audiotapes of their sessions. This has the advantage that clients can replay segments of the tape as many times as they find valuable to clarify their understanding of what transpired between them and their counsellors. When this technique is suggested counsellors should preferably encourage clients to write down any issues they wish to discuss in their following counselling session, and in particular to make a note of any doubts they may have about the invalidity and self-defeating nature of their irrational beliefs.

Some clients do not find listening to tapes of their therapy sessions very useful. These are often clients who blame themselves for their lack of understanding as demonstrated in the session, or for the sound of their voice. Although it is sometimes helpful to suggest that such clients use the tapes as stimuli to dispute their irrational beliefs about these two features, counsellors should preferably not insist that clients listen to these tapes when doing so is not helpful for them.

Structured disputing

There exist a number of forms that structure the disputing process for clients to use between counselling sessions. A good example is *DIBS*

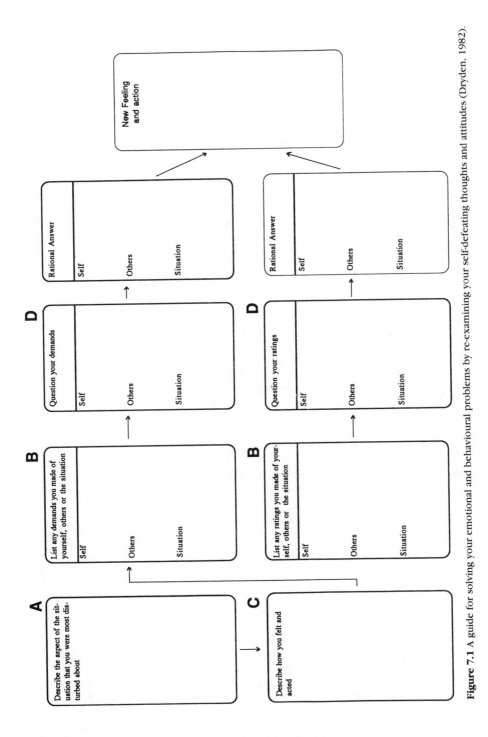

Figure 7.1 A guide for solving your emotional and behavioural problems by re-examining your self-defeating thoughts and attitudes (Dryden, 1982).

RET SELF-HELP FORM

Institute for Rational-Emotive Therapy
45 East 65th Street, New York, N.Y. 10021
(212) 535-0822

(A) ACTIVATING EVENTS, thoughts, or feelings that happened just before I felt emotionally disturbed or acted self-defeatingly: _____

(C) CONSEQUENCE or CONDITION—disturbed feeling or self-defeating behavior—that I produced and would like to change: _____

(B) BELIEFS—Irrational BELIEFS (IBs) leading to my CONSEQUENCE (emotional disturbance or self-defeating behavior). Circle all that apply to these ACTIVATING EVENTS (A).	(D) DISPUTES for each circled IRRATIONAL BELIEF. Examples: "Why MUST I do very well?" "Where is it written that I am a BAD PERSON?" "Where is the evidence that I MUST be approved or accepted?"	(E) EFFECTIVE RATIONAL BELIEFS (RBs) to replace my IRRATIONAL BELIEFS (IBs). Examples: "I'd PREFER to do very well but I don't HAVE TO." "I am a PERSON WHO acted badly, not a BAD PERSON." "There is no evidence that I HAVE TO be approved, though I would LIKE to be."
1. I MUST do well or very well!	....	....
2. I am a BAD OR WORTHLESS PERSON when I act weakly or stupidly.	....	....

Figure 7.2 RET self-help form (Sichel and Ellis, 1984). (Reproduced with the permission of the Institute for Rational-Emotive Therapy, New York, USA. © Institute for RET, 1984.)

(OVER)

3. I MUST be approved or accepted by people I find important!

4. I am a BAD, UNLOVABLE PERSON if I get rejected.

5. People MUST treat me fairly and give me what I NEED!

6. People who act immorally are undeserving, ROTTEN PEOPLE!

7. People MUST live up to my expectations or it is TERRIBLE!

8. My life MUST have few major hassles or troubles.

9. I CAN'T STAND really bad things or very difficult people!

Figure 7.2 (continued)

10. It's AWFUL or HORRIBLE when major things don't go my way!

11. I CAN'T STAND IT when life is really unfair!

12. I NEED to be loved by someone who matters to me a lot!

13. I NEED a good deal of immediate gratification and HAVE TO feel miserable when I don't get it!

<u>Additional Irrational Beliefs:</u>

14.

15.

Figure 7.2 (continued)

16.

17.

18.

(F) FEELINGS and BEHAVIORS I experienced after arriving at my EFFECTIVE RATIONAL BELIEFS: _____

I WILL WORK HARD TO REPEAT MY EFFECTIVE RATIONAL BELIEFS FORCEFULLY TO MYSELF ON MANY OCCASIONS SO THAT I CAN MAKE MYSELF LESS DISTURBED NOW AND ACT LESS SELF-DEFEATINGLY IN THE FUTURE.

Figure 7.2 (continued)

(disputing irrational beliefs) and Ellis (1979c, pp. 79–80) has outlined its form thus:

Question 1: What irrational belief do I want to dispute and surrender?
Answer: I must be as effective and sexually fulfilled as most other women.
Question 2: Can I rationally support this belief?
Answer: ....
Question 3: What evidence exists of the truth of this belief?
Answer: ....
Question 4: What evidence exists of the falseness of my belief that I must be as orgasmic as other women are?
Answer: ....
Question 5: What are the worst possible things that could actually happen to me if I never achieved the orgasm that I think I must achieve?
Answer: ....
Question 6: What good things could happen, or could I make happen, if I never achieved the heights of orgasm that I think I must achieve?
Answer: ....

As a homework exercise DIBS is best used after a general Socratic and/or didactic disputing sequence has been successfully completed, and after the counsellor has demonstrated the use of DIBS in the session, taking the irrational belief that has been successfully disputed as an example.

Apart from DIBS, there exist a number of structured disputing exercises that can be suggested for use as cognitive homework assignments. Two examples of these appear in Figures 7.1 and 7.2. The major purpose of these forms is to help clients to identify, challenge and change their irrational beliefs and they appear to have a number of shared components. They encourage clients to identify activating events (or inferences about these events); irrational feelings and/or self-defeating actions that occur in the context of these events; and their mediating irrational beliefs. Furthermore, these forms invite clients to ask for evidence that supports their irrational beliefs and provide spaces for them to identify rational alternatives to that irrational belief; and likely emotional and/or behavioural effects of these new rational beliefs. It is recommended that rational–emotive counsellors demonstrate the use of these forms in counselling sessions before asking clients to use them in their daily lives.

Rational self-help material

Rational–emotive counsellors frequently suggest that clients read or listen to self-help materials between sessions in order to build upon and reinforce the rational intellectual insight that clients gain within sessions. Since there is a wide range of such aids available, counsellors are recommended to monitor clients' reactions to these so that they can suggest material that is most appropriate to the client's level of understanding of rational concepts. Frequently suggested books include Ellis and Harper's (1975) *A New Guide to Rational Living*, Ellis and Becker's (1982) *A Guide to Personal Happiness*, and Dryden and Gordon's (1990) *Think Your Way To Happiness*. When using these books, counsellors, in the first instance, are advised to assign chapters that reinforce the message that beliefs determine emotions and actions, and thereafter recommend particular chapters relevant to the client's problem(s). It is helpful to encourage clients to note points for future discussion in counselling sessions, particularly those which they do not understand and those with which they disagree. If clients find the three books mentioned difficult to understand, they can be asked to read less complex material such as Young's (1974) *A Rational Counseling Primer* or Kranzler's (1974) *You Can Change How You Feel*.

In addition, RET-orientated books are available that are devoted to particular client problems, such as depression, anger, anxiety, procrastination etc., and in this regard Paul Hauck's books in the Sheldon Press *Overcoming Common Problems* series are particularly popular with British clients.

In addition to reading material, there exist numerous audiotapes on general and specific applications of rational–emotive theory that clients can use for the same purposes as the books we have mentioned. Again, counsellors are advised to elicit clients' reactions to such material, paying particular attention to doubts and disagreements, which can then be discussed in regular sessions.

While the achievement of rational *intellectual* insight is an important stage for clients in the counselling process, as noted earlier, it is rarely sufficient for meaningful psychological change to occur. For such change to take place clients need to achieve *emotional* rational insight, and the next chapter is devoted to its promotion.

Chapter 8
Promoting Emotional Rational Insight

Overview

In this chapter, we deal with issues concerning the promotion of emotional rational insight. First, we note that helping clients to achieve this type of insight is difficult, and list a number of reasons why this is so. Then we highlight standard and vivid techniques which are used during this stage of rational-emotive counselling. Thus, we describe cognitive, imagery and behavioural techniques, most of which have a decided emotive quality. Finally, we outline a number of vivid cues that counsellors can use to encourage clients to initiate the process of promoting emotional rational insight.

Promoting Emotional Rational Insight is Difficult

When clients have achieved intellectual but not emotional insight into rational concepts, they typically make such statements as, 'Yes, I see that what you say makes sense, but I don't believe it yet', or 'I understand it up here in my head, but not down here in my gut'. It is important to explain to clients that gaining intellectual rational insight is an important step in the change process but one which is usually insufficient to bring about meaningful emotional and behavioural change. Rational-emotive counsellors further explain that, in order to achieve significant attitude change that affects feelings and actions, i.e. emotional rational insight, clients will usually have to employ repeatedly and persistently a variety of cognitive, emotive and behavioural techniques.

As rational-emotive practitioners note (e.g. Grieger, 1985), helping clients to move from intellectual to emotional rational insight is often a difficult painstaking process, for a number of reasons. First, as Ellis (1976) in particular has argued, humans have a distinct biologically based tendency towards irrational thinking and often have a hard time working against this tendency.

Secondly, even those rational–emotive counsellors who adopt a social learning perspective, rather than a biological perspective on human irrationality, acknowledge that changing irrational beliefs is a difficult process. Such theorists (e.g. Grieger, 1985) note that once clients have learned to think irrationally and to act in accordance with their irrational beliefs, they become habituated to these ideas and 'changing anything so well learned, therefore, requires repeated energetic efforts, even for those who are willing and committed to change' (Grieger, 1985, p. 144).

Thirdly, many clients have a philosophy of low frustration tolerance (LFT) and believe that they should not have to work so hard to effect meaningful psychological change and, as Grieger (1985, p. 145) notes, 'left to their own devices, they drift, goof and act on their acknowledged irrational, self-defeating beliefs even though they know better'. Attacking clients' LFT beliefs is a prominent feature of promoting emotional rational insight.

Fourthly, and related to the above, clients often become habituated to their problems and become used to the 'comfortable discomfort' that these problems bring. They fear that change may bring more acute discomfort and therefore will not risk changing. Rational–emotive counsellors need to help clients understand that they may indeed feel more uncomfortable in the short term, but if they work at tolerating such discomfort the long-term rewards will usually outweigh the short-term rewards of avoiding discomfort.

Fifthly, as Fransella (1985) has shown, clients often give their psychological problems a central position in their sense of identity (e.g. a person who stammers sees himself as 'a stammerer') and they cannot imagine how they would lead their lives if they did not, for example, stammer. Here rational–emotive counsellors may choose to employ general semantic methods, such as helping clients to use more precise and accurate language (e.g. changing 'I am a stammerer' to 'I am a person who stammers under certain conditions and not under other conditions'). In addition, they would help such clients construct a view of what life might be like if they did not stammer as often.

In a related vein, one of us (J.Y.) has noted that clients with a strong self-created 'need' for other people's approval may be quite tuned in to what they think significant others want and prefer, but are out of touch with their own wants and preferences. Such individuals often have a difficult time envisioning a future existence in which they have given up their primary agenda of 'people pleasing', as this agenda historically provided them with a set of goals and behavioural guidelines (albeit dysfunctional ones) for structuring their daily lives. These clients can benefit from counselling interventions designed to help them develop their awareness of their own personal likes and dislikes. Once identified, these likes and dislikes can then be translated into new life goals to be striven for.

134   Counselling Individuals: A Rational-Emotive Handbook

Sixthly, clients may experience sources of secondary gain as a result of having their problems. Thus a woman who wishes to lose weight in order to be more attractive to men might find, if she is successful, that she has to be assertive in declining to sleep with men, which she would find difficult. An advantage of being fat for this woman, then, is that she does not place herself in situations where she might act promiscuously, which she would evaluate very negatively. It is clear then that rational–emotive counsellors need to focus particular attention on assessing potential obstacles to the change process and deal with these as they become relevant during this stage of counselling. This issue will be discussed more fully in Chapter 11.

Seventh, as Grieger, among others has noted, clients often make unrealistic predictions of what their lives might be like if they adhered to a rational philosophy of life: these include 'fear of losing one's identity or becoming a phony . . .; fears of becoming emotionally dulled or machine-like by thinking rationally; and fears of becoming mediocre and losing one's specialness by giving up perfectionistic ideas' (Grieger, 1985, p. 144). One of W.D.'s clients recently announced that she didn't think much of life according to rational-emotive philosophy because it meant never falling in love! It is important that rational-emotive counsellors be aware that clients may well misinterpret rational-emotive philosophy and be ready to correct such misconceptions. We advise rational-emotive counsellors to ask clients directly about how they would construe their lives if they indeed achieved what they hoped to gain from counselling, rather than waiting for clients to disclose such constructions. In such exploration counsellors should pay particular attention to misinterpretations of rational-emotive philosophy and deal with them accordingly.

Finally, clients may find it difficult to put their intellectual rational insights into consistent practice because the balance of their outside relationships would be disturbed if they did. For example, asserting oneself with one's spouse may lead to marital problems; getting over one's depression may be a trigger for one's partner to become depressed, etc. Rational-emotive counsellors need to be sensitive to the fact that clients in individual counselling have a wide variety of interpersonal relationships in their daily lives which may exert a positive or negative influence on their attempts to achieve their counselling goals. Rational-emotive counsellors may indeed suggest to clients that they involve their significant others in counselling, particularly if these others may wittingly or unwittingly sabotage clients' attempts to change. Since this book is concerned with counselling individuals, we refer the reader to Ellis and Dryden (1987) for a discussion of the practice of RET in its other modalities. In the final analysis, however, if significant others do react negatively to clients' attempts to change and do not want to become involved in counselling, then rational-emotive counsellors encourage their clients to view this situation as another troublesome A in the ABC framework to be coped with using rational thinking.

Techniques to Promote Emotional Rational Insight

The remainder of this chapter will focus on methods and techniques that clients can use to achieve emotional rational insight. In addition to using repeatedly and persistently the disputing methods outlined in the previous chapter, clients are encouraged to use a variety of cognitive, behavioural and emotive assignments in the service of achieving emotional and behavioural changes. We will focus especially on methods and techniques which are most frequently used in rational–emotive counselling, and those which are particularly vivid. In this latter respect, Ellis (1958, p. 45, italics added) from RET's inception strongly recommended that clients undertake 'some kind of activity which itself will act as a *forceful* counterpropagandist agency against the nonsense they believe'. Ellis continues to stress that for clients who will agree to do them, *dramatic*, *forceful* and *implosive* activities remain the best forms of promoting emotional insight. This is due to the fact that since clients, according to Ellis, have a pronounced tendency to think irrationally, they need to counter this tendency forcefully and repeatedly.

Cognitive techniques

Clients are encouraged to use cognitive techniques to convince themselves outside counselling sessions that rational philosophies, which they can acknowledge as correct in counselling, are indeed correct and functional for them. The emphasis here is particularly on clients weakening their adherence to irrational beliefs and strengthening their adherence to rational beliefs. We have found that techniques that encourage clients to provide evidence in favour of rational beliefs are particularly helpful at this stage of rational–emotive counselling, and these will be discussed first.

Building your rational portfolio

Here, as noted above, counsellors encourage clients to focus on evidence in favour of rational beliefs. Thus a client who can see that there is no evidence in support of her irrational belief 'I *must* control my emotions in public' is asked to explain in detail why it would be better but not essential if she could control her emotions in public. The role of the counsellor in this process is to encourage the client to find a variety of different reasons in support of the rational belief and to suggest others when the client has exhausted her own supply. We call this technique 'Building your rational portfolio'.

Devil's advocate disputing

Once a client has sufficiently built up her portfolio in the above manner and shows some skill at disputing her irrational beliefs, the counsellor can adopt the role of a devil's advocate and attack the client's rational thinking. The client's role is to point out flaws in the reasoning of the devil's advocate and destroy his arguments, thus strengthening further her rational belief:

Counsellor: (as devil's advocate) But how can you possibly say that you don't need a man in your life? Look at all your friends, they do and they're normal. Aren't you abnormal for trying to deny your needs?

Client: Just because my friends believe they need a man in their life doesn't mean that I have to believe the same. Most of them are anxious when they don't have a man and anxious when they do in case he leaves them. I don't want that for myself. Also I'm not denying my need, I'm trying to challenge it and if I am abnormal in this regard I'm abnormally healthy, not sick as you seem to imply.

In devil's advocate disputing the counsellor looks for issues that the client does not deal with and feeds this back into the discussion. Thus in the above example, if the client did not deal with the issue of abnormality the counsellor in his role of devil's advocate would have raised this issue again.

When beginning devil's advocate disputing, the counsellor should preferably raise one issue at a time until the client shows some skill at this procedure. The example provided above is with a client who has previously demonstrated a high level of skill at this form of disputing. Thus, the counsellor, in the example, can raise two or three issues at once.

Another major counsellor goal in devil's advocate disputing is to find vulnerable points in the client's rational thinking so that these can be dealt with. Here the counsellor presents irrational beliefs to the client to which she experiences difficulty in responding. When this occurs it is best to stop the procedure and discuss the new irrational belief in a more traditional manner.

Devil's advocate disputing is one example of what Kassinove and Di-Giuseppe (1975) call rational role reversal, where the counsellor adopts an irrational role and the client adopts a rational role. Although we have focused on devil's advocate disputing where the counsellor attacks the client's thinking, rational role reversal can take different forms. For example, the counsellor plays the irrational part of the client and supplies the client with irrational messages. The client's task is to respond rationally to these irrational messages. In another version the counsellor plays a naive client with an emotional problem that is usually similar to the client's, and presents an irrational belief identical to the one targeted for change. The client is encouraged to adopt the role of the rational–emotive counsellor and help the 'client' to dispute his or her irrational belief.

It should be reiterated that all versions of rational role reversal are best used when the client has demonstrated a fair measure of skill at disputing her own irrational beliefs using more traditional methods, as described in the previous chapter. As noted above, they can also all be used to identify weaknesses in the clients' rational arguments in response to irrational beliefs articulated in 'reversed role' by counsellors.

The courtroom evidence technique

In the courtroom evidence technique the client is asked to play the roles of prosecuting attorney and defence attorney, providing evidence for and against the client's rational belief in one 'trial', and doing the same with the client's irrational belief in another 'trial'. The goal, of course, is to provide more compelling evidence in favour of the rational belief and to contradict the 'evidence' in favour of the irrational belief. At the end of this procedure the client is asked to play the role of judge and sum up all the evidence presented and provide a verdict, which hopefully is: 'I thus conclude that the rational belief is valid and the irrational belief is invalid'. If the client concludes otherwise the counsellor is provided with useful information concerning the client's doubts and reservations about the relevant rational belief. These are then discussed once the 'trial' has been concluded. After these have been discussed the counsellor calls for an appeal against the previous verdict and the procedure is repeated.

Rational essays

Another technique that can be used under the heading of strengthening rational beliefs is to suggest that the client write an essay on a theme suggested by a rational belief, e.g. 'Why I cannot legitimately give myself a global rating'. Here is an extract from an essay written by one of W.D.'s clients on the above theme:

> I have many different roles in my life. But let me take one, 'mother', to show how complex this role is. Breaking this role down into its component parts, I find there are many different aspects of mothering. But let me take one, 'disciplining'. Even this has different components including 'setting limits', 'working with my husband', 'voice tone', etc. Let me take one: voice tone. Even this has different components including firmness, gentleness, harshness, etc. Yesterday, in the space of an hour I used what I consider to be a good voice tone (firmness) with my child and a bad voice tone (harshness). Can I say I have a good voice tone? Hardly. How stupid it is then for me to say 'I'm a good or bad disciplinarian with my child'. If that is stupid how even more stupid for me to say 'I'm a good or bad mother'. Looking at it this way how can I possibly say that I'm a good or bad person? Obviously I can't. As Dr Dryden suggested I will undertake to use the sentence 'I am a person who . . .' whenever I can. But if I don't and I do rate myself, I won't rate *myself* badly for rating myself.

Rational proselytising (Bard, 1973)

Here clients are encouraged to teach rational–emotive principles to their friends and relatives. In teaching others to live more rationally it is hypothesised that clients will become more convinced of rational–emotive philosophy, and in our experience this often happens. In the process of teaching these principles to significant others, clients learn to counter their objections and thus learn to think 'on their feet' when confronted with their own irrational beliefs. In addition, when clients report being unable to counter objections from significant others these are discussed further in regular counselling sessions. This technique, however, is best used with caution and clients should be warned against playing the role of unwanted counsellor to friends and relations.

Tape-recorded disputing

In this technique clients are encouraged to put a disputing sequence on tape and instructed to play both the rational and irrational parts of themselves. They are further encouraged to try and make the rational part more persuasive and more forceful in responding to the irrational part. Clients then play excerpts of these tapes to their counsellors, who check whether their clients have indeed successfully disputed their irrational beliefs and listen carefully to the tone of the dialogue. When clients do not dispute their irrational beliefs forcefully and persuasively this may be attributed to two factors. First, this may indicate their difficulties in responding to certain elements of their irrational philosophy, in which case their doubts and lack of intellectual insight should be targets for discussion in sessions. Secondly, it may indicate that clients find it difficult to be forceful in adopting the rational role. When clients experience such difficulty, counsellors should model appropriate ways of disputing forcefully and encourage clients to practise responding to their irrational beliefs in similar ways.

Passionate rational self-statements

Clients who are intellectually unable to do cognitive self-disputing in the traditional sense can be encouraged to use passionate rational self-statements instead. Here clients and counsellors work together to develop appropriate rational self-statements that clients can use in their daily lives. Clients are then encouraged to repeat these statements in a very forceful manner instead of in their normal voice tone. Another variation of this technique is to encourage clients to say rational self-statements to their reflection in a mirror, using a passionate tone and dramatic gestures to reinforce the rational message.

Encouraging clients to go against their irrational action tendencies

In Chapter 2, we introduced the concepts of action tendencies and response options. In Chapter 4 we argued that different emotions lead to different action tendencies and that, given a certain tendency to act, a person will choose certain response options and avoid others. We also argued that irrational emotions lead to irrational action tendencies which in turn influence individuals to choose responses that tend to be self-defeating. It follows that if clients are to be encouraged to act rationally, then counsellors need to encourage them to go against irrational action tendencies. Also, as is argued in the next section, behavioural change is often the best way of encouraging clients to change their irrational beliefs. In order to encourage such behavioural change, rational–emotive counsellors often have first to help clients to dispute the irrational beliefs that are implicit in their irrational action tendencies.

For example, one of W.D.'s clients experienced anxiety about asking girls to dance at a discotheque. His irrational belief in this situation was 'I would be worthless if they refused to dance with me'. This client was helped to dispute this belief and to achieve intellectual rational insight. However, he still would not ask any girls to dance and work toward rational emotional insight due to his tendency to avoid anxiety (irrational action tendency). Implicit in this action tendency was another irrational belief . . . 'I must be comfortable when I ask girls to dance'. Thus, in order to help this client to achieve emotional rational insight it was necessary first to help him to challenge this latter belief and change it to 'I prefer being comfortable when I ask girls to dance but I can still do so even though I feel uncomfortable'. Then, he was encouraged to push himself to act on this latter belief and choose a different option from his response repertoire, i.e. ask girls to dance rather than avoid the situation. He did this repeatedly and achieved emotional rational insight on both the aforementioned beliefs.

When action tendencies encourage clients to avoid situations rather than to confront them constructively, activities which help them to reverse this trend have been called 'stay in there' activities by Grieger and Boyd (1980).

Another example: one of J.Y.'s clients wanted to overcome her car-driving phobia. She would, however, make herself anxious about the possibility of breaking down in some remote spot where assistance would not be readily available. In order to avoid this possibility and the distressing anxiety she experienced whenever she thought about its occurrence, she would almost never venture more than a few blocks away from home in her car. After her irrational ideas had been elicited and disputed in traditional verbal dialogue, she was encouraged to drive a lengthy distance in order to visit an old friend whom she had not seen for some time. She did indeed make herself anxious while travelling in her car to this friend's neighbourhood but, as agreed in session, disputed her belief that 'I *can't stand* feeling this way' and resisted her urge to flee homeward. She reached her destination and later returned home without mishap, and was thus able to re-evaluate her overestimation of the probability of having a breakdown while out driving. More importantly, she proved to herself that she could 'stay in there' and tolerate her anxious feelings, even though they were quite uncomfortable for her.

The same methods can be used when action tendencies encourage clients to act in self-defeating ways other than avoidance. However, whatever action tendencies are involved in clients' problems, the following principle can be recommended: whenever clients find it difficult to choose appropriate options from their repertoire, and in fact choose to act in accordance with their irrational action tendencies, look for their low frustration tolerance (LFT) ideas, since clients often have these in such situations.

Behavioural techniques

As shown above, one of the best ways of encouraging clients to achieve emotional rational insight is to have them change their self-defeating behaviour in relevant situations. We wish to reiterate this point, since many people believe wrongly that rational–emotive counsellors only employ cognitive techniques to help clients change irrational beliefs. However, behaviour change should ideally be enacted while clients are simultaneously working cognitively to change their irrational beliefs. Thus in the example we introduced in the previous section, the client asked girls to dance while convincing himself: 'I can do this even though I feel uncomfortable and I'm not a worm if I'm rejected'. With this point in mind we will discuss in this section certain behavioural techniques that rational–emotive counsellors particularly favour.

Ellis (1983c) has criticized some popular behavioural techniques on the grounds that they do not necessarily encourage clients to achieve emotional rational insight as efficiently as possible. In particular, he criticises those methods that encourage clients to confront dreaded events in a gradual manner. He argues that 'gradualism' may indeed reinforce some clients' low frustration tolerance ideas, e.g. 'I do need to go slowly; you see, even my counsellor believes I can't stand feeling anxious'. Wherever possible then, rational–emotive counsellors encourage their clients to act in dramatic and vivid ways because they believe significant attitude change is more likely to follow the successful completion of such tasks. In addition, dramatic behavioural assignments are recommended to help clients overcome their LFT beliefs. Here the focus is oriented toward clients changing their irrational beliefs concerning their internal experiences of anxiety or frustration, such that they are able to see that they can tolerate these feelings.

Shame-attacking exercises

Here clients are encouraged to act in a manner which they regard as 'shameful' while disputing their shame-creating beliefs. Clients are encouraged to act in ways that will encourage other people in the environment to pay attention to them and criticise them negatively, without bringing harm to themselves or the other people, and without unduly alarming others. Clients are encouraged in particular to engage simultaneously in vigorous disputing such as, 'They may think I'm an idiot but I choose to accept myself even though I may be acting stupidly'. Examples of shame-attacking exercises that some of our clients have undertaken include: asking for directions to a street along which one is already walking; asking for a bar of chocolate in a hardware store; and wearing clothes back to front. One of the difficulties with shame-attacking exercises for clients is actually eliciting the aversive responses from others that clients predict will occur. For example, if a client is anxious about a shopkeeper laughing at him for acting stupidly, then the client may have to carry out shame-attacking exercises several times before he encounters such a shopkeeper. However, this actual encounter is important if the client is going to have the experience of disputing his shame-inducing belief in the context of the feared event. Otherwise the client may make an inferentially based change, i.e. he may come to learn 'it is unlikely that shopkeepers will laugh at me when I act stupidly'. While this change is not to be decried, it is less preferable than evaluative belief change, e.g. 'If shopkeepers laugh at me, I can still accept myself'.

Risk-taking exercises

In risk-taking exercises clients are encouraged to do something they regard as being 'too risky'. These exercises are particularly helpful in encouraging clients to dispute discomfort-related irrational beliefs relating to certainty. For example, a client may be encouraged to take the risk of acting in an unpredictable manner not knowing how others will respond, while disputing his belief 'I can stand the uncertainty of not knowing what will happen'.

Step-out-of-character exercises

Wessler (1984) has modified this exercise from Kelly (1955). Clients are encouraged to identify desired behavioural goals which are not currently enacted with frequency, and are encouraged to practise these behaviours while tolerating the accompanying feelings of 'unnaturalness' and to continue doing this until the new behaviour becomes habitual. For example, one of W.D.'s clients chose the goal of eating more slowly, which for him was a desirable, non-shameful, non-risky exercise, but one that involved monitoring of eating habits and cognitive disputing of low-frustration-tolerance ideas.

In vivo desensitisation

These methods require clients to repeatedly confront their fears in an implosive manner. For example, clients with elevator phobia are asked to ride in elevators 20–30 times a day at the start of treatment instead of gradually working their way up to this situation either in imagery or in actuality. Again, simultaneous cognitive disputing is urged. Neuman (1982) has written on and presented tapes of short-term group-oriented treatment of phobias. In his groups, clients are encouraged to rate their levels of anxiety. The most important goal is for clients to experience a 'level 10', which is extreme panic. Neuman continually points out to people that it is important to experience 'level 10' because only then can they learn that they can survive and live through such an experience. Similarly, if inroads to severe phobic conditions are to be made, it is important for rational–emotive counsellors to work toward helping clients tolerate extreme forms of anxiety before helping them to reduce this anxiety.

There are occasions when clients refuse to undertake such assignments. When this occurs, compromises should preferably be made, as discussed in Chapter 11.

Repetition of behavioural assignments

Some clients tend to do dramatic exercises once or twice and then drop them from their repertoire. Counsellors are often so glad and so surprised that their clients will actually do these assignments that they do not show them the importance of continuing to do them. One of the reasons for continued practice has already been mentioned, namely that clients are more likely to make inferential changes than belief changes by doing these assignments infrequently. This is largely because the 'dreaded' event has a far lower probability of occurring than clients think. However, sooner or later, if clients consistently and persistently put into practice the above assignments, they may well encounter such events that will provide a context for disputing of irrational beliefs. Thus, if counsellors really want to encourage clients to make changes at B as well as at A, they had better be prepared to consistently encourage clients to do these dramatic assignments over a long period of time.

Rewards and penalties

Ellis (1979c) has consistently employed rewards and penalties to encourage clients to take responsibility for being their own primary agents of change. Here, clients are encouraged to identify and employ positive reinforcements for undertaking assignments, and penalties when they do not do so. While not all clients require such encouragement, difficult and resistant clients, whose resistance is due to low frustration tolerance ideas, can be encouraged to take full responsibility for not putting into practice assignments that would stimulate change. Thus, dramatic experiences like burning a ten pound note, throwing away an eagerly awaited meal, and cleaning a dirty room at the end of a hard day's work are experiences that are designed to be so aversive that clients would choose to do the assignment previously avoided rather than undergo the penalty. Of course clients can, and often do, refuse to do the assignment and refuse to employ operant-conditioning methods. However, many clients who have been resistant to this part of the change process have, in our experience, begun to move when the counsellor adopts this no-nonsense approach.

Imagery techniques

Lazarus (1989) has criticised rational–emotive counselling for under-emphasising the imagery modality in working with clients. This criticism does have some merit in that RET practitioners prefer, whenever possible, to encourage clients towards emotional rational insight through action rather than through imagination, believing action to be a more powerful medium for promoting such insight than imagery. Perhaps the exception to this is the technique known as rational–emotive imagery (REI) which was pioneered by Maultsby (1975) and modified by Ellis. The purpose of REI is to promote emotional rational insight while vividly imagining troublesome events at A.

REI (Ellis version)

In Ellis' version of REI the client is asked to imagine a vivid example of the context A in which the client's emotional problems occur, and to 'get in touch with' her irrational emotion at C. She is then asked to change her irrational emotion to its rational alternative (e.g. anxiety to concern) while still vividly imagining the same situation at A. When the client executes the procedure successfully, she does so by changing her irrational belief to its rational alternative. However, counsellors are recommended to check this, since clients can achieve this feeling change by modifying inferences or by distraction. When this occurs, the counsellor encourages the client to repeat the exercise, but this time without changing inferences and without using distractions. Once the client has learned how to execute REI in the counselling session she is instructed to practise it for 30 days (three times a day for a minimum of ten minutes on each occasion).

REI (Maultsby version)

In Maultsby's version of REI, the client is again asked to imagine vividly the situation at A, but this time she is instructed to repeat forcefully the relevant rational belief at B in order to experience a rational emotion at C. Repeated practice is again recommended after the client has understood the procedure.

It is worthwhile noting that some clients experience difficulty creating images and may have to be trained in stepwise fashion to utilise this ability. Furthermore, while helpful, it is probably not necessary for clients to imagine with clarity in order to benefit from both versions of REI.

Imagery rehearsal

Imagery rehearsal can be used in rational–emotive counselling to build a bridge between the client's intellectual insight into a rational concept and his or her attempt to act on that insight in the world. For example, one client gained intellectual insight into her shame-based philosophy and understood intellectually, but not emotionally, that she was not a fool for acting foolishly; rather she was a fallible human being who acted foolishly. In order for her to begin to act on and internalise this rational belief, she was encouraged to act foolishly in public while practising the new rational philosophy. Imagery rehearsal was used with this client, as with others, prior to the behavioural assignment because she doubted her ability to execute the assignment in the real world. Thus:

Counsellor: OK. You say that you see the sense of doing that (Here the assignment was for her to go into a confectionery shop and ask for one brand of chocolate bar, leave the shop and return to exchange the bar for another brand. She was to practise simultaneously the rational belief: 'I'm a fallible human being even though I may appear stupid to others').

Client: Yes, but I don't know whether I can do it.

Counsellor: OK, but let's see. Let's try it out in your mind's eye first. Do you think imagining yourself doing it will help you to do it?

Client: It might.

Counsellor: OK. Now close your eyes and imagine that you've begun the exercise by going into the shop and buying the first bar. Can you picture that?

Client: Yes.

Counsellor: OK, and how do you feel in this image?

Client: Fine at this point.

Counsellor: Good. Now imagine you've bought the bar and you've left the shop. Picture yourself deciding to go back to exchange the bar. How do you feel now?

Client: Anxious.

Counsellor: OK. Now see yourself using that anxiety as a cue to vigorously say to yourself your new rational belief: 'I'm a fallible human being even though I may appear stupid to the shopkeeper'. Can you imagine yourself doing that?

Client: (Pause) Yes.

Counsellor: Now keep that new belief in mind and picture yourself going into the shop and see yourself ask for a swap and imagine that the shopkeeper's attitude implies that he thinks you are stupid. Really work on keeping the new philosophy in the front of your mind even in the face of his critical attitude and even though it's a struggle. Now really work on doing that. (Pause). Can you do that?

Client: (Pause). Yes, but it's difficult.

Counsellor: Now go over that scene in your mind's eye several times a day. Keep on assuming that the shopkeeper's attitude will be critical and see yourself accept yourself in the face of his attitude. Do you think that will help you to do that in reality?

Client: Yes, I think that may well help.

It is important to offer clients a coping rather than a mastery model of themselves in imagery rehearsal. Thus note that the counsellor stressed both that it was a struggle to keep the new belief in her mind's eye and that she could do it even though it was difficult.

Rational role construction

We have found it helpful to draw upon Kelly's (1955) 'fixed role therapy' method to help clients to construct a new attitude. Let us assume that a client has once again gained intellectual insight into the rational concept of unconditional self-acceptance as a psychologically healthy alternative to the irrational concept of conditional self-esteem. What we do is to have the client select a relevant situation in which she can practise the new rational philosophy. We then say the following:

> Now imagine someone with whom you can identify, who is like you in many ways apart from the fact that, at the moment, she is more self-accepting than you. What kind of thoughts will the person have about herself, others, and the situation she finds herself in? What will she say in this situation, what will she be feeling and what will she be doing?

After this material has been collected and modified to represent a realistic rational model, i.e. one that is not perfectly rational and thus outside the client's scope, we suggest that the client imagines in her mind's eye for a week or two that she is that person, to see how the role fits. When the client has done this, we discuss her reactions and make appropriate adjustments to the new rational role. We then suggest that the client practises in imagery the modified role for a further week. Assuming that no further adjustments are necessary, we suggest that the client tries out the new role in action as an experiment. The client's reactions to this experiment are then discussed in counselling, with the counsellor helping the client to dispute any further irrational beliefs and suggesting modifications to the role as appropriate.

A variation of this method is to use the client as her own model and to contrast her present irrational self with a perfectly rational self and a fallible, i.e. imperfect, rational self. We particularly emphasise the latter distinction with clients who demand that they must be perfectly rational.

Vivid Cues for Encouraging Clients to Initiate the Process of Promoting Emotional Rational Insight

Although some clients conscientiously do the homework assignments that they and their counsellors have negotiated, other clients do not. It is true that some clients do not follow through on these assignments because of low frustration toleration ideas; still other clients do not follow through, particularly early on in the process of promoting emotional rational insight, because they require some vivid reminders to initiate this process. With such clients, we have found it particularly helpful to ask them what they generally find memorable in everyday life experiences. For example, some people find the printed word memorable while others have visual images on which they cue. Yet others focus primarily on auditory stimuli. We find that it is profitable to capitalise on whatever channel the client finds most memorable.

Vivid visual cues

There are a number of ways clients can remind themselves to initiate the disputing process. A number of rational–emotive counsellors encourage clients to carry around small cards with rational self-statements written on them to which they can refer at various times. Other counsellors have encouraged clients to write reminders to themselves either to initiate a homework assignment or to refer to a rational message. These clients are encouraged to pin up such messages at various places around the home or in their work situation.

We find it helpful to encourage those clients who find visual images powerful to associate a particular dysfunctional feeling with a visual image that would enable them to initiate the disputing process. Thus one client found it helpful to conjure up a sign in her mind that said 'Dispute' when she began to feel anxious. Another client, who was depressed, began to associate the onset of depression with a road sign on which was written 'Act Now'.

Another strategy we have used is to ascertain from clients what, if any, in-session experiences they have found particularly memorable. We try to help them encapsulate some of these experiences as a cue either to initiate the disputing process or to remind themselves of the relevant rational principle to which this experience referred. One client who was prone to thinking himself an idiot for acting idiotically, found it memorable when W.D. made strange faces at him to help him get the point that concluding he was an idiot for acting idiotically was an overgeneralisation. Whenever he began to make such an overgeneralisation in everyday life, he would get the image of his counsellor making faces and quickly remember to what this referred. This helped him accept himself for any idiotic act he actually made, or thought he might make in the future.

Another client who did virtually no cognitive disputing or behavioural assignments outside the sessions was helped in the following manner: first, this issue was made the focus of counselling. Instead of asking her traditional disputing questions, W.D. asked her to imagine what he would say to her were he to respond to her irrational beliefs. She in fact had understood rational principles because her answers were very good. Her problem was that she would not employ these principles. W.D. then asked her if there was any way she could conjure up a picture of him giving her rational messages at various emotionally vulnerable times in her everyday life. She hit on the idea of imagining that he was perched on her shoulder whispering rational messages into her ear. Additionally she began to carry around a small card that said 'Imagine that Dr Dryden is on your shoulder'. This proved a particularly effective technique where all else had failed.

Vivid language

Wexler and Butler (1976) have argued in favour of counsellors using expressive language in counselling. We have found that one of the major benefits of using vivid non-profane language is that clients remember these vivid expressions, or catchphrases, and use them as shorthand ways of disputing irrational beliefs in their everyday lives. For example, several of our clients find phrases like 'just too bad', 'tough luck', 'hard cheese' as helpful vivid reminders to practise the rational philosophy of high frustration tolerance. Concerning self-worth problems, W.D. helped one of his clients who was ashamed of urinating in public toilets to move from intellectual to emotional insight by encouraging him to remind himself that he was a 'fallible human peeing' while he was urinating.

In a related technique, the counsellor can ask the client to give his or her own distinctive name to a faulty psychological process. Wessler and Wessler (1980) give such an example where a client came to refer to himself as 'Robert the Rule Maker' to describe his tendency to make demands on himself and other people. A knowledge of clients' subcultural values is particularly helpful here. W.D. used to work in a working-class area in Birmingham, England, and one word his clients frequently used which was unfamiliar to him, was the word 'mither'. (This is pronounced 'my-the' and means to be worried or bothered.) W.D. helped one client who was angry with her mother to see that her mother was a fallible human being with a worrying problem, and that she could be accepted for this rather than be damned for it. The client suddenly laughed and said, 'Yes! I guess my mother is a mitherer'. She was encouraged to remember this catchy phrase whenever she began to feel angry toward her mother.

Auditory cues

As has been shown, rational–emotive counsellors often make tape recordings of their sessions for clients to replay several times between sessions. This serves to remind clients of rational principles they have understood in the session but may have since forgotten. Using personal recording systems, clients can also be encouraged to develop auditory reminders to initiate either cognitive or behavioural homework assignments. In addition, they can be encouraged to put forceful and emphatic rational statements on cassettes and play these while undertaking behavioural assignments. For example, W.D. once saw a client who was anxious about other people looking at her for fear they might think her strange. He suggested that she do something in her everyday life that would encourage people to look at her so that she could dispute some of her underlying irrational beliefs. She decided to wear a personal stereo system in the street, which she thought would encourage people to look at her. It was suggested that while walking she play a tape on which she had recorded the rational message 'Just because I look strange doesn't mean that I am strange'.

The use of rational songs in counselling has already been described. Several of our clients have found that singing a particular rational song at an emotionally vulnerable time has been helpful for them. It has reminded them of a rational message they might not ordinarily have been able to focus on while being emotionally distressed. Another client reported that her counselling sessions reminded her of a particular song, and whenever she hummed this song to herself it helped to bring to mind the fact that she could accept herself even though she did not have a man in her life. The song ironically was 'You're No-one Till Somebody Loves You'. In fact she rewrote some of the words and changed the title to 'You're Someone Even Though Nobody Loves You'.

Olfactory cues

It is possible for clients to use various aromas as cues to remind themselves to do a homework assignment or to initiate the disputing process. One of W.D.'s clients said that she found his pipe tobacco particularly aromatic and distinctive. Since he and the client were both seeking a memorable cue, he suggested an experiment whereby she purchased a packet of his favourite tobacco and carried this around with her to smell at various distressing times. This aroma was associated in her mind with a particular rational message. This proved helpful and indeed the client claimed that by saying to herself the phrase 'Pipe up' she now no longer had to take the tobacco out of her handbag to smell. Just the phrase was enough to remind her of the rational message.

While we have outlined a number of techniques in this chapter which encourage clients to initiate and sustain the process of moving from intellectual to emotional insight, once again we wish to stress that it is important for counsellors to use their own creativity in devising and implementing new techniques to help their own clients to initiate the change process.

Chapter 9
The Rational–Emotive
Counselling Sequence

Overview

The preceding chapters of this volume have presented the essential elements involved in the theory and practice of rational–emotive counselling. This chapter will provide a synthesis of these elements by describing the rational–emotive counselling sequence, which illustrates the application of RET to an actual client problem.

The rational–emotive counselling sequence consists of 13 important steps (Figure 9.1) that are typically part of the process of helping clients to overcome their emotional problems. In particular, it illustrates the manner in which RET's ABC model can be used as a vehicle for helping counsellor and client to assess and reach a common understanding of the client's problems before intervention (i.e. disputing of irrational beliefs) is attempted. The counselling sequence further specifies the importance of teaching clients the relationship between their thoughts and feelings, the central place of homework assignments within RET, and the desirability of helping clients to approach the goal of 'becoming their own therapists'.

The general format of this chapter is as follows: each step of the counselling sequence is described in detail, and then illustrated through presentation of actual case material, drawn from work that J.Y. did with a 25-year-old female secretary who presented with work-related difficulties. In order to preserve this client's right to confidentiality she has been given a pseudonym ('Monica'), and identifying information has been omitted or altered.

The material that follows is used to demonstrate an orderly and organised implementation of the various critical components of RET. Counsellors are advised, however, that it is not always possible (or desirable) to adhere to the framework provided by the counselling sequence in such a neat, stepwise progression. As an example, early on in counselling a given client may appear to grasp the notion that her shoulds and musts are self-defeating; subsequent sessions, however, may reveal to the counsellor that the client is actually reluctant to surrender her absolutistic demands because she regards them as a source of motivation for impelling herself to higher levels of personal achievement. When this is the case, the counsellor may have to do considerable backtracking in order to resolve this issue so that counselling will be able to proceed in an effective manner. Hence the counselling sequence is perhaps best regarded as representing

Step 1:	Ask for a problem	
Step 2:	Define and agree upon the target problem (set goals in line with problem as defined)	
Step 3:	Assess C	Assess the target problem (set goals in line with the problem as assessed)
Step 4:	Assess A	
Step 5:	Identify and assess any secondary emotional problems	
Step 6:	Teach the B–C connection	
Step 7:	Assess iB	
Step 8:	Connect iB and C	
Step 9:	Dispute iB	
Step 10:	Prepare client to deepen her conviction in her rational beliefs	
Step 11:	Homework: encourage client to put her new learning into practice	
Step 12:	Check homework assignments	
Step 13:	Facilitate the working-through process	

Figure 9.1. The rational–emotive counselling sequence: A = activating event (and inference); B = belief; iB = irrational belief; C = emotional consequence.

a set of guidelines for the effective and efficient practice of RET. Counsellors are cautioned against attempting to utilise these guidelines in a rigid, compulsive manner, and to watch out for their own perfectionistic demands that counselling *should* proceed in a tidy fashion!

Finally, it is noted that the counselling sequence material presented in this chapter focuses on the treatment of only one particular client problem. It does not deal with issues pertaining to case management and the entire *process* of rational–emotive counselling. Such issues will be discussed in Chapter 10, 'The Rational–Emotive Counselling Process'.

The initial step of the counselling sequence is presented below.

Step 1: Ask for a Problem

After dealing with certain practicalities (e.g. determining a fee appropriate to the client's situation), counsellors are advised to establish a problem-solving orientation at the outset of counselling by immediately asking the client to describe the problem that she would like to discuss first. By doing so, counsellors can indirectly communicate a number of therapeutically important messages to the client. First, quickly requesting a problem helps to emphasise that counsellor and client are not meeting merely in order to socialise and have a pleasant conversation; rather, they are going to work together in order to assist the client in overcoming her emotional problems. Secondly, it can serve to highlight the fact that RET is a relatively efficient and focused approach to emotional problem solving. Finally, it conveys the message to the client that the counsellor is going to be quite active in the counselling process, and will tend to operate in such a way as to keep a problem-focused stance throughout this process.

Two main strategies: client choice versus client's most serious problem

Two basic strategies are recommended for counsellors to utilise when attempting to elicit a target problem from a client. The first of these relies upon client choice, and involves simply asking a question such as 'What problem would you like to work on first?' The client's response to this question may or may not be her most serious problem, but it can nevertheless provide a starting point for the counselling. The second strategy is somewhat more directive, as it involves asking the client to start with her most serious problem. Here, for example, the counsellor might ask, 'What are you most bothered about in your life right now?'

When clients fail to quickly identify a target problem

Occasionally, clients will appear to experience difficulty in identifying a target problem to focus on. When this is the case, there are a number of strategies that counsellors can employ to encourage such clients to describe a problem area. First, the counsellor can remind the client that it is not essential to choose a serious problem to work on. It can be made clear that it is perfectly appropriate to begin the counselling process with an issue that may be impeding the client in some slight way. Here, it can be helpful to point out that there is almost always something that individuals can work on in counselling, as human beings tend to operate at a less than optimal level.

Secondly, the client can be encouraged to identify feelings and behaviours she would like to either increase or decrease. This approach can be particularly useful for clients who are largely naive about the counselling process, and who may be in some confusion as to just how counselling might be of help to them. With respect to this issue, the reader will recall that Chapter 6 detailed the importance of attending to induction procedures within rational-emotive counselling as a means for mitigating client misunderstandings and eventual disillusionment with the counselling process (see pp. 73–77).

Another, less direct, means of helping the client to identify a problem area involves making an inquiry as to what she would like to accomplish through counselling. After the client has stated a particular goal, the counsellor can then ask her to describe the ways in which she is failing to achieve this goal at the present time. In many instances, such questioning can lead to fruitful discussion of inappropriate feelings and behaviours that may serve as impediments to goal attainment. The counsellor can then explore these factors with the client, without necessarily labelling them as 'problems'. Some individuals (even after they have gone to the trouble of entering counselling) have difficulty owning up to the fact that they have problems; thus, they may be discouraged from becoming engaged in a problem-focused approach such as RET. When this appears to be the case with a particular client, the counsellor can attempt to identify and employ alternative terminology that may be more acceptable to the client.

Step 1: Monica

After greeting Monica and determining how she came to be referred to me, we discussed her expectations for counselling and agreed upon a fee appropriate to her circumstances. In order to quickly establish a problem-solving focus for the counselling, I then asked her what problem she would like to deal with first. She replied that she had started a new secretarial job in a small office approximately one month ago, and noted that her boss was quite demanding. She had, in fact, seen him yell at employees who made mistakes in their work. She related that she found herself constantly worrying about committing some error that would lead to her dismissal, as this would result in significant financial hardship. She stated that she felt particularly anxious and intimidated whenever in her boss's presence, and that she tended to avoid contact with him as a result.

Recently, Monica's boss had instructed her to learn how to operate the office's personal computer, which was used for billing and word-processing purposes. Monica was completely inexperienced with personal computers, and did not believe she was up to the task she had been assigned. Despite the fact that she had had numerous opportunities to read the operating manual, obtain assistance from fellow employees, and practise word processing and billing applications, she avoided this learning process and the machine that she had made her adversary. She lived in daily dread that her boss would learn of her failure to follow his directive and fire her on the spot. She described herself as 'computer phobic'.

It appeared that Monica had several problems that could be addressed in counselling, and I suggested that we list them so that they could be dealt with one at a time. Monica agreed to this suggestion, and together we generated the following problem list:

1. Avoidance of the task of learning how to operate the office computer.

2. Anxiety about being in the presence of her employer.
3. Worries about financial security.

I asked Monica which problem she would like to focus on first, and she decided she would like to work on overcoming her avoidance of the office computer. She picked this particular problem because she viewed it as having immediate relevance to her continued employment. Rather than questioning her view that she would immediately be fired for not following her boss's directive, I agreed to work on this problem with her.

Step 2: Define and Agree Upon the Target Problem

Frequently, the nature of the client's problem will be clear after some initial discussion during the very first session of counselling. When this is the case, the counsellor may proceed to assess the problem as per steps 3, 4 and 5 of the RET counselling sequence. If, however, the nature of the client's problem remains unclear, it is desirable to reach an agreed definition of it prior to implementing the assessment stage. In addition, when a client discloses a number of problems in close succession, it is important to reach agreement as to which one will receive treatment first.

Arriving at a common understanding of a target problem and agreeing to work upon it together is an important component of rational-emotive counselling, as it helps to solidify the therapeutic alliance. Concurrence on these issues enables counsellor and client to function as a more effective team, and also helps the client to feel understood and to have confidence in the counsellor's expertise. In our experience as supervisors of counsellors in training, we have often reviewed audiotapes of counselling sessions in which counsellor and client seemed to drift along aimlessly, in large part because the novice counsellor failed to establish with the client a particular problem area to focus on.

Distinguish between emotional and practical problems

It is useful to make a distinction with clients between *practical* problems (e.g. 'I might not have enough money to pay the rent') and *emotional* problems (e.g. 'I'm worried to death that I might not have enough money to pay the rent') when conducting rational–emotive counselling. Bard (1980) has noted that RET is an approach to counselling that is designed to assist clients in overcoming the latter type of problem; it is not designed to directly assist clients with problems falling in the former category. When clients have an emotional problem about a practical difficulty, however, this emotional problem may well become the focus of therapeutic exploration. In addition, as clients make progress in removing the emotional obstacles they create for themselves, they may experience greater success in resolving their particular practical issues (Ellis, 1985a).

Target inappropriate but not appropriate negative emotions

As noted in Chapter 2, irrational beliefs will tend to lead an individual to experience inappropriate negative emotional responses when faced with negative life events. Rational beliefs, on the other hand, will usually lead an individual to experience appropriate (although still negative) emotional responses to these same events. Chapter 4 elaborated upon the distinctions between inappropriate and appropriate negative emotions by presenting descriptions of the various irrational feelings and their rational alternatives. Feelings such as anxiety, hurt, anger, guilt and depression are considered to stem from irrational beliefs and to represent inappropriate negative emotions, whereas feelings such as concern, disappointment, annoyance, remorse, regret and sadness are viewed as the products of rational beliefs, and regarded as appropriate negative emotions.

Rational-emotive counsellors do not encourage their clients to change their appropriate negative emotions, as these are regarded as psychologically healthy reactions to negative events. Such emotions can motivate individuals to act on unfortunate or undesirable life circumstances in a constructive fashion, and are unlikely to impair adjustment to situations that may be largely unmodifiable. Clients *are* encouraged to change their inappropriate negative emotions, as these are more likely to stand in the way of healthy adjustment and goal attainment. In this vein, it is wise to make sure that clients understand the distinctions between appropriate and inappropriate negative emotions. Asking the question, 'How is this a problem for you?' can often lead to a useful discussion which will help counsellor and client to identify and define a 'real' emotional problem.

Operationalise vague problems

Clients will sometimes discuss their target problems in vague or confusing terms. When this is the case with a particular client, it is important for the counsellor to help her to operationalise the problem. This involves defining the elements of the problem in terms that will assist the counsellor in applying RET to it.

To cite an example, a given client might state, 'My boss is a royal pain in the arse'. The counsellor can assist the client to specify the meaning of this statement by asking a question such as, 'What specifically does your boss do that leads you to this conclusion, and how do you feel when he acts this way?' This type of question can help the counsellor to begin formulating the client's problem according to RET's ABC model. The first part of the question may elicit descriptions of relevant activating events (As), while the second part may prompt the client to report on the emotional consequences (Cs) she experiences in the face of these As.

Focus on helping clients to change C, not A

Clients may often wish to focus their counselling on a discussion of means to change A, rather than on their feelings (Cs) about A. Changing the A constitutes a practical solution, while changing C is the emotional solution. When counsellors encounter this situation, they can utilise certain strategies to encourage their clients to work at changing C before attempting to change A. First, they can attempt to show clients who already possess adequate practical problem-solving skills that they may be able to more effectively deploy these skills to change A if they are not emotionally disturbed at C. Secondly, they can attempt to show clients who lack an adequate repertoire of problem-solving skills that they will probably experience greater success in acquiring the skills needed to modify problematic As if they remove the emotional obstacles they have at C.

Dealing with failure to identify a target problem

When counsellors have reached this stage of the assessment process and have not yet reached agreement with the client as to the nature of the problem to be targeted for change, they can recommend that the client keep a *problem diary*. The client would utilise this to monitor and record disturbed feelings experienced between counselling sessions, with written notes concerning the types of feelings involved and when and where they were experienced.

Aim for specificity in assessing the target problem

It is important to be as specific as possible in defining and agreeing upon the target problem with clients. Clients experience emotional problems and hold related irrational beliefs in specific contexts, so that being specific will help the counsellor to obtain reliable and valid data about A, B and C. Providing clients with a sound rationale for specificity can aid this endeavour, particularly with those who tend to discuss their problems in vague terms. Clients can be taught that being specific about their target problem can help them to deal with it more constructively in the situations about which they disturb themselves. Counsellors can model specificity for clients by asking for a recent or typical example of the target problem (e.g. 'When was the last time A happened?').

In some cases, clients who remain unable to provide specific examples of their target problems may have secondary emotional problems about their primary emotional problem. When this appears to be the case, counsellors are advised to investigate further, as per Step 5 below.

Step 2: Monica

As stated earlier, Monica decided that she first wanted to focus on her avoidance of learning how to operate the office computer. I encouraged her to tell me a bit more about this problem, and the following dialogue ensued:

Monica: Well, I know I really should be making efforts to learn how to operate the computer, but it seems I've made the task into a monster. I've thumbed through the operating manual a bit, but that's about it. It's gotten so that I can't even stand to be in the same room with the bloody machine!

Joe: But let's suppose that you *were* in the same room with the computer. In fact, imagine that you're actually sitting in front of it, with the intent of turning it on and exploring its functions. What feelings do you think you might experience at that point?

Monica: I think I'd feel tense and jumpy. That's the way I feel whenever I even *think* about working on the computer.

Joe: Okay – so when you think about the computer and start to feel that way, what do you tend to do next?

Monica: [Humorously] Well, I certainly don't make a rush for the computer! I'll usually get myself busy doing some other task in the office. I feel better when my mind is on something else.

Joe: So you try to shy away from even thinking about the computer – right? Would it be safe to say that your busying yourself with other tasks represents a means by which you avoid experiencing the unpleasant feelings you described?

Monica: Yes, I think so.

Joe: Right. So in order to overcome your 'computer phobia', would it then make sense for us to focus on those negative feelings and help you come to terms with them so that you'll be better able to work on the task you've been assigned?

Monica: Yes – that sounds like a reasonable approach. If I could feel more comfortable about working on the computer, I probably wouldn't tend to avoid it so much.

Step 3: Assess C

As stated in Chapter 6, A and C are typically assessed prior to B. At this stage of the counselling sequence counsellors may assess either A or C, depending upon which element of the target problem the client initially describes. For the purposes of this discussion, however, issues involved in the assessment of C will receive treatment first.

Re-check for an inappropriate negative emotion

In assessing C, counsellors are advised to keep in mind that clients' emotional problems are conceptualised as inappropriate (disturbed) negative emotions, not as appropriate (non-disturbed) negative emotions. Inappropriate negative emotions are targeted for change because they are strongly dysphoric, contribute to self-defeating behaviours, and block goal attainment.

Chapter 4 contained a compendium of feeling words used in rational–emotive theory to distinguish between appropriate and inappropriate negative emotions. It is important to recognise, however, that clients may not tend to employ these terms in the same way as their rational–emotive counsellors. Thus, a given client may make reference to feelings of anger when she is really experiencing annoyance, or vice versa. Counsellors should take steps to ensure that they have identified an inappropriate negative emotion, and that they are using the same terminology as the client when referring to it (Dryden, 1986). Here, the counsellor can try to teach RET's 'emotional vocabulary' to the client, or may choose to adopt the client's own particular use of feeling language. Regardless of the alternative chosen, it is helpful for counsellors to be consistent in their vocabulary throughout the course of treatment.

Focus on an emotional C

A client's Cs can be emotional or behavioural in nature. Dysfunctional behaviours often serve a defensive function, however, and may exist to help clients avoid experiencing certain inappropriate negative emotions. This discussion of the counselling sequence will therefore deal with the assessment of inappropriate negative emotions rather than the assessment of dysfunctional behaviours.

It is suggested that counsellors in training adopt the practice of attempting to identify (and treat) the inappropriate negative emotions that contribute to the dysfunctional behaviours that clients may present. Thus, if a given client states her desire to stop smoking, the counsellor can regard smoking as a defensive behaviour and encourage the client to identify the problematic emotions she might experience if she were to refrain from it.

Clarify C

A client's inappropriate negative emotions at C can provide valuable clues concerning the nature of the irrational beliefs to which she subscribes. It is therefore important for counsellors to gain clarification as to the Cs that clients experience.

If a client is vague or unclear in attempting to describe C, there are a number of specific techniques that can be used to clarify its nature. Gestalt exercises such as the empty-chair technique (see Passons, 1975) and Gendlin's (1978) focusing technique are sometimes helpful in this regard. In addition, imagery methods can be employed wherein the client is asked to imagine an example of her problem and to identify any associated feelings that are experienced. Albert Ellis will sometimes encourage his clients to 'Take a wild guess' when they have difficulty in identifying a specific emotion; surprisingly, this method can yield useful information about C in some instances.

Frustration is an A, not a C

Clients will sometimes refer to feeling frustrated at C. Here, it is important to note that some RET counsellors prefer to regard frustration as an activating event rather than a feeling (Trexler, 1976). As a C, frustration in RET theory is usually regarded as an appropriate negative emotion that clients experience when they are blocked from attaining their goals. When a given client reports feeling frustrated, however, it is possible that she is referring to an inappropriate negative emotion. Counsellors can often determine whether a client's reported feeling of frustration is an appropriate or inappropriate negative emotion by asking if the feeling is bearable or unbearable. If the client responds to such an inquiry by describing the feeling as unbearable, she may well be experiencing an inappropriate negative emotion that could be targeted for change.

Assess client motivation to change C

Clients sometimes experience inappropriate, disturbed negative emotions that they are not motivated to change. This absence of motivation can occur when clients fail to recognise the destructive, self-defeating nature of the emotion in question. This situation arises most often in the case of anger; it may also occur with feelings of guilt and depression. As such, counsellors are advised to assess clients' understanding of the dysfunctional aspects of the target emotion (C). If a particular client does not understand why her disturbed emotion is inappropriate, it is beneficial to devote as much time as necessary to helping her see this point. This can be accomplished with the following three steps:

1. Assist the client to assess the consequences of the inappropriate negative emotion. What happens when she feels this way? Does she tend to act constructively or self-defeatingly?
2. Emphasise that the goal is to replace the inappropriate negative emotion with its appropriate, more rational counterpart (e.g. replacing anxiety with concern). Making this point can be difficult, particularly if the client has rigidly entrenched ideas concerning the ways she is 'supposed' to feel when confronted with negative As (see DiGiuseppe, 1984, for a more extended discussion of this issue). If provided with appropriate models, however, the client will usually be able to see that she can experience the appropriate emotion in a given context. To cite an example, a client with public speaking anxiety can be helped to identify individuals she knows who experience feelings of strong concern, but not anxiety, prior to giving a lecture in front of an audience.
3. Finally, work with the client to assess the consequences that would occur if she experienced the corresponding appropriate emotion when confronted with a problematic situation. As the client probably has not

thought in these terms before, help her to imagine how she would behave and how the outcome might be different if she felt the appropriate emotion in the face of a negative A. Then, compare the outcomes of experiencing appropriate versus inappropriate emotions. As an example, a given client could be encouraged to imagine how he might act (and what types of results he might get) if he felt merely annoyed (instead of angry) when his teenage son breaks his evening curfew. This may help the client to better understand the advantages of the appropriate emotion, and this insight may well increase his motivation to change C.

Avoid potential pitfalls in assessing C

Counsellors may encounter a number of potential difficulties as they work to assess clients' problematic emotions at C. These difficulties may be avoided by implementing the following suggestions:

1. Avoid using questions that reinforce the notion that A causes C. Novice rational–emotive counsellors may make the error of asking clients questions such as 'How does the situation *make you* feel?' As an alternative, counsellors might ask 'How do you feel *about* the situation?' This question can serve to elicit descriptions of problematic Cs, and does not implicitly convey the message that A *causes* C.
2. When clients respond to inquiries concerning their feelings about A with terms such as 'bad', 'upset', 'miserable' etc., do not attempt to work with these vague descriptions of emotions. Instead, work with clients to help them clarify exactly what feelings they experience at C. Also, do not accept statements such as 'I feel trapped' or 'I felt rejected' as descriptions of emotions occurring at C. Trapped and rejected are not emotions. These terms probably refer to combinations of A, B and C factors, and it is important to discriminate between these three and ensure that clients' C statements really do refer to feelings. To illustrate, if a client states 'I felt rejected', she can be helped to see that rejection is an A and then asked how she felt about the rejection at point C (e.g. hurt, ashamed, etc.).

Step 3: Monica

In Step 2, I established with Monica that her avoidance behaviour served as a means for warding off the unpleasant feelings she experienced whenever she thought about working on the computer. She seemed to understand that it made sense to target these feelings for change, and that a change in her feelings could help her to face the task her boss had given her. As such, my next task was to more fully assess the nature of her negative feelings:

Joe: You mentioned that you feel tense and jumpy whenever you think about working on the computer. Those terms – tense and jumpy – are usually used

Monica: to describe *physical* feelings or sensations a person might experience. What type of *emotional* feelings do you think you experience when you think about working on the computer?

Monica: I have a bad case of nerves – I feel nervous.

Joe: Meaning you feel anxious?

Monica: No, not anxious – if I were anxious to learn the computer. I would have done it already!

Joe: Oh, I see. You're using the term 'anxious' to mean 'eager'. When I used the word 'anxious', I meant it in the sense of having anxiety. Behavioural scientists have done a lot of research which demonstrates that anxiety can interfere with a person's performance on complex tasks. Would it be correct to say that you experience anxiety with respect to the idea of working on the computer?

Monica: When you use the word that way – yes, that would be correct. That's what I feel.

Joe: So if we helped you to overcome your anxiety – which probably contributes to your feeling tense and jumpy and interferes with your getting down to the task – you would stand a better chance of becoming computer-proficient. Is that right?

Monica: Yes – I can see that.

Note that, as I worked with Monica to determine the precise nature of the feeling she experienced at C, it became apparent that she viewed the term 'anxious' as being synonymous with 'eager'. I thus took steps to clarify my use of the term, and obtained her agreement that 'anxiety' was an appropriate word to describe the uncomfortable emotion she felt with respect to learning to operate the office computer. As mentioned earlier, it is important to ensure that counsellor and client are employing language in the same way in order to avoid misunderstandings that may bog down the counselling process.

Step 4: Assess A

If C is assessed first, the next step in the counselling sequence is to assess A. As noted earlier, A can refer to activating events that may be regarded as confirmable reality (i.e. neutral observers could confirm a given client's descriptions of A). In this presentation, however, A will also be used to stand for clients' inferences or interpretations about the activating event.

As with assessments of C, aim for specificity when assessing A. This can be accomplished by asking the client to provide the most recent occurrence of A, a typical example of A, or the most relevant example the client can recall.

Identify the part of A that triggers B

In the process of assessing A, it is important to help the client to identify the most relevant aspect of A (i.e. the part that generally serves to trigger irrational beliefs at B). Identifying this trigger can sometimes be complicated by inferences the client makes about the situation. As these inferences are often linked (or chained) together, the technique referred to as *inference chaining* (described in Chapter 6) can be used to identify the particular inference in the chain that functions as the trigger.

By way of illustration, imagine a client who experiences anxiety at point C. Initial inquiry reveals that she is due to give a class presentation. Giving the class presentation thus represents an activating event, but the counsellor will wish to determine just what it is about the presentation that is anxiety-provoking in the client's mind. The following dialogue might then ensue:

Counsellor: What is it about giving the presentation that you are anxious about?
Client: Well, I'm afraid I may not do a very good job.
Counsellor: For the moment, let's just assume that you don't. What's anxiety-provoking in your mind about that?
Client: Well, if I don't do a good job in class, then my teacher will give me a poor grade.
Counsellor: Let's assume that as well. What would you be anxious about there?
Client: That I might flunk the course.
Counsellor: And if you did?
Client: Oh, my God, I couldn't face my father!
Counsellor: Imagine telling your father that you had failed. What would be anxiety-provoking about that in your mind?
Client: I can just picture his reaction – he would be devastated!
Counsellor: And how would you feel if that happened?
Client: Oh God, that would be terrible! I really couldn't stand to see my father cry – I'd feel so very sorry for him!

The class presentation was initially identified as A by the client. Through inference chaining, however, the counsellor has discovered the client's fearful anticipation of her father's upset upon hearing of her presumed failure.

To test whether a given inference in a chain genuinely represents the most relevant aspect of A in a client's emotional problem, the counsellor might write down the inference chain, review it with the client, and ask her to identify the point she thinks is most important. Another technique for confirming whether the newly identified aspect of A is central is to 'manipulate' A and then check the client's responses at C. Thus, for example, the counsellor could say to the client, 'Let's suppose you told your father that you flunked the course, and he wasn't devastated – in fact, he coped quite well with the news. Would that different turn of events have any impact on your anxiety about giving the class presentation?' If the client responds in the affirmative, the counsellor can be more confident that the problem has been accurately assessed. If the client indicates that she would still be anxious, this could indicate that the prospect of seeing her father cry (at A) is not the most relevant factor in her anxiety problem.

Once the most relevant aspect of A has been established, it is important to reassess any changes in the client's feelings at C since the initial analysis of the problem. Assuming that the new aspect of A revealed in the above illustration is indeed the central factor, it would be important to encourage the client to see that her anxiety is more closely associated with the overwhelming pity for her father she would feel at C, than with any general fears of failure she might have. Two alternative courses then present themselves in terms of treatment: the first would involve focusing on the client's feelings of anxiety at C about the future prospect of her father's emotional devastation. The second would involve asking the client to assume that the new A (the father's upset) had already occurred, and then dealing with the feelings of other-pity that would presumably occur at C.

A can refer to many things

Rational–emotive counsellors generally agree that A can be a thought, an inference, an image, a sensation, or a behaviour, as well as an actual event in the client's environment that can be confirmed by neutral observers. In addition, a client's *feelings* at C may also serve as an A. A given client may, for example, experience guilt feelings at C. This guilt could then serve as a new A, and the client may feel ashamed (a new C) about feeling guilty. Here, the client has a secondary emotional problem about a primary emotional problem. Not all clients will present such secondary problems, but the process of determining whether or not they exist is an important part of assessment in the counselling sequence (see Step 5).

Assume (at least temporarily) that A is true

In the course of assessing A, it sometimes becomes apparent to counsellors that the client's most relevant A is a clear distortion of reality. When this is the case, it can be tempting to dispute A in order to correct the client's misinterpretations.

Generally, counsellors are advised to resist this temptation and to encourage the client to temporarily assume that A is correct. In the case previously described, for example, it is not essential to determine whether or not the client's father would truly be devastated upon hearing about her failure. Rather, it is important to treat A as if it is an accurate depiction of reality, in order to assist the client in identifying the irrational beliefs that lead to particular feelings at C.

Avoid pitfalls in assessing A

A number of potential pitfalls that counsellors may encounter in assessing A may be avoided by implementing the following suggestions:

1. Refrain from obtaining too much detail about A. Allowing clients to speak at length about A can turn counselling into a gripe session, which will make it difficult to maintain a problem-solving approach to overcoming emotional difficulties. With clients who tend to ramble or provide compulsive details concerning their As, counsellors can attempt to abstract the most salient theme, or what appears to be the major aspect of A. At times, it is appropriate to tactfully interrupt clients in order to re-establish a specific focus. A counsellor might say, for instance, 'I think you may be providing me with more detail than I require. Can you tell me what it was about the situation that you were most upset about?'
2. Discourage clients from describing A in vague terms. Attempt to obtain as clear and specific an example of A as possible. An example of a vague A would be, 'My husband was really on my case last night'. In contrast, a specific A would be, 'My husband told me I was lazy and inept for not having dinner ready and waiting for him when he arrived from work'.
3. Discourage clients from talking about several As at one time. Some individuals will jump from event to event within a given counselling session; in RET, it is important to work on one A at a time. Clients can be encouraged to deal with the A they consider to best illustrate the context within which they make themselves disturbed, and can be assured that their other As can be dealt with later on.
4. If at this point of the counselling sequence a given client still has not identified a clear A, encourage her to start a diary prior to the next session. This diary can be used to record examples of activating events about which she makes herself disturbed.

Agree on Goals

It has been emphasised that it is important for counsellor and client to develop a common understanding of the client's target problem. Likewise, it is desirable to reach agreement as to the client's goals for change, as this will facilitate the development of a sound therapeutic alliance between the two parties involved in the individual counselling process.

When to agree on goals

There are two main points at which counsellors will want to assess a given client's goals for change. The first point occurs when counsellor and client have defined and reached agreement concerning the client's target problem (Step 2). Here, it is recommended that the counsellor help the client to set a goal in line with the problem as initially assessed. Thus, if a particular client's problem relates to being overweight, an initial goal would be for her to achieve and maintain a specific target weight.

Counsellors may, however, wish to reconsider and reformulate the client's goal at the assessment stage (Steps 3, 4 and 5). For example, after agreeing that the client's goal is to achieve and maintain a specific weight, assessment may reveal that she becomes anxious and overeats when she is bored. At this point, the client's goal might be reformulated so that it focuses on her ability to deal more appropriately with boredom, so that she less often resorts to the (self-defeating) coping strategy of overeating. The client can be encouraged to work at feeling concerned (rather than anxious) about being bored, and to use that feeling of concern to deal with boredom in more constructive ways. Generally, it is helpful to encourage clients to select an appropriate negative emotion as a goal, and to assist them in understanding why such an emotion represents a realistic and constructive response to a negative activating event at A.

Help clients take a long-term perspective

When discussing goals with clients, it is useful to make them cognisant of the distinction between long-term goals and short-term goals. At times, clients may wish to settle upon a short-term goal that may in the long term be self-defeating and therefore irrational (e.g. in the case of a shoplifting client, the desire to steal without experiencing guilt feelings). Counsellors are advised to help clients adopt a broader perspective and to obtain their commitment to work towards productive long-term goals.

Avoid pitfalls when agreeing on goals

Several potential difficulties may be encountered when working with clients to establish goals. The following suggestions may prove helpful in avoiding them:

1. Do not accept clients' goal statements when they express a desire to experience less of an inappropriate negative emotion (e.g. 'I want to feel less anxious', or 'I want to feel less guilty'). Rational–emotive theory maintains that the presence of an inappropriate negative emotion (such as anxiety or guilt) indicates that the client experiencing that emotion is subscribing to an irrational belief. As such, it is advisable to help clients to distinguish between the inappropriate negative emotion in question and its appropriate counterpart. Clients can be encouraged to set the latter type of emotion as their goal. They can therefore work at feeling concerned instead of anxious, or sorry rather than guilty and self-downing.

2. Do not accept client goals that express the wish to feel neutral, indifferent or calm with respect to events about which it would be rational to experience an appropriate negative emotion. Emotions indicating indifference (e.g. calmness in the face of an unfortunate event) would mean that a given client did not have a rational belief about the event in question, whereas in reality the client would probably prefer that the

event not occur. Acquiescing to the client's goal to feel calm or indifferent about a negative event may actually encourage her to deny the existence of her desires, rather than to think rationally.

3. For similar reasons, do not accept client goals that involve experiencing positive feelings about a negative A. It would be unrealistic for an individual to feel happy about a negative life event she would prefer not to encounter. Accepting the goal of feeling positive about a negative event may encourage clients to believe that it is good that a particular negative A occurred. This is undesirable, as it fails to promote rational thinking. To reiterate an earlier point, clients who become better able to experience an appropriate (as opposed to inappropriate) negative feeling in the face of a negative life event may be more psychologically prepared to either accept it or modify it.

4. Do not accept vague goals, such as 'I want to be happy'. The more specific you can encourage your client to be in setting goals, the more likely it is that she will be motivated to do the hard work of changing her irrational beliefs in the service of achieving these goals.

Step 4: Monica

At this point I used inference chaining as a means of identifying the part of Monica's A that served to trigger her anxiety:

Joe: Okay - our next task is to figure out just what you're anxious about. Close your eyes and picture yourself actually sitting in front of the computer. You begin to feel very tense and jumpy. Now, what do you think you would be feeling anxious about?

Monica: I'd be anxious that I wouldn't be able to get it right - I'd make all sorts of mistakes. [Inference 1]

Joe: Okay. For the moment, let's assume that's the case - you try to operate the machine, and you make all sorts of errors. In your mind, what would be anxiety-provoking about that?

Monica: Well, I would regard it as evidence that I'd never be able to become proficient with it. [Inference 2]

Joe: That probably wouldn't be the case, but let's just assume that it is. Thinking about it now, what would be anxiety-provoking in your mind about that?

Monica: Well, it would mean that I'd be fired - and that would mean that I'd failed at my job. [Inference 3]

Joe: And if it were true that you had failed at your job . . .?

Monica: If I failed at my job . . . I'd feel like an incompetent.

Joe: So looking at it now, the real issue is not that you're afraid of making errors on the computer or of never being able to master it - what's *really* anxiety-provoking for you is the idea of failing at your job and having to regard yourself as an incompetent person. Does that sound accurate to you?

Monica: Yes, it does.

My next step was to establish a goal we would work on with regard to Monica's target problem and anxiety at C:

Joe: Okay – now, we've already touched on how anxiety can interfere with task performance, right? So we can be pretty sure that as long as you're anxious, you'll have difficulty getting yourself to work on learning how to operate the computer.

Monica: Right.

Joe: Now if anxiety gets in your way, what sort of feeling could you work at replacing it with that might help you in your learning process?

Monica: I wish I could be completely relaxed about it.

Joe: Well, at first glance that looks like a good alternative – but if you were *completely* relaxed, do you think you'd be very motivated to do a good job?

Monica: I think I see what you mean – I might just have an 'I don't care' attitude.

Joe: Right – that could be a possibility. How about aiming to feel *concerned* instead of anxious? Anxiety just gets in your way by contributing to avoidance behaviour, but a feeling of concern will very likely help you to face the difficulties involved in the task and motivate you to try your best.

Monica: I've never thought about it like that before – I could try to feel only concerned instead of anxious. That sounds reasonable, but how do I do it?

As sometimes happens, Monica expressed the desire to replace her feeling of anxiety at C with a feeling of being completely relaxed. This probably would not have proven to be a productive goal, for two reasons: first, it is unlikely that RET would be able to help Monica achieve such a feeling state given the circumstances with which she is faced; secondly, being 'completely relaxed' may have resulted in an apathetic approach to completing the task her boss had assigned her. As such, the goal of working to feel concerned rather than anxious was presented to her.

Step 5: Identify and Assess any Secondary Emotional Problems

Clients can frequently have secondary emotional problems about their primary emotional problems. If a particular client's primary problem is anxiety, for instance, the counsellor can check for the presence of a secondary emotional problem (such as shame about feeling anxious) by asking a question such as, 'How do you feel about feeling anxious?'

When to attend to the secondary emotional problem first

It is suggested that counsellors attend to the client's secondary problem if any of the following conditions are met:

1. The client's secondary problem significantly interferes with the work being done on her primary problem.
2. From a clinical perspective, the secondary problem appears to be the more important of the two.
3. The client can see the sense of working on her secondary emotional problem first.

It can be important to present clients with a plausible rationale for working on the secondary problem first. If the client still wishes to work on the primary problem first, even after a reasonable explanation has been provided, then it is advisable to do so. To do otherwise could jeopardise the therapeutic alliance between client and counsellor.

Check for an emotional problem about an appropriate negative emotion

In the course of assessing a client's *stated* primary problem, it may become evident that she is in fact experiencing an appropriate negative emotion (e.g. sadness in the face of an important loss). If this is the case, check to see whether your client has a problem with this appropriate emotion. A client may, for example, feel ashamed about feeling sad. Work to reach agreement that the secondary emotional problem (shame) will be the client's target problem and proceed to assess this agreed-upon problem.

Assess for the presence of shame

As noted above, clients who are reluctant to disclose an emotional problem may feel ashamed about having the problem, or about admitting it to a therapist. Counsellors can attempt to surmount this difficulty by asking such clients how they would feel if they *did* have an emotional problem about the activating event under discussion. With clients who provide indications that they would feel ashamed, the counsellor can attempt to reach agreement to work on shame as the target problem before encouraging disclosure of the original problem?

Step 5: Monica

Monica's question at the end of Step 4 suggested that she was ready to discuss the means by which she might change her anxiety to a feeling of concern. Prior to beginning such discussion, however, I briefly checked for the presence of a secondary emotional problem:

Joe: You've asked a good question, and we'll begin coming up with some answers in just a minute. But before we do, I wanted to check on something with you. Earlier, as you were describing your problems at work, I started to get the sense that you might be kicking yourself for having these difficulties. People will often do that to themselves – they'll give themselves a problem about having a problem. Is it possible that you're telling yourself you *shouldn't* have a problem?

Monica: No, I don't really think I'm kicking myself for having this problem. I think anybody who had to face the circumstances I deal with at work every day would feel anxious!

Monica's response appeared to indicate that she did not have a secondary emotional problem. It is noted, however, that she expressed the belief that any individual would experience anxiety if faced with circumstances similar to her own. As will be seen in Step 6, I was able to use this erroneous belief as a vehicle for teaching the B–C connection.

Step 6: Teach the B–C Connection

By this stage the A and C elements of a client's primary or secondary emotional problem have been assessed. The next step is for the counsellor to teach the client the *B–C connection*, that is, the concept that emotional problems are largely determined by beliefs rather than by the activating event that has previously been assessed. This step is critical, because unless the client understands that her emotional problems are determined by her beliefs, she will not understand why those beliefs are being assessed during the next step of the treatment process. Utilising an example unrelated to the client's problem can often be helpful in explaining this concept (see for example, the 'teaching dialogue' appearing on pp. 91–92). Alternative exercises and metaphors for conveying this idea are described in a number of the other available RET texts (e.g. Walen, DiGiuseppe and Wessler, 1980; Ellis and Dryden, 1987).

Step 6: Monica

As noted earlier, Monica voiced her belief that all individuals would feel anxious if they were in her position at work. I was able to utilise this misconception as a vehicle for teaching her the B–C connection:

Joe: Okay – it sounds like you're not putting yourself down for being anxious about learning how to operate the computer at work. That's good. I'm struck, however, by the fact that you seem to think that anxiety is inevitable under the circumstances you face. It sounds like you believe that those circumstances are *making* you feel anxious.

Monica: Well . . . they are, aren't they?

Joe: If that were true, then you'd *have to* continue to feel anxious at work until circumstances somehow changed for the better. I'd like to suggest that your anxiety isn't caused by circumstances; it's caused by the way you *think* about those circumstances.

Monica: Hmm . . . the way I think? What do you mean?

Joe: Let me use an example to illustrate. Suppose we take two individuals who are strangers to each other, but happen to be going to the same party on a given Saturday night. Imagine that their circumstances are identical insofar as it's the same party, and neither of them knows any of the other partygoers except for their host. Are you with me so far?

Monica: Yes.

Joe: Okay. Now, Person A walks into the party with the following belief in mind: 'I *must* make a good impression on the people I'm going to meet, and it would be absolutely awful if I committed some faux pas and they disapproved of me'. Person B, on the other hand, enters the party with a different sort of attitude: 'I would certainly *like* to make a good impression, but if I commit some social error and they don't accept me, it's not the end of the world'. Now, which of these two people do you think will be more likely to experience anxiety at the party?

Monica: Um . . . Person A.

Joe: Right – that will very likely be the case. Do you see why?

Monica: It's because of what he believes about making a good impression.

Joe: Right again. More specifically, it's because he's escalating a desire to the level of an absolute *must*. If he just stuck with his desire – like Person B – he would still feel concerned about making a good impression, but not anxious. Does that make sense to you?

Monica: Yes, it does seem to make sense.

Step 7: Assess Beliefs

In assessing B, it is important for counsellors to keep in mind the distinction between clients' rational and irrational beliefs, and to help clients understand the differences between these two types of thinking.

Assess both premise and derivative forms of irrational beliefs

Chapter 2 introduced the reader to the differences between rational and irrational beliefs, and Chapter 3 noted that irrational beliefs are often comprised of a premise and certain derivatives that tend to stem from that premise. To briefly review, the premise component of irrational beliefs embodies absolutistic shoulds, musts, have to's, etc.; these can be expressed as demands directed at self, others or the world and life conditions. The three main irrational derivatives are awfulising, I-can't-stand-it-itis and damnation.

At this stage of the counselling sequence, counsellors will want to carefully assess both the premise and the derivative components of their clients' irrational beliefs. With respect to irrational derivatives, counsellors may either teach and use the RET terms for these processes, or use clients' own language. If the latter alternative is chosen, however, it is advisable to make sure that the terms used by clients accurately reflect irrational beliefs. This decision can be based upon client feedback concerning the strategy perceived to be most helpful.

Distinguish between absolute shoulds and other shoulds

Rational–emotive counsellors can become highly attuned to indications that clients are harbouring particular irrational beliefs in their thinking. It is important to bear in mind, however, that every client utterance of the word 'should' does not constitute evidence for the presence of an irrational belief. Most expressions of the word *should*, in fact, will be unrelated to a given client's emotional problems, as this word has multiple meanings in the English language. These include shoulds of preference (e.g. 'I *should* get to work on time'); empirical or probabilistic shoulds (e.g. 'When two parts of hydrogen and one part of oxygen are combined, you *should* get water'); and shoulds of recommendation (see p. 17 for an example).

Rational–emotive theory hypothesises that only *absolute shoulds* are related to emotional disturbance. When clients find the different meanings confusing, it can sometimes be useful to substitute the word *must* in cases where an irrational belief in its premise form may be operative (compare, for instance, 'I *should* be admired by my colleagues' and 'I *must* be admired by my colleagues'). Our own clinical experience (as well as that of Albert Ellis) suggests that the word *must* conveys the meaning of absolute demand-ingness better than the word *should*. In particular, clients can be helped to distinguish between absolute shoulds and shoulds of preference.

Use questions to assess irrational beliefs

Counsellors are advised to employ questions when assessing clients' irrational beliefs. An example of a standard question used by rational-emotive counsellors is 'What were you telling yourself about A to make yourself disturbed at C?' This type of *open-ended question* offers both advantages and disadvantages.

One advantage of such a question is that it embodies and may convey several important elements of the rational–emotive theory of emotional disturbance. In essence, it reinforces for the client the concept that A does not cause C: it is B that determines whether appropriate or inappropriate negative emotions are experienced at C. An additional advantage of the above type of enquiry is that it is unlikely to put words in the client's mouth concerning the content of her beliefs.

The main disadvantage of using this type of question is that clients (particularly those who are new to RET) will frequently not respond to it by articulating an irrational belief. Instead, they may respond by providing further inferences about A – and in some cases, these inferences may well be less relevant than the one previously selected at Step 4.

Imagine, for example, that a given client is particularly anxious that other people will think she is a fool if she stammers in public. If her counsellor asks, 'What were you telling yourself about other people's criticism to make yourself anxious at C?' she may conceivably respond by stating 'I thought they wouldn't like me'. Note that this response is actually an inference about A, and that it fails to reveal the client's irrational belief. Here, the counsellor would try to help the client see that her statement does not describe an irrational belief, and then educate her to look further for her anxiety-provoking irrational belief about A. This can be done by judiciously combining the use of open-ended questions with didactic explanation.

Walen, DiGiuseppe and Wessler (1980) list a number of other open-ended questions that may be used to assess clients' irrational beliefs. These include: 'What was going through your mind?'; 'Were you aware of any thoughts in your head?'; 'What was on your mind then?' and 'Are you aware of what you were thinking at that moment?' Again, clients will not necessarily disclose irrational beliefs in response to these questions; they may require further help of a didactic nature.

Theory-driven questions represent an alternative to the use of open-ended questions for assessing irrational beliefs. Such questions are directly derived from rational–emotive theory, and are more specific with respect to identifying the type of response that is desired. As an example, a counsellor attempting to elicit a response concerning a client's operative must (i.e. a premise) might ask, 'What *demand* were you making about other people's criticism to make yourself disturbed at point C?' By way of further illustration, the following question could be used to assess for a particular derivative of an irrational premise: 'What kind of person did you think you were for stammering and incurring other people's criticism?'

Theory-driven questions are useful insofar as they orient the client to look for her irrational beliefs. In using them, however, the counsellor runs the risk of putting words in the client's mouth and encouraging her to look for irrational beliefs that she may not actually hold. This risk is minimised when careful assessment has already established that the client has an inappropriate negative emotion at point C.

Step 7: Monica

Joe:	Okay – so it's not circumstances that determine whether a person feels anxious or not; it's the beliefs that a person holds about those circumstances. One's desires and preferences are unlikely to cause serious emotional trouble, but making those desires into absolutistic musts, shoulds and have-tos will often result in significant upsets and self-defeating behaviours. Now, as we go back to your own situation, see if you can keep in mind this distinction between desires and absolutistic musts. Okay?
Monica:	Okay.
Joe:	Now, with respect to the problem we've been discussing, what's your desire?
Monica:	To overcome my anxiety and learn how to use the computer with a minimum of hassle.
Joe:	Okay. And what *must* are you bringing to the situation that results in your feeling anxious?
Monica:	I must succeed!
Joe:	Right! And with that must in place, how will you tend to label yourself if you actually *don't* succeed?
Monica:	As an incompetent loser.

Step 8: Connect Irrational Beliefs and C

After assessing clients' irrational beliefs in both premise and derivative form, counsellors should take care to ensure that clients grasp the connection between their irrational beliefs and their disturbed emotions at point C. This step should precede any attempts at disputing these beliefs.

A simple enquiry can be used to determine whether a given client understands this very important connection. Thus, a counsellor might say, 'Can you understand that as long as you demand that other people must not criticise you, you are bound to make yourself anxious about the possibility that this might occur?'. With respect to an irrational derivative, the counsellor may ask, 'Can you see that as long as you believe that you are no good for being regarded by others as a fool, you will be anxious about being criticised?'. If the client responds in the affirmative, the counsellor can then attempt to elicit from the client the B–C connection: 'So, in order to change your feeling of anxiety to one of concern, what do you need to change first?' Eliciting this connection is likely to be more productive than simply telling the client that such a connection exists. If the client fails to see the connection, it is strongly advised that the counsellor spend time helping her to understand it before proceeding to dispute her irrational beliefs.

Step 8: Monica

Joe: So, do you see that as long as you believe that you *must* succeed and that you would be an incompetent loser if you didn't, you'll tend to feel anxious and avoid working on the computer?

Monica: Yes, that connection seems to make sense.

Joe: Right. So, if you want to change your feeling of anxiety to a feeling of concern and stop avoiding – assuming that circumstances remain the same – what do you need to change?

Monica: My belief that I must succeed.

Joe: Right – and also, the idea that not succeeding would mean you're an incompetent loser.

Step 9: Dispute Irrational Beliefs

After conducting a thorough assessment of the target problem, identifying and assessing any secondary emotional problems, and teaching the B–C connection, the next step in the counselling sequence is to begin the process of disputing clients' irrational beliefs.

The goals of disputing

A major goal of disputing at this point is to help clients to understand that the irrational beliefs to which they subscribe are unproductive (in the sense that they lead to self-defeating emotions and behaviours), illogical and inconsistent with reality. Counsellors attempt to teach clients that the alternatives to these beliefs (i.e. rational beliefs) are productive, logical and consistent with reality.

Even if a given client provides evidence that she has reached such an understanding, it would probably be an error for the counsellor to assume that her conviction in the alternative rational belief will be strong. In this vein, it can be helpful to teach the client the distinction between *light conviction* and *deep conviction* in a rational belief. As noted in Chapters 7 and 8, the former state is considered characteristic of intellectual rational insight, while the latter state is characteristic of emotional rational insight. Clients can be encouraged to view even a light conviction in an alternative rational belief as a sign of progress, albeit usually insufficient in itself to promote emotional change.

With specific regard to the target problem, the goals of disputing are to help the client to understand the following:

1. Preferences versus musts: human beings quite frequently escalate their preferences to the level of absolute demands (i.e. irrational beliefs). It is very likely that there is no evidence in support of the absolute demands embodied in irrational beliefs, whereas evidence can be found to support preferences.
2. Awfulising: individuals experiencing emotional disturbance are often defining their negative As as being absolutely awful (i.e. 101 per cent bad). This constitutes magical nonsense, since in reality all experience lies within a 0–99.9 per cent range of badness.
3. I-can't-stand-it-itis: human beings can virtually always tolerate and survive that which they think they cannot stand, and can find some degree of happiness even if their negative As persist.
4. Damnation: this is a concept that is illogical and inconsistent with reality and will lead to emotional trouble. The preferable alternative to damnation is for human beings to accept themselves, other people and the world as imperfect and complex – too complex to be given a single global rating

As treatment proceeds, counsellors can pursue the goal of helping clients to internalise a broad range of rational beliefs so that they become part of a general philosophy of rational living. This process, however, is beyond the scope of the present chapter.

Use questions during disputing

In the first stage of the disputing sequence, counsellors typically ask clients to provide evidence in support of their musts. To review material presented in Chapter 7, some standard questions used for this purpose include, 'Where is the evidence that you *must* under all conditions?'; 'Where is the proof?'; 'Is it true that you absolutely *must*?'; and 'Where is it written that you *must*?'

It is important for counsellors to ensure that clients actually answer the disputing questions asked of them. For example, in response to the question

'Why *must* you succeed?' a given client might answer, 'Because succeeding will bring me certain advantages'. Note that the client has really not addressed herself to the question that was asked; rather, she has actually provided a response to the question, 'Why is it *preferable* for you to succeed?' Generally, it is good practice to anticipate that clients will not immediately provide correct responses to initial disputing questions.

As per RET theory, the only valid answer to the question 'Why *must* you succeed?' is 'There is no reason why I absolutely *must*, although it would be preferable'. When clients provide any other answer, it is likely that they need to be educated as to why their answer is (1) incorrect with respect to the question that was asked, or (2) a correct answer to a different question. During this process a combination of questions and short didactic explanations may be used to help clients attain an understanding of the correct answer.

It is usually helpful at this point to assist clients in distinguishing between their rational and irrational beliefs. One means for accomplishing this is to write down two questions, such as the following:

1. Why *must* you succeed?
2. Why is it preferable but not essential for you to succeed?

When clients attempt to answer these questions, it is often the case that they will give the same answer to both. When this occurs, they can be helped to see that the reasons they provided in their response constitute evidence for their rational belief, but not for their irrational belief. Here, the goal is to help clients to comprehend that the only answer to a question concerning the existence of musts is – to paraphrase Ellis – 'There are probably no absolute musts in the universe'.

Persistence in disputing

As noted earlier, it is important to dispute both the premise and the derivative forms of a given client's irrational beliefs. If, however, the counsellor has started this process by disputing the irrational premise, it is important to persist in this endeavour until the client is able to see that there is no evidence in support of this premise before beginning to dispute a derivative from the premise.

Switching too quickly from premise to derivative (and vice versa) during disputing can be confusing for the client. If, however, disputing is initially aimed at an irrational premise and it becomes clear that the client is not finding this helpful, it can make sense to redirect the focus toward a derivative and monitor the client's reactions. Some clients appear to have an easier time understanding why their derivatives are irrational than why their musts are irrational.

Use a variety of disputing strategies

As noted in Chapter 7, there are three main foci for disputing irrational beliefs. It is probably preferable to use all three of these strategies whenever possible:

1. *Focus on illogicality:* here, clients are helped to understand why their irrational beliefs are illogical. They are shown, for instance, that simply because they may *want* something to happen, it does not logically follow that it absolutely *must* happen. Counsellors can show clients that their irrational beliefs often represent illogical non sequiturs.
2. *Focus on empiricism:* the goal of this strategy is to demonstrate to clients that their musts and irrational derivatives are almost always inconsistent with reality. To accomplish this goal, counsellors use questions which ask clients to provide evidence in support of their irrational beliefs (e.g. 'Where is the evidence that you *must* succeed?'). A given client could be helped to see that if there were evidence to support her belief that she *must* succeed, then she would have to succeed no matter what she believed. If she is not succeeding at present, that fact constitutes evidence that her irrational belief is empirically inconsistent with reality.
3. *Focus on pragmatism:* with this strategy, counsellors focus on showing clients the pragmatic consequences of holding irrational beliefs. The goal is to help clients see that as long as they subscribe to their irrational musts and their derivatives, they will remain disturbed. Here, questions such as, 'What is believing that you *must* succeed going to get you other than anxious and depressed?' are used.

After disputing an irrational belief, clients need to learn how to replace their irrational belief with a new, rational belief. Counsellors work together with clients to construct a rational belief that appears to be most adaptive with respect to A. After an alternative rational belief has been formulated, the three disputing strategies described above can be applied to it in order to demonstrate to clients that rational beliefs are in fact rational. It is much better for clients to see for themselves the evidence that rational beliefs are more valid and helpful, than for counsellors to simply tell them that this is so.

Use a variety of disputing styles

While seasoned practitioners of rational–emotive counselling tend to develop their own individual disputing styles, four basic styles for disputing irrational beliefs will be emphasised here. These four styles are termed Socratic, didactic, humorous and self-disclosing.

Socratic style

When utilising the Socratic style of disputing, counsellors set themselves the task of asking clients questions concerning the illogical, empirically inconsistent and dysfunctional aspects of their irrational beliefs. Such questions are intended to prompt clients to think for themselves, as opposed to simply accepting the counsellor's viewpoint because it stems from a background of expertise. Although the Socratic style emphasises the use of questions, it can be supplemented with brief explanations designed to quickly correct client misconceptions that may arise along the way.

Didactic style

Although a good number of rational–emotive counsellors seem to prefer using the Socratic style, it is acknowledged that the use of questions does not always prove productive. When this is the case, counsellors can shift to utilising direct, didactic explanations as to why irrational beliefs are self-defeating and rational beliefs are more productive. It is quite likely that almost all counsellors find it helpful to use didactic explanations at various points in the treatment process.

When didactic explanations are employed, it is good practice to check whether clients have understood the message conveyed. One means of doing this is to request that they paraphrase the points made. Here, the counsellor might make a statement such as 'I'm not quite sure I'm making myself clear to you – perhaps you could put into your own words what you think I've been saying to you'. It can be a mistake to accept clients' non-verbal and paraverbal signs of understanding (e.g. head nods, mm-hmms) without questioning them. Clients will sometimes evince understanding even when they actually have not understood a word the counsellor has said (Dryden, 1986).

Humorous style

With some clients, the use of humour or humorous exaggeration (see 'Reduction to Absurdity' on pp. 123–124) can represent a productive vehicle for making the point that there is no evidence to support irrational beliefs. The use of humour as a disputing strategy, however, is advised only when the following conditions are met: (1) the counsellor has established a good working relationship with the client; (2) the client has already provided some evidence that she has a good sense of humour; and (3) the humorous interventions are directed at the irrationality of the client's belief and *not* at the client as a person. In addition, Ellis (1983b) has noted that it is important for counsellors to refrain from overusing techniques that they find enjoyable at clients' expense.

Self-disclosing style

Counsellor self-disclosure can represent another useful means of disputing clients' irrational beliefs. Generally, the coping model (as opposed to the mastery model) of self-disclosure is viewed as having features which are likely to be helpful to clients. In using the coping model, counsellors reveal that: (a) they have experienced a problem that in some sense is similar to the client's problem; (b) they once held an irrational belief that is similar to the one the client maintains; and (c) they worked at changing this belief and thus no longer have the problem.

In contrast to the coping model of self-disclosure, the mastery model would involve telling the client that the counsellor has never experienced a problem similar to the client's because he or she has always thought rationally about the issue at hand. Although this approach can highlight the fact that rational thinking helps an individual to avoid particular emotional problems, it can be disadvantageous insofar as it accentuates the differences between counsellor and client. In our experience, the mastery model is less productive than the coping model in encouraging clients to challenge their irrationality. We would note, however, that some clients will not even find the coping model useful. Particular clients, for instance, will tend to condemn the counsellor when the latter displays any signs of 'weakness'. If it becomes apparent that attempts at self-disclosure are failing to benefit the client (and are perhaps damaging the therapeutic alliance), other disputing strategies may be used instead.

Creative disputing

As noted earlier, counsellors tend to develop their own individual styles as they gain experience in disputing clients' irrational beliefs. Typically, they build up a repertoire of stories, metaphors, aphorisms and examples which are used to demonstrate why irrational beliefs are indeed irrational, and why rational beliefs will tend to promote psychological health. As these various vehicles can serve to increase counselling's impact on the client, it is desirable for counsellors to work at accumulating their own repertoire of creative disputing strategies.

The 'Terrorist Dispute' (described on pp. 109–110) can be considered as an example of a creative approach to working with clients who believe that they absolutely cannot stand the discomfort involved in changing long-standing patterns of self-defeating emotions and behaviours. Another creative disputing strategy, termed the 'Friend Dispute', can be useful for pointing out the existence of irrationally demanding self-standards. If, for example, a given client has failed at an important endeavour and is engaging in self-damning (stemming from the irrational belief 'I *must* do well and I'm no good if I don't'), she can be asked if she would condemn a close friend for a similar failure in the same manner that she condemns herself. When she responds in the negative, she can be shown that she has one set of standards for herself and another set of quite different standards for her friend. She can then be helped to see that if she were as accepting of herself as she is of her friend, she would be less prone to emotional disturbance.

Additional creative strategies for disputing clients' irrational beliefs can be found in the discussion of vivid disputing methods presented in Chapter 7. Counsellors are cautioned, however, to work toward mastery of basic disputing skills before attempting to be too creative.

Step 9: Monica

Joe: Okay – we've identified two beliefs that result in your feeling of anxiety and your avoidance of the task of learning to operate the computer. The first belief is, 'I *must* succeed'. The second belief, which stems from the first one, is 'I'm an incompetent loser if I don't succeed'. Now, in order to change those beliefs we have to question and challenge them through a process called *disputing*. Let's dispute these beliefs one at a time – even though they're really linked to each other – because that way we can be more sure we're not missing anything. Okay?

Monica: Okay – how do we proceed?

Joe: Let's start with the first belief: 'I *must* succeed'. There are basically three ways we can challenge this belief. First, we can ask whether or not it's logical. Second, we can put it to the test to see whether it's consistent with reality. Finally, we can consider the consequences of holding the belief – does it help you or hinder you?

Let's look at the logical argument first. Now, your desire, or preference, is to be able to learn how to operate the computer with a minimum of difficulty. That's how you would define succeeding at the task – right?

Monica: Right.

Joe: But – is it sound logic to conclude that because you would prefer to succeed, you *must* succeed?

Monica: No . . .

Joe: Why not?

Monica: Well . . . it sort of reminds me of the old saying: 'If wishes were horses, then beggars would ride'. Just because I might prefer a particular outcome, that doesn't mean that that outcome must occur.

Joe: That's right – demanding that a particular outcome *must* occur because we want it to occur is equivalent to believing in magic.

Monica: And magic doesn't really exist – I've never believed in it, anyway!

Joe: Right! Now, let's see if your belief is consistent with reality. Do you believe that the universe is governed by particular laws and principles? I'm making reference here to the kinds of 'laws' that physicists and other scientists are interested in studying.

Monica: Yes, I believe that.

Joe: Okay – these 'laws' generally state that if a particular set of conditions exists, then a particular outcome will follow. If there were a law of the universe that stated, 'You *must* succeed', then what outcome would have to follow?

Monica: I would succeed! But of course, there really is no guarantee that I'll succeed –

	so my belief amounts to demanding an outcome that could possibly not occur.
Joe:	Right – if it were true that you *must* succeed, then you would have no choice but to succeed. And that isn't consistent with reality, is it?
Monica:	No, it's not.
Joe:	Now let's take the third way of challenging this belief. Let's examine the consequences of holding it, and determine whether those consequences are useful to you or not. As long as you maintain the belief, 'I *must* succeed', what are you going to experience?
Monica:	Anxiety and avoidance, which aren't going to help me.
Joe:	That's correct – the 'must' will create emotional and behavioural difficulties for you. Now, we've challenged your belief by asking, 'Is it logical?'; 'Is it consistent with reality?'; and 'Will it get me good results?' As we've seen, the answer to all three of these questions is 'no'. It's important, however, for you to continue thinking this through for yourself – you can practise challenging your must on your own. Also, it's a good idea to apply these three questions to your non-absolute preference as well – that way, you can show yourself that your preference is more logical, consistent with reality and useful than the absolute must.
Monica:	Right – I can see that it would be good for me to review what we've gone over here.
Joe:	That will really be helpful. Now, let's use the same three questions to challenge your second belief: 'I would be an incompetent loser if I didn't succeed'. First, is it logical to conclude that you would be an incompetent loser if you failed at this particular task?
Monica:	Well, it *feels* that way – I mean, I could lose my job if I don't succeed.
Joe:	But let's suppose that came to pass – you actually did lose your job. How could that one failure make you an incompetent loser? Does failing at something logically make you a failure?
Monica:	I think I see what you mean now – I would be condemning my entire self because of one screw-up.
Joe:	That's right – you would be negatively rating the whole on the basis of just one part. Now, is that logical?
Monica:	No, certainly not.
Joe:	That's right – in fact, it's a good idea to work at giving up the idea of trying to place one all-encompassing rating on your*self*. You can rate parts of the whole, but as a human being you are far too complex to be subsumed under any one label. You're made up of thousands – maybe millions – of parts! Now, let's look at the second argument. If the belief 'I'm an incompetent loser' were consistent with reality, what would that mean about your ability to succeed at other endeavours?
Monica:	I'd be doomed to fail at everything – and that's not true! Even with my present job, I'm able to handle most of my responsibilities quite well.
Joe:	That's right – but if you were truly an incompetent loser, you would fail at everything you attempted. Now, what's more true – that you're an incompetent loser if you fail, or that you're a fallible human being with both strong points and weak points – too complex to be given a single rating?
Monica:	The second is definitely more true!
Joe:	Right. Now let's move to the third point – if you continue to believe that

Monica: failing to learn how to operate the computer means you're an incompetent loser, what kinds of emotional and behavioural consequences will you get?

Monica: Well, if I'm basing my entire view of myself on how I do with this one task, I'll be terrified to even try! I'll continue to feel anxious and to avoid getting down to business with the computer.

Joe: That could very well be the outcome. If, on the other hand, you hold the view that you're a fallible, unratable human being, what types of consequences will you be more likely to experience?

Monica: Going back to what we discussed earlier, I'd still feel concerned – but not anxious. And if I did away with my anxiety, I'd probably stand a better chance of getting down to task.

Step 10: Prepare Clients to Deepen Their Conviction in Rational Beliefs

Once clients have acknowledged that (a) there is no evidence in support of irrational beliefs, but rational beliefs can be supported by evidence; (b) it is more logical to think rationally; and (c) rational beliefs will lead to more productive emotional results than irrational beliefs, counsellors are in a position to help them deepen their conviction in their new, alternative rational beliefs.

Emphasise that weak conviction in a rational belief is unlikely (on its own) to promote change

As noted in Chapter 8, intellectual rational insight is usually insufficient to bring about meaningful emotional and behavioural change. As such, at this stage of the counselling sequence, counsellors help their clients to see that weak conviction in rational beliefs – although important – is unlikely to help them reach their counselling goals. This can be accomplished with brief discussion of the rational–emotive view of therapeutic change. Through the use of Socratic questioning and brief didactic explanations (as per Step 9), clients can be helped to understand that they will strengthen their conviction in their new rational beliefs by disputing irrational beliefs (and replacing them with their rational alternatives) within and between counselling sessions. Clients should also understand that this process will require them to *act* against their irrational beliefs as well as to dispute them cognitively. Teaching this concept now will make it easier for counsellors to encourage clients to put their new learning into practice (Steps 11 and 12) and to facilitate the working-through process (Step 13).

Dealing with the 'head–gut' issue

As clients learn to think more rationally, they may sometimes make statements such as, 'I understand that my rational belief will help me to achieve my goals, but I don't really believe in it yet'. Counsellors can anticipate that clients will often experience some difficulty in crossing the bridge between intellectual and emotional insight, and can initiate discussion on this point as a prelude to consideration of ways to deepen conviction in rational beliefs and weaken conviction in irrational ones. As an example, a counsellor might ask a client, 'What do you think you'll have to do in order to get your new rational belief into your gut?'

It is good practice to encourage clients to commit themselves to a process of therapeutic change that will require repeated and forceful disputing of irrational beliefs, as well as efforts to practise rational thinking within relevant life contexts. Here, clients are helped to design and undertake a variety of homework assignments, as described in Step 11.

Step 10: Monica

Joe: Now, how often do you think you'll have to challenge your self-defeating beliefs in order to more strongly subscribe to their alternatives?

Monica: Quite often, I suppose.

Joe: I would agree – but why do you see it that way?

Monica: Well, because it probably takes a lot of work to change the way you're accustomed to thinking about something.

Joe: Right. Let's consider an example – you have secretarial skills, right?

Monica: Right.

Joe: Okay. Imagine that when you were learning how to type, you had a teacher who taught you all wrong. Nevertheless, you eagerly practised the incorrect technique because you didn't realise that it was wrong. As time went on, you noted that your typing speed was not improving, and that you were indeed much slower than other typists. As a result, you decided to consult with a second teacher who was able to diagnose your problems and show you the correct way to type. Now, would that be all you needed to improve your typing?

Monica: No . . .

Joe: Why not?

Monica: I'd have to keep practising the correct technique.

Joe: That's right – but would practising the new technique feel comfortable to you at the start?

Monica: I guess not.

Joe: Why is that?

Monica: Because I'd developed some bad habits. The incorrect way would still feel more comfortable.

Joe: Right – the incorrect technique would feel more natural to you. But would that 'natural feeling' have to stop you from correcting your technique once you realised it was wrong?

Monica: No.

Joe: That's right. It's the same thing with your beliefs. The next time you think about sitting down to try and learn how to operate the computer, it's quite likely that your beliefs, 'I must succeed; to do otherwise would prove I'm an incompetent loser', will still be operative. That's because you've subscribed to those beliefs for some time, and at this point they're fairly natural to you. But if you resist that natural feeling you can work at identifying, challenging and changing these beliefs until the new, alternative way of thinking comes more naturally to you. Also, the more you *act* in accordance with your new beliefs, the more likely it is that you'll become convinced of their validity and usefulness. Does that make sense to you?

Monica: Yes, it does. It's important for me to continually challenge my old way of thinking, and to act as if I subscribed to the new beliefs.

Joe: That's it. Keep practising the new beliefs until you've really internalised them. It's a process of moving beyond intellectual understanding to a point where you can really feel the truth of the new beliefs in your gut. Once they're at that gut level, you'll be better able to act spontaneously on them.

Step 11: Encouraging Clients to Put New Learning into Practice

At this point, clients should be ready to put their rational beliefs into practice. They can be reminded that, as per the rational–emotive theory of therapeutic change, they will have greater success in deepening conviction in their rational beliefs if they work at disputing irrational beliefs and strengthening rational ones in situations that are the same or similar to the activating event previously assessed. RET advocates a variety of homework assignments for accomplishing this end. As described in Chapter 8, these assignments can be categorised according to whether they have a cognitive, behavioural or imagery focus. In using homework assignments with clients, counsellors should bear in mind the following important points:

1. *Ensure that homework assignments are relevant.* Counsellors are advised to develop homework activities that are relevant to the irrational belief targeted for change. Enacting the homework assignment will help the client to weaken conviction in this irrational belief and deepen conviction in the alternative rational belief.

2. *Collaborate with clients.* It is good practice to enlist clients' active collaboration when discussing appropriate homework assignments. In order to increase the likelihood that a particular assignment will be enacted, the counsellor should ensure that the client (a) sees the sense of doing the homework assignment; (b) agrees that carrying out the assignment will help in the attainment of desired goals; and (c) has some degree of confidence in her ability to carry out the assignment. The probability of client compliance with homework assignments can be further maximised by establishing when, where and how often the particular activity will be implemented.

3. *Be prepared to compromise.* Ideally, homework assignments involve having clients actively and forcefully dispute their irrational beliefs in the most relevant life contexts possible. If this is not feasible, however, cilents can be encouraged to (a) dispute their irrational beliefs in situations that approximate the most relevant A, or (b) use imagery to

dispute irrational beliefs while vividly imagining A. Doing these less-than-ideal assignments can sometimes increase the likelihood that clients will eventually take on more challenging homework activities.

4. *Assess and troubleshoot obstacles.* Counsellors can work with clients to specify in advance any obstacles that may serve as impediments to homework completion. Clients can be encouraged to find possible ways of overcoming these obstacles before carrying out the assignment.

5. *Use homework at different times during counselling.* The present discussion has focused on homework assignments that help clients to strengthen conviction in their rational beliefs. It should be noted, however, that homework assignments can be useful at various points and for various purposes throughout the treatment sequence. Thus, homework assignments can be designed to help clients (a) specify their problematic emotions at C; (b) detect their irrational beliefs at B; and (c) identify the most relevant aspect of A about which they have made themselves disturbed. In addition, homework assignments can also be used as a means for educating clients about the ABCs of RET. Clients can be encouraged to read particular books (bibliotherapy), or to listen to RET lectures on audio tape. When suggesting such assignments, it is wise to select material that is relevant to the target problem and readily understandable. Counsellors can consider creating their own written materials or audio tapes to use with particular clients when appropriate material is not available.

Step 11: Monica

Joe: Now, since changing your beliefs usually takes a lot of effort, it's desirable to practise between sessions what you learn within sessions. Does that idea make sense to you?

Monica: Yes, it does.

Joe: Okay, good. What do you think you could do along those lines?

Monica: I'm not sure – I suppose I could practise applying the three arguments we went over to my self-defeating beliefs.

Joe: That sounds like a good idea. Specifically, you could use those arguments to challenge the idea that 'I *must* succeed; failing would prove that I'm an incompetent loser'. Also, you can apply those same three points to the more constructive, alternative beliefs we've discussed: 'I would prefer to succeed, but that doesn't mean that I must' and 'If I don't succeed I'm not an incompetent loser; I'm a fallible, unratable human being who happened to fail at a particular task'. Again, the idea is to weaken your conviction in your old beliefs, and strengthen your conviction in your new beliefs.

Monica: Right.

Joe: Now, how often would you like to review those arguments?

Monica: Oh . . . I think once in the morning – before going to work – and once in the evening.

Joe: That sounds fine. Do you anticipate any obstacles to doing this?

Monica: No, it sounds quite manageable.

Joe: Good. Why don't we just make some written notes on the three types of arguments that you can refer to as you practise?

Step 12: Check Homework Assignments

It is good practice to review previously negotiated homework assignments at the start of each session. Failure to do so may inadvertently communicate to clients that the counsellor does not consider these assignments to be an integral part of the change process. This is undesirable, as homework assignments are central to helping clients achieve their counselling goals.

Confirm that clients faced A

Unfortunately, clients can be quite creative in developing strategies to avoid problematic As. As such, it is advisable for counsellors to ascertain that clients actually faced the As they committed themselves to confronting. When clients genuinely *have* faced their As, they typically report that they first made themselves disturbed and then managed to become undisturbed (without simply escaping from the situation) by utilising the disputing techniques discussed in counselling. When clients fail to carry out their homework assignments in this manner, counsellors can help them to identify and deal with any obstacles that may have been involved. They can then encourage clients to again confront their troublesome situations and use vigorous disputing to make themselves undisturbed within that context. As necessary, appropriate disputes can be modelled and rehearsed in the session before clients make another attempt to confront the A in question.

Verify that clients changed B

When clients report success in implementing homework assignments, it is good practice to determine whether this success can be attributed to (a) changing an irrational belief to its rational alternative; (b) changing either A itself or inferences about A; or (c) the use of distraction techniques. If enquiry reveals that a given client utilised the latter two methods, the counsellor can acknowledge the client's efforts but then point out that these strategies may not be helpful in the long term. Practical solutions (i.e. changing A) or distractions are merely palliative, as they do not require clients to change the irrational beliefs that produce inappropriate negative emotions when A is faced. Many As are unavoidable; as such, the emotional problem will tend to reassert itself again and again. Counsellors can attempt to convey these points to clients, encourage them to again face the situation at A, and elicit their commitment to dispute their irrational beliefs and practise acting on the basis of the new rational beliefs.

Deal with failure to complete homework assignments

When clients fail to execute agreed-upon homework, rational-emotive counsellors accept them as fallible human beings and help them to identify the reasons the assignment was not carried out. The ABC framework can be used to help clients identify possible irrational beliefs that interfered with homework completion. In particular, counsellors will want to assess for irrational beliefs that contribute to low frustration tolerance (e.g. 'I shouldn't have to work so hard at changing – it's too damn hard!'). When clients hold such beliefs, they can be helped to challenge and change them prior to reassignment of the homework.

Step 12: Monica

The following exchange occurred one week later, during Monica's next session:

Joe: So, how did you make out with your homework assignment? You were going to work at challenging your self-defeating beliefs twice a day . . .

Monica: Well, I did okay at first, but as the week wore on I became rather inconsistent. I'd miss a morning, or an evening, or maybe even an entire day.

Joe: So you were doing well at first – let's give you some credit for that! But let's take a closer look at how you got yourself off track. When was the first morning when you didn't do your homework exercise?

Monica: Um . . . Thursday, I think.

Joe: Okay, imagine it's Thursday morning once again. What were you telling yourself at that time to make yourself miss your practice?

Monica: 'This is getting sort of boring'.

Joe: Well, wait a minute – that wouldn't be enough to stop you from practising. After all, you could have told yourself, 'This is getting boring. Too damn bad – I'll push myself to do it anyway, because I know that it will benefit me'. You then probably would have gone on to do the exercise.

Since you didn't do the exercise, you were probably telling yourself something *about* the boredom that dissuaded you from practising. What do you think that might have been?

Monica: Oh! Now I see it: 'It must not be boring!'

Joe: Right – that belief may well have been in operation. Also, you may have been adding this: 'I *can't stand it* if it's boring!' How could you challenge those two beliefs?

Monica: Well, I could make use of the same sorts of challenging questions we discussed last week.

Joe: Right! 'Is it logical?' 'Is it consistent with reality?' 'Does it produce helpful outcomes for me?' You can show yourself that it doesn't *have to* be stimulating, and that even if it isn't, you can still stand it.

Monica: That second part sounds important to me – I can tolerate the practice even if I do find it boring.

Joe: And perhaps you can experiment with ways to make it more interesting for yourself. Want to try the assignment again during the coming week?

Monica: Yes – I'm determined to keep working at it.

The session continued with further discussion of Monica's work-related problems and consideration of activity-oriented exercises that she could undertake to challenge her irrational beliefs.

Step 13: Facilitate the Working-through Process

It is unlikely that clients will achieve enduring therapeutic change unless they repeatedly and forcefully challenge their irrational beliefs in relevant contexts at A. By engaging in this process, they will further strengthen their conviction in rational beliefs and continue to weaken their conviction in irrational ones. The working-through process represents a means by which clients integrate rational beliefs into their emotional and behavioural repertoires.

Suggest a variety of homework assignments targeted at the same irrational belief

When clients have experienced some success in disputing particular irrational beliefs in relevant situations at A, they can be encouraged to use different types of homework activities to further erode the degree to which they subscribe to these same beliefs. Doing so teaches clients that a variety of methods can be used to dispute their targeted irrational beliefs, as well as others. In addition, introducing this sort of variety can help to sustain clients' interest in the change process.

Discuss the non-linear model of change

Counsellors can explain that change is a non-linear process in order to prepare clients for the difficulties they may encounter as they try to dispute irrational beliefs within a wide variety of contexts. Potential setbacks can be identified, and clients can be helped in advance to develop ways of dealing with them. Specifically, clients can be given assistance in identifying and challenging the irrational beliefs that might underpin their relapses.

In addition, counsellors can teach clients to evaluate change on the following three major dimensions:

1. Frequency: are inappropriate negative emotions experienced less often than before?
2. Intensity: when inappropriate negative emotions *are* experienced, are they less intense than before?
3. Duration: do inappropriate emotional episodes last for shorter periods than before?

Clients can be encouraged to keep records of their disturbed emotions at point C, using these three criteria for change. In addition, clients may find it helpful to read the booklet, *How to Maintain and Enhance Your*

Rational-Emotive Therapy Gains (Ellis, 1984c). This publication (which is reproduced in Chapter 10) contains many useful suggestions that clients may use to facilitate the working-through process.

Encourage clients to take responsibility for continued progress

At this stage, clients can be helped to develop their own homework assignments to change their target beliefs and to change other irrational beliefs in different situations. If, for example, a given client has been successful in disputing an irrational belief about approval in a work-related situation that involves criticism, she might be encouraged to dispute this belief in other situations in which criticism is encountered (e.g. with family members or friends). As clients develop confidence in designing and carrying out their own homework assignments, they are likely to experience increasing success in acting as their own therapists. This accomplishment is most important, as the long-term goal of rational–emotive counselling is to encourage clients to internalise the RET model of change and to take responsibility for further progress after therapy has ended.

Step 13: Monica

At the close of her second session, Monica agreed to take on the activity-oriented assignment of getting to work a half-hour earlier in order to have time to develop her skills on the office computer. She took on this assignment in addition to the cognitive exercise of challenging her irrational beliefs with the three types of disputing arguments she had learned in session. It was emphasised that she could utilise these arguments if she began to feel anxious while working with the computer.

With respect to working to overcome her 'computer phobia', Monica was generally more consistent in implementing her activity-oriented disputing exercises than her cognitive disputing exercises. Nevertheless, she did continue to use and benefit from the latter. As she progressed in therapy she began to tackle some of her other problem areas, including her fear of being criticised by her employer and her worries about financial security. With regard to the former, she successfully utilised rational–emotive imagery to help herself reach a point where she could remain in her boss's presence without experiencing anxiety. With respect to the latter issue, she was able to take steps toward internalising a personal philosophy wherein the possibility of temporary unemployment (with its attendant financial hardships) was regarded as a definite inconvenience, but certainly not a horror.

Monica also followed up on some of my suggestions for bibliotherapy assignments, and as a result sharpened her awareness of the broad range of emotional and behavioural problems to which RET can be applied. It seemed apparent that she was taking important steps toward becoming her own counsellor, as she often spontaneously reported instances in which she had utilised rational–emotive techniques to deal with upsets other than those that were included on her original problem list. We jointly decided that it was appropriate to end regularly scheduled contacts after we had met for a total of 14 sessions. Monica seemed pleased with the progress she had made in counselling, and understood that she could return for additional sessions if she encountered difficulty in coping on her own.

Chapter 10
The Rational–Emotive
Counselling Process

Overview

In Chapter 9 we presented the rational-emotive counselling sequence, which provides guidelines for helping clients to deal with a specific problem area. In this chapter we review the rational-emotive counselling *process*, and review treatment issues relevant to the beginning, middle and ending stages of counselling. Of particular note, we discuss issues pertaining to the formation of a sound therapeutic alliance, assisting clients in dealing with multiple problem areas, dealing with obstacles to therapeutic change, and encouraging clients to become their own counsellors. We conclude by presenting a brief account of a typical case in rational-emotive counselling.

It is noted that dividing the counselling process into beginning, middle and ending phases is a somewhat artificial convention we have chosen to employ in order to provide structure for the material presented in this chapter. Actually, it is impossible to differentiate so clearly between the various components of the counselling process. Issues pertaining to the therapeutic alliance between counsellor and client, for instance, will have importance throughout a course of treatment, and in reality are not restricted to the beginning stage of counselling. As such, we would advise the reader to approach the material that follows with a flexible frame of mind.

The Beginning Stage

Establishing a therapeutic alliance

Within the counselling field, the quality of the therapeutic alliance between counsellor and client is generally regarded as an important determinant of treatment outcome. Bordin (1979) provides a useful framework for conceptualising the therapeutic alliance by breaking it down into three major components: bonds, goals and tasks. The *bond* between counsellor and client refers to the nature and quality of the interpersonal relationship that exists between the two individuals. *Goals* are the purposes that counsellor and client would like to see achieved through counselling. *Tasks* are the respective activities that counsellor and client take responsibility for in the service of approaching counselling goals.

Bonds

If a productive bond fails to form between counsellor and client, the likelihood of therapeutic failure may be increased. In the service of promoting a productive bond, rational–emotive counsellors will attempt to identify the style of interaction most suitable for a given client. At the outset of counselling, for instance, counsellors can make enquiries concerning the client's view of what constitutes helpful versus unhelpful counsellor behaviour. Here, questions concerning the client's experiences with any previous counsellors can be particularly helpful. Some counsellors like to employ Lazarus's (1981) 'Life History Questionnaire', which contains the following questions:

1. In a few words, what do you think counselling is all about?
2. How do you think a therapist should interact with his or her clients?
3. What personal qualities do you think the ideal therapist should possess?

It is important to recognise that certain qualifications apply to the issue of counsellors modifying their interactional style to suit the client. Rational–emotive counsellors are willing to be flexible concerning the manner in which they relate to clients, but only insofar as this does not interfere with the attainment of counselling goals.

First, as mentioned in Chapter 5, it may be wise for counsellors to take the client's own personality style into account when trying to identify an optimal style of therapeutic interaction. It may be best, for example, to avoid an overly cognitive, intellectualised style when working with clients who appear to have obsessive–compulsive personality traits. Alternatively, some variant of this sort of style may prove quite suitable with clients who tend to be excitable and histrionic. As RET is a psychoeducational approach to counselling, a good rule of thumb is to find an interactional style that promotes an optimal learning environment for the particular client.

Secondly, some clients – either because of their own personality make-up or their prior experiences with counselling – may strongly prefer that their counsellor adopt a passive role within sessions. They may convey this preference directly through verbal statements, or indirectly through passive–aggressive responses to the counsellor's ministrations. It is important to bear in mind, however, that an active–directive counsellor style tends to be the preferred vehicle for implementing the problem-solving approach to counselling which is characteristic of RET. Thus, with clients who prefer counsellor passivity, rational–emotive counsellors would attempt to structure therapeutic conditions such that these clients become more receptive to a high degree of counsellor activity and directiveness. Initially, this could mean overtly presenting clients with a sound rationale for the counsellor's active-directive stance. If this fails, less direct strategies can be employed. These might include a gradual increase in the counsellor's verbal activity level over the course of the beginning stage of counselling, or the use of well-chosen, well-timed questions which promote a high degree of *client* verbal activity, while structuring sessions in a productive way. A minority of clients will remain 'allergic' to active-directive counsellor behaviour; for such individuals, a judicious referral to a practitioner who utilises a more passive approach to counselling may be in order.

It is noted that rational-emotive counsellors attempt to put into practice a philosophy of unconditional acceptance in their work with clients; this can also contribute to the formation of a good bond between counsellor and client. Translated into actual behaviour, a philosophy of unconditional acceptance means that counsellors refrain from responding in a judgmental, condemning fashion when clients report acts that society would consider unethical or morally wrong, or when clients behave inconsiderately toward their counsellor. When confronted with such things, rational-emotive counsellors generally attempt to respond to clients in a reasoned, matter-of-fact and objective manner. This can promote an air of trust and openness within counselling, and can indirectly convey to clients that they do not have to condemn themselves for their 'bad' acts. Counsellors will, however, sometimes opt to bring obnoxious behaviour to a client's attention, as when it appears that the client's negative behaviour toward the counsellor is representative of a larger pattern that impairs her ability to form good relationships with others.

Goals

It is important for counsellor and client to be working mainly toward the same goals within counselling. Failure to agree upon goals can lead them to operate at cross-purposes with each other, which will probably result in eventual dissolution of the therapeutic alliance.

Assessment of client attitudes about counselling

At the start of counselling, counsellors can promote congruence in the goal domain by initiating a discussion on the client's views as to whether and how counselling might be helpful to her. Just because a given client has presented herself at the counsellor's office, it should not be assumed that the client regards counselling as a potentially useful endeavour. Some clients, for instance, are pushed into counselling by significant others or the judicial system. Needless to say, special steps need to be taken to engage reluctant clients in the counselling process. Sociopathic individuals, for example, may not be open to counselling until the counsellor has presented strong arguments that it can help them to more effectively avoid legal problems and attain desired ends.

A number of clients willingly enter into counselling, but harbour misconceptions concerning how it might assist them. As discussed in Chapter 6, it is often advisable for counsellors to educate clients as to what counselling can and cannot provide. Clients should, for instance, understand that rational–emotive counselling is focused upon helping them with their psychological problems, as opposed to their practical problems. They can be helped to see, however, that improved psychological functioning may facilitate their ability to resolve practical issues. Counsellor utilisation of induction procedures can be a worthwhile investment of session time with clients who are largely naive about the ways in which counselling works.

Use of a problem list

Congruence in the goal domain can be further enhanced by encouraging clients to generate a 'problem list'. This is an inventory of problems for which the client is seeking help during counselling. It can be suggested to clients as an initial homework assignment to be completed prior to the next scheduled appointment, although it can be perfectly legitimate to devote session time to its production. Ideally, the list should exist in written form with copies for both counsellor and client to keep.

When counsellor and client are ready to start focusing on a problem, the client is invited to choose an item from the problem list. This item may be the client's most pressing problem, the problem which is easiest to solve, or one which – if progress is achieved – engenders most hope for the client. The guiding principle here is that counsellor and client work together on problem selection and agree on the chosen issue, which, in practice, usually tends to be the client's most pressing problem.

When a client chooses an item from her problem list to focus upon, it will often be necessary for the counsellor to work with the client on translating that problem into an appropriate goal for rational–emotive counselling. Counsellor/client collaboration in this venture also helps to ensure that both individuals are working together to achieve the same outcome in counselling.

It is noted that allowing the client to choose the problems to be dealt with in counselling can enhance the therapeutic alliance by indirectly conveying that the counsellor is sensitive to the client's concerns and priorities. In addition, encouraging client choice can serve to set the stage for the client's active involvement in the counselling process. On occasion, however, it will be evident to the counsellor that the client's choice of a problem area to focus upon is not entirely appropriate. Such a situation can arise when the counsellor obtains evidence (through enquiry and observation) that the client has a secondary problem *about* the chosen problem. In such cases, it is generally good practice for the counsellor to bring the secondary problem to the client's attention and to present a rationale for dealing with it first. If, however, the client expresses a strong preference to work on the chosen problem rather than the secondary problem, it may be wise for the counsellor to assent to this wish. To do otherwise could compromise the therapeutic alliance.

Use of a session agenda

When counsellors work with clients to establish a session agenda (see Beck, Rush, Shaw and Emery, 1979) at the start of each counselling contact, they can help to promote goal congruence on a per session basis. A session agenda constitutes an agreement between counsellor and client as to what will be discussed during a particular session, and can serve as a means for structuring the proceedings. It can, for example, discourage either counsellor or client from jumping unhelpfully from problem to problem without making significant progress on any given one.

The following excerpt from *Daring to be Myself* (Dryden and Yankura, 1992) illustrates how W.D. introduced the concept of establishing session agendas to his client, Sarah:

Dr Dryden: What I usually like to do at the beginning of every interview is to set up an agenda with you. I'll make suggestions about any items I might want to bring up, but it's mainly for any items that you want to talk about. This way, we can actually get the sense that we're working together on the same agenda. Okay?

Today, I'd like to discuss the problem list you were going to do – did you bring it with you?

Sarah: I did it very quickly last night.

Dr Dryden: Okay. Also, did you research any places to go [for social contacts]?

Sarah: Well, I phoned up social services.

Dr Dryden: Okay – we'll go into that in a minute. But first, what would you like to spend the bulk of today's session talking about? What particular issue or problem?

Sarah: Well, to put it in a nutshell, I'd like to talk about why I'm sort of frightened to get on with people.

Dr Dryden: So it's mainly your fear with other people?

Sarah: Mostly people I know, funny enough.

Dr Dryden: Okay. (Writing) 'People I know . . .'. Do you think that will take up the whole of the session?

[The session proceeds with review of the client's reactions to the last session and discussion of current agenda items.]

It is advisable for counsellors to exercise flexibility in using session agendas, and to avoid conveying the impression that an agenda *must* be thoroughly covered in any particular session. In this vein it is usually wise to avoid agendas that contain a long list of items, especially when it seems likely that one item will require a large portion of session time.

Tasks

Counsellors can avoid a particular threat to the therapeutic alliance by taking steps to ensure that clients understand the respective tasks of counsellor and client within rational–emotive counselling. Generally, rational–emotive counsellors will take the role of active–directive problem-solvers, and will collaborate with clients to dispute their irrational beliefs and design potentially helpful homework assignments. Clients, on their part, will ideally become active participants in their counselling and accept the task of working with counsellors to identify and challenge their irrational beliefs. Hopefully, they will also take an active hand in designing homework assignments for themselves and take responsibility for enacting these homework assignments between sessions.

Counsellors can utilise both direct and indirect means to educate clients as to the respective tasks of counsellor and client. With respect to direct means, counsellors can make statements early on in counselling (and at various points later on, as appropriate) which describe the tasks for which they will take responsibility. These statements may take a form such as the following:

Okay – as you've already noted, we've spent much of our first session together discussing your *attitudes* about your current job. As you've seen, some of these attitudes are causing you to experience feelings of anxiety and depression. As your counsellor, I propose to help you by sharpening your awareness of the attitudes that contribute to your upsets, and by showing you how you can *change* those unhelpful attitudes to more helpful ones. If you agree, we'll get down to working on that the next time we meet.

Similarly, counsellors can make direct statements that outline the tasks that clients are encouraged to take on.

Indirect means for communicating counsellor and client tasks include the following:

1. The counsellor's stance as an active–directive problem-solver through-out the course of counselling, conveyed through a high level of focused verbal activity.
2. The use of techniques such as Socratic questioning which prompt the client to engage in the task of actively examining and questioning her beliefs.
3. The use of prompts which encourage the client to play an active role in the design of relevant homework assignments (e.g. 'What do you think you could do during the coming week to put your new philosophy of self-acceptance into practice?').
4. Counsellors consistently devoting session time to designing and then subsequently following up on homework exercises.

The activities listed here are probably best viewed as vehicles for sup-plementing more direct communications concerning counsellor/client tasks. Conceivably, clients could fall into confusion and doubt if these activities are introduced into counselling sessions without direct verbal statements describing their purpose.

It is important to note that counsellors' and clients' respective tasks will change somewhat over the course of rational-emotive counselling. Counsellors attempt to gradually decrease their activity level such that clients are encouraged to take on more of the responsibility and effort involved in making progress and maintaining gains. This issue is dealt with again in the forthcoming section on the middle stage of counselling.

Monitoring clients' reactions

As an additional means of promoting a sound therapeutic alliance, we have found it helpful to monitor clients' reactions to counselling throughout the course of treatment. Thus, we will routinely ask clients at the end of a given session if they found any of our statements or suggestions particularly helpful or unhelpful. At the start of the next scheduled session, we inquire of clients whether they had any additional reactions to the preceding session. The feedback resulting from these enquiries allows us to identify and correct any misunderstandings or misconceptions which clients may have developed, and helps us to modify our strategies and interventions so that they are more likely to promote beneficial change for individual clients.

Some clients will be reluctant to provide their counsellor with negative feedback, as they are afraid of losing the counsellor's approval and acceptance. When a given client only provides glowing responses to counsellor enquiries concerning her reactions to sessions, it may be appropriate to consider the hypothesis that this individual has a self-created need for the counsellor's approval. If this appears to be the case, it is generally good practice for the counsellor to directly (but tactfully) broach this issue and devote session time to exploring it with the client. In doing so, the counsellor may be able to identify and dispute any irrational beliefs (e.g. I *must* maintain my counsellor's approval; to lose this approval would *really* prove that I'm a worthless and unlovable person!') that could interfere with the counselling process.

Teaching the ABC model

In order for clients to make sense of their rational-emotive counsellor's approach to helping them overcome emotional problems, they will require a foundation in rational-emotive concepts and techniques. Thus, during the beginning stage of counselling, counsellors need to teach clients the three main insights of RET and the means by which emotional problems can be analysed and remediated with the ABC model.

With respect to RET's first main insight, it is important for clients to understand that their emotional problems are largely determined by their irrational beliefs, and not directly by the troublesome life events that they have experienced. This should be considered a fundamental point for counsellors to convey to clients; if clients do not attain this understanding then they will probably fail to grasp why their counsellors focus so much attention on their thinking. As a result, they may make continued efforts to focus discussions upon the details of the current negative circumstances that they face, and may be put off by the counsellor's limited interest in this material.

RET's second major insight holds that individuals remain disturbed by continually reindoctrinating themselves in the *present* with the irrational beliefs to which they subscribe. Thus, detailed exploration of the historical antecedents of a client's irrational beliefs is eschewed within rational–emotive counselling, and a focus is placed upon identifying currently held musts, shoulds and have to's. It is important for clients to understand that it is not essential for them to determine precisely where their irrational beliefs came from, as long as they see that continuing to hold these beliefs will increase their vulnerability to emotional upsets and dysfunctional behaviour.

RET's third main insight emphasises that clients will need to work consistently and diligently at challenging and replacing their irrational beliefs if they are to derive significant, lasting benefits from counselling. Clients who possess this understanding are in a position to be active participants within their counselling, and will be able to see the desirability of putting into practice the knowledge they gain during counselling sessions.

Clients are taught both directly and indirectly to utilise the ABC model as a means for analysing and understanding their emotional upsets. Didactic explanations represent a direct means for teaching clients about the model's components, and can be useful at various points throughout the course of counselling. The model can also be conveyed indirectly through the Socratic questioning technique, which can be used to prompt clients to identify the relevant activating events, consequent emotions and behaviours, and operative irrational beliefs involved in their emotional episodes. Brighter clients may often be able to learn how to independently analyse their upsets through the counsellor's use of Socratic questioning, and may require fewer didactic explanations. In our own practices, however, we will generally employ a didactic presentation of the ABC model at some early point in the counselling process, rather than assuming that clients will pick it up indirectly.

Given that rational–emotive counselling has a psychoeducational focus, it is important for counsellors to take steps to ensure that clients grasp the material they are trying to teach them. One way to accomplish this is to ask clients periodically to convey their understanding of critical points that have been covered. This can be tactfully done when counsellors use questions such as the following: 'We've been discussing how you don't have to rate yourself as either a good or a bad person, but I want to be sure I've been expressing myself clearly. Can you restate to me – in your own words – what you've understood me to be saying?'

In addition to utilising periodic checking, counsellors are advised to avoid jumping from problem to problem within any given counselling session. Remaining focused on one problem at a time (and covering the essential steps of the counselling sequence) is usually the best means for teaching clients the elements of rational–emotive problem-solving.

By the end of the beginning stage of counselling, clients should have learned the three main insights of RET. They will also have had some initial experience in identifying and disputing the irrational beliefs that underpin their emotional problems. Counsellors will also have introduced clients to the concept of homework assignments, which will serve as an important vehicle for facilitating client movement from intellectual to emotional rational insight as counselling continues. Bibliotherapy assignments (which involve suggesting that clients obtain and read some of the relevant RET self-help texts) given at an early point in counselling can often help clients to become accustomed to the idea of devoting time and effort to working on their problem areas between sessions.

Dealing with client doubts

During the beginning stage of counselling, some clients may express doubts as to whether the rational–emotive approach will be able to help them solve their own particular set of emotional problems. In responding to these expressed doubts, the counsellor is advised to first assess and correct any misunderstandings about the approach that a given client may have. If the client still appears doubtful after this intervention, the counsellor can suggest that she try a brief 'trial' of counselling (consisting of five or so sessions) as a means for determining through direct experience whether she finds the rational–emotive approach helpful. At the end of this trial counsellor and client can review and discuss any remaining doubts that the client may have. If the client still maintains strong doubts at this point, it may be wise to make a judicious referral to another mental health professional who practises an alternative form of counselling. Such a referral would take into account the client's views concerning the type of counselling approach most likely to promote therapeutic gains.

It should be noted that some clients may harbour doubts about counselling because they are confusing the rational–emotive approach with the counsellor's interactional style. Thus, it can be important for counsellors to make enquiries which will help them to determine whether client objections are focused on issues pertaining to the counselling or the counsellor. If a given client is having a negative reaction to the counsellor's style of interaction within sessions, an appropriate modification in style may resolve this issue so that counselling may proceed.

The Middle Stage

As clients move into the middle stage of counselling, they may experience some initial success in disputing their irrational beliefs and dealing with particular episodes of emotional disturbance. At the same time, however, they may begin to see that their irrational beliefs are deeply entrenched and that they adversely affect a number of different areas of their functioning. In a related vein, they may find that it is difficult to work in a consistent and determined manner at modifying the thinking habits that contribute to their psychological problems. Thus, the middle stage of counselling presents the rational–emotive practitioner with a number of significant challenges germane to promoting continued therapeutic progress. The sections that follow will provide guidelines for counsellors to follow as they attempt to facilitate client movement from intellectual to emotional rational insight.

Dealing with multiple problem areas

Typically, clients present more than one problem area during a course of counselling. In some cases these multiple problem areas will be identified and targeted for change at an early point in the counselling process. Frequently, however, new problem areas will emerge as counselling proceeds. This can occur for several reasons:

1. The client develops a level of trust in the counsellor such that she becomes comfortable in disclosing problems previously considered 'too embarrassing' for discussion.
2. The client develops an awareness of how particular irrational beliefs are adversely affecting a number of different areas of her life.
3. The client experiences additional unfortunate activating events during the course of counselling (such as the loss of a job) that serve to trigger 'new' upsets.

Rational–emotive counsellors prefer to deal with a particular problem area until the client is able to cope with it reasonably well. It will sometimes happen, however, that during the course of working on one problem area, the client wishes to change the focus to another problem area that is experienced as more pressing or important. Alternatively, circumstances may arise which lead the counsellor to wonder whether a change in tack would be desirable from a therapeutic perspective. When confronted with such situations, counsellors will find it useful to have a set of guidelines to which they can refer in deciding whether to switch to discussion of the new problem area.

First, it is important to consider the effect that persisting with treatment of the original problem area will have on the therapeutic alliance. If a client maintains a strong desire to switch to a new problem area after the counsellor has presented a rationale for staying with the original problem until it is resolved, it may be wise to accede to the client's preference and begin to work on the new problem. To do otherwise could communicate the unfortunate message that the counsellor is more interested in following his or her own agenda than in responding to the client's concerns. This, of course, could damage the working relationship between counsellor and client.

Secondly, clients will sometimes experience crisis situations during the course of counselling which serve as triggers for new, additional upsets. When this occurs, efforts to resolve the original targeted problem may temporarily become irrelevant until the new upset has been dealt with. To cite an example, a given counsellor/client dyad may have been working to help the client overcome the feelings of anger and hurt he typically experiences in the face of his wife's harsh criticisms. While attending to this problem area, the client loses his job and makes himself depressed through negative self-rating and self-pity. As this depression significantly interferes with a number of areas of this client's functioning (including his ability to engage in the immediate task of job-hunting), it is appropriate for the counsellor to shift attention away from the original problem in order to focus attention to the new problem area. When the new problem area has received adequate treatment (such that the client is able to manage his depressed moods and function more effectively), counsellor and client may decide to return to their work on the original problem area.

Thirdly, counsellors may see that it is advisable to switch attention to a 'new' emotional problem that the client is experiencing when it becomes apparent that this upset is impeding the client's ability to concentrate on the original problem area under consideration. In such a situation it would make little sense to continue working on the original problem area, as the client is not in a state to benefit from such efforts. Again, counsellor and client may decide to put aside their work on the original problem until the client is able to cope reasonably well with the new one.

Finally, there may be some circumstances in which it becomes evident to the counsellor that the client has an ongoing problem – currently not the focus of treatment – that pervades numerous areas of her life. Here, the counsellor may wish to suggest to the client that they shift their attention to this other problem area. A given client may, for instance, exhibit problematic drinking behaviour that interferes with her functioning at work and within her interpersonal relationships. Conceivably, however, she might not regard her drinking as being central to many of the difficulties she encounters and could express a preference to work on a more circumscribed area of her functioning (e.g. being more assertive with co-workers).

It would be wise in such a situation for her counsellor to bring to her attention the way in which her drinking negatively affects numerous areas of her life, and to present a rationale for working to modify this behaviour. In this scenario, counsellor and client could proceed to work at identifying and disputing the irrational beliefs that contribute to episodes of overdrinking, and later attend (if necessary) to other, more circumscribed problem areas of concern to the client.

Whenever counsellor and client switch from one problem area to another, it is important for the counsellor to encourage the client to maintain a focus on this new problem until a coping criterion has been attained. Frequent jumping from problem to problem is likely to interfere with the counselling process, as it will make it difficult for clients to learn the emotional problem-solving techniques that are part and parcel of RET.

Occasionally, counsellors will encounter a client who tries to touch upon numerous problem areas during any given session, as opposed to focusing on only one or two. If a counsellor presents a rationale for dealing with one problem at a time but the client persists in this pattern, it may be appropriate for the counsellor to exercise flexibility on this issue in order to avoid endangering the therapeutic alliance. In some cases, however, the client's frequent switching can represent avoidance behaviour. Some individuals, for instance, will try to get on to a different topic when they begin to experience strong negative emotions during the course of discussing a particular problem area. If this occurs frequently, the counsellor may choose to bring it to the client's attention as another problem area to work on. Again, it is incumbent upon the counsellor to exercise an appropriate degree of flexibility with respect to the issue of switching problems, and to recognise that it may be quite difficult for some clients to face and deal with their dysfunctional avoidance of upsetting feelings.

Identifying core irrational beliefs

As counsellors work with clients on the various problem areas targeted for intervention within counselling, they are advised to watch for common themes among the irrational beliefs that underpin these problems. By looking for common themes, counsellors can often identify core irrational beliefs to which clients subscribe. When core irrational beliefs are identified, it becomes possible to show clients that various problem areas (perhaps previously regarded by clients as being largely independent of one another) have similar underlying cognitive dynamics. During the middle stage of counselling, these core irrational beliefs – as opposed to specific problems – can receive more attention with respect to therapeutic exploration.

To illustrate the usefulness of identifying and dealing with core irrational beliefs, consider the case of a client who presents for counselling with complaints of non-assertiveness with friends and family, anxiety in social situations, and an unsatisfying marital relationship. As counselling with this individual proceeds, it is possible that her counsellor will identify the following irrational belief as being central to her problem areas: 'I *must* have the approval of others in order to consider myself a worthwhile person'. With respect to her non-assertiveness with friends and family, this irrational belief may make it difficult for her to refuse unreasonable requests for favours out of fear that significant others will reject her. With regard to her social anxiety, her *must* may result in worries about saying or doing 'the wrong thing' in interpersonal situations. As concerns her unsatisfying relationship with her husband, her irrational belief may cause her to make unreasonable efforts to please him while sacrificing her own set of wants and preferences.

Once this client's counsellor has assembled a reasonable body of evidence to support the hypothesis that a particular irrational belief is at the root of many of her interpersonal difficulties, she can be shown the common theme that runs through her problem areas. This insight can help the client to have a better understanding of her own individual psychology, and can simplify the work of counselling for her to a considerable degree. Now, instead of working on the 'separate' areas of non-assertiveness, shyness and an unsatisfying marriage, she can focus her efforts on overcoming her self-created need for others' approval.

With respect to the process of identifying themes across problems, counsellors are cautioned to guard against assuming that all of a client's problems can be explained with reference to a single irrational belief. In our experience, it is more typically the case that clients will subscribe to two or three core irrational beliefs. As a potentially helpful rule of thumb, counsellors are advised to bear in mind that RET identifies two broad categories of disturbance: ego disturbance and discomfort disturbance. Since it is relatively rare for clients to present for counselling with only one of these two categories of disturbance, counsellors can remain alert to manifestations of both forms. They can then work to identify the central irrational beliefs that underpin the manifestations of these two forms of disturbance for a particular client.

Encouraging clients to engage in relevant tasks

A primary task for counsellors during the middle stage of counselling is to assist clients in approaching emotional rational insight by encouraging them to strengthen their conviction in their rational beliefs. As noted previously, emotional rational insight – as opposed to intellectual rational insight – is likely to lead to significant emotional and behavioural changes for clients.

As described in Chapter 8, there is a variety of cognitive, behavioural and imagery techniques used within rational–emotive counselling to help clients move from intellectual to emotional rational insight. Although counsellors may initiate the use of some of these techniques, it is important that by the middle stage of counselling clients see the role that *they* can play in promoting the change process. In particular, they need to see the usefulness of working hard to overcome their problems outside counselling sessions via homework assignments. Thus, by this stage of counselling, counsellors should have presented clients with a plausible rationale for homework assignments and should also have dealt with any objections or questions that clients may have had about undertaking such assignments.

Some clients will show that they understand the importance of their own efforts and homework assignments within counselling, but will harbour doubts about their ability to execute relevant tasks (i.e. those that will promote emotional rational insight) outside sessions. Counsellors can respond to these doubts in a number of different ways.

First, counsellors can work collaboratively with clients to design homework assignments that they are willing to do. Novice rational–emotive counsellors will sometimes make the error of pushing behavioural 'flooding' homework assignments on clients, since they know that RET views such assignments as representing the most efficient vehicle for promoting swift and meaningful modifications of irrational beliefs. Many clients will, however, make themselves anxious when they think about enacting flooding assignments, and will thus avoid doing them. As an example, a counsellor might insist that an agoraphobic client take on the exercise of spending an afternoon alone at a shopping mall, as a means for powerfully countering the client's self-created needs for security and comfort. The client may very well avoid implementing this assignment because the mere image of being in a crowded store (in combination with the irrational belief, 'I *must* feel emotionally comfortable at all times') leads to anxiety. Rather than suggesting assignments that clients are unlikely to implement because of the emotional obstacles they create for themselves, counsellors can work with them to design homework activities that are 'challenging but not overwhelming'. Here, clients are encouraged to take on assignments involving behaviours not currently engaged in with frequency or complete ease (that are thus 'challenging'), but that are not regarded as too difficult or threatening (i.e. 'overwhelming'). With reference to the example described above, the counsellor could work with the client to design a homework assignment – such as going to a neighbourhood shop to complete a quick errand – that may stand a better chance of being completed. In the process of designing this assignment the counsellor can explain that tasks involving some degree of difficulty are more likely to facilitate the process of belief change.

As a second means of dealing with clients' doubts concerning their ability to execute homework assignments, counsellors can help clients to practise implementation of these assignments within counselling sessions. Certain behavioural assignments can be readily rehearsed within sessions, such as assertively requesting a rise in pay from one's employer. With other types of assignments – such as certain shame-attacking exercises – rehearsal of the behaviours involved would be more difficult. In such cases, however, the counsellor can help the client to rehearse the assignment in imagery. Whether an assignment is practised through overt behaviour or imagery, the counsellor can use the rehearsal to assist the client in identifying emotional 'trouble spots' (i.e. points at which the client might create anxiety or some other upset for herself) in advance of actual implementation, and can then devote time to dealing with the irrational beliefs responsible for these upsets.

A third way of increasing the likelihood of homework enactment is for counsellors to work with clients to identify when, where and how particular homework assignments will be implemented. Although this would seem to be a rather minimal standard of practice in the design of homework assignments, our experiences as counselling supervisors suggest that it is often neglected by even the more experienced RET practitioners. A fairly large number of clients (particularly those who have difficulty in keeping themselves organised) will fail to do homework assignments because they do not plan when they will fit them into their weekly schedules. Counsellors can prompt clients to do such planning by simply asking them on what days, and at what times of day, they will engage in homework activities. In addition, counsellors can establish with clients the place or context within which homework assignments will be implemented, and can make sure that they are aware in advance of all the component steps that may be involved in the completion of a particular assignment.

It is also important that homework assignments be of a practical nature, meaning that clients are able to implement them without experiencing a great deal of inconvenience. Many individuals in counselling may be highly motivated to work at overcoming their disturbance; the fact remains, however, that they also have daily lives to attend to. The tasks of daily living can take up a good part of the day, and will impose limits on the amounts of time and effort that clients will be able (and willing) to devote to counselling-related activities. As such, homework assignments that require extraordinary investments of time, money or energy will stand a much lower chance of completion.

Given the central place of homework assignments within rational-emotive counselling, it is important for counsellors to check up on clients' experiences in executing them. Failure to follow-up on homework assignments may indirectly communicate the unfortunate message that such activities are not so significant a part of the change process.

With respect to thoroughgoing follow-up on homework assignments, counsellors will want to keep the following suggestions in mind:

1. Make an enquiry as to what the client learned through enactment of the assignment. Is this learning beneficial in terms of countering an irrational belief that the client holds, or will it serve to somehow reinforce the client's irrational thinking?
2. Reinforce the client's success in enacting the homework assignment. If the assignment was not successfully implemented (e.g. the client did only part of it), then recognise and reinforce any efforts that *were* made to complete it.
3. Identify and deal with the client's reasons for not attempting or completing the homework assignment (see Appendix I). Help the client to identify and dispute any irrational beliefs that may have been involved here.
4. If appropriate, encourage the client to try the assignment again if she was not fully successful with it. Even if the criterion for success was attained, bear in mind that repetition of particular homework activities can be helpful.

As a final note, it is recommended that counsellors assess the reasons for the apparently therapeutic changes that clients may report. In some cases, clients may enact homework assignments and describe seemingly positive changes in their usual patterns of behaviour that occur for the 'wrong' (i.e. non-therapeutic) reasons. As an example, a young male client seen by J.Y. reported at one point during his counselling that he was no longer fearful about approaching and starting conversations with women. Upon enquiry, it was learned that he had adopted the following attitude as a means for countering his approval anxiety: 'If they reject me, it doesn't mean that I'm a loser; it means that *they* are losers'. Although the first part of this statement may be logically and empirically correct, the second part is irrational as it embodies a person-rating philosophy. Conceivably, such a philosophy could lead this individual to reject other people too readily.

Dealing with obstacles to change

A number of significant obstacles to change may be encountered during the middle stage of counselling. Clients may, for instance, have had some success at this point in terms of disputing their irrational beliefs, but will typically experience recurrences of their emotional problems. This is because they are still in the process of approaching emotional rational insight. When clients bring a philosophy of low frustration tolerance (LFT) to bear upon their failure to remain free of upsets, they may block themselves from persisting with their efforts to internalise a new rational philosophy. Here, it is important for counsellors to help their clients to identify and dispute the beliefs that produce their LFT. Such beliefs may take numerous forms, including 'Change must not be difficult' and 'I shouldn't have to work so hard in counselling'.

Also, it is important to note that change itself can be an uncomfortable experience for clients. Maultsby (1984) has described a state which he refers to as *cognitive-emotional dissonance*, in which clients experience feelings of 'strangeness' as they work to strengthen their conviction in their irrational beliefs. Counsellors can encourage their clients to accept such feelings as being a natural part of the change process, and if necessary can dispute their irrational demands to feel natural and comfortable all of the time.

A minority of clients will develop a state of 'pseudo-rationality', which can interfere with their ability to effect meaningful emotional and behavioural changes in their lives. Such clients become avid consumers of rational-emotive books and audiotapes, and make themselves extremely knowledgeable about RET's theory and practice. They can quote extensively from the RET literature and are able to give all the 'right' answers to counsellors' disputing questions during sessions, but fail to put their knowledge into practice between sessions. Such lack of effort may again be attributable to a philosophy of low frustration tolerance; alternatively, it may stem from the erroneous belief that intellectual insight is sufficient to bring about lasting changes. In either case, counsellors need to help clients to challenge and change the attitudes that block them from working to approach emotional rational insight.

Counsellors may sometimes encounter bright, achievement-oriented clients who are able to understand the B–C connection, but who nevertheless evince a reluctance to surrender their musts. With such clients, an enquiry may reveal that they view their musts as an important source of motivation for achieving their goals, and that they worry that giving up their musts will lead them into apathy and inertia. Counsellors can emphasise the distinction between strong desires and absolutistic demands with these clients, and can show them that their strong desires will provide sufficient motivation for working toward attainment of the goals they value. Further, they can be shown particular ways in which their musts create emotional obstacles that may function to block goal attainment.

The material presented in this section is intended to highlight some of the obstacles to client progress that are particularly germane to the middle stage of counselling. In Chapter 11 we present a broad overview of obstacles to progress, along with recommendations concerning ways of overcoming them.

Encouraging clients to maintain and enhance their gains

It is usually the case that clients will display the greatest variability in their rates of progress during the middle stage of counselling. They will at times appear to make significant gains with respect to approaching emotional rational insight; they will, however, also experience periodic backsliding.

During this stage, counsellors need to help their clients to deal with setbacks, maintain the progress they have made, and explore ways to enhance their therapeutic gains. Ellis (1984c) has written an excellent pamphlet on these issues which is reproduced below, with minor modifications. It can be helpful for counsellors to provide clients with a copy of this handout when the issues it covers become salient during the course of counselling.

How to maintain your improvement

1. When you improve and then fall back to old feelings of anxiety, depression, or self-downing, try to remind yourself and pinpoint exactly what thoughts, feelings, and behaviours you once changed to bring about your improvement. If you again feel depressed, think back to how you previously used rational–emotive principles to make yourself undepressed. For example, you may remember that:
   (a) you stopped telling yourself that you were worthless and that you couldn't ever succeed in getting what you wanted;
   (b) you did well in a job or in a love affair and proved to yourself that you did have some ability and that you were lovable;
   (c) you forced yourself to go to interviews instead of avoiding them and thereby helped yourself overcome your anxiety about them.
   Remind yourself of thoughts, feelings, and behaviours that you have changed and that you have helped yourself by changing.
2. Keep thinking, thinking and thinking rational beliefs or coping statements, such as: 'It's great to succeed but I can fully accept myself as a person and enjoy life considerably even when I fail!' Don't merely parrot these statements but go over them carefully many times and think them through until you really begin to believe and feel that they are true.
3. Keep seeking for, discovering, and disputing and challenging your irrational beliefs with which you are once again upsetting yourself. Take each important irrational belief – such as, 'I have to succeed in order to be a worthwhile person!' – and keep asking yourself: 'Why is this belief true?', 'Where is the evidence that my worth to myself, and my enjoyment of living, utterly depends on my succeeding at something?', 'In what way would I be totally unacceptable as a human if I failed at an important task or test?'
   Keep forcefully and persistently disputing your irrational beliefs wherever you see that you are letting them creep back again. And even when you don't actively hold them, realise that they may arise once more, bring them to your consciousness, and preventively – and vigorously! – dispute them.
4. Keep risking and doing things that you irrationally fear – such as riding

in elevators, socialising, job hunting or creative writing. Once you have partly overcome one of your irrational fears, keep acting against it on a regular basis. If you feel uncomfortable in forcing yourself to do things that you are unrealistically afraid of doing, don't allow yourself to avoid doing them - and thereby to preserve your discomfort forever! Often, make yourself as uncomfortable as you can be, in order to eradicate your irrational fears and to become unanxious and comfortable later.

5. Try to see clearly the difference between rational negative feelings - such as those of sorrow, regret, and frustration, when you do not get some of the important things you want - and irrational negative feelings - such as those of depression, anxiety, self-hatred, and self-pity, when you are deprived of desirable goals and plagued with undesirable things. Whenever you feel *over*concerned (panicked) or *unduly* miserable (depressed) acknowledge that you are having a statistically normal but a psychologically unhealthy feeling and that you are bringing it on yourself with some dogmatic *should*, *ought* or *must*. Realise that you are invariably capable of changing your irrational (or *must*urbatory) feelings back into rational (or preferential) ones. Take your depressed feelings and work on them until you *only* feel sorry and regretful. Take your anxious feelings and work on them until you *only* feel concerned and vigilant. Use rational-emotive imagery to imagine unpleasant activating events vividly even before they happen: let yourself feel irrationally upset (anxious, depressed, enraged or self-downing) as you imagine them; then work on your feelings to change them to rational emotions (concern, sorrow, annoyance or regret) as you keep imagining some of the worst things happening. Don't give up until you actually do change your feelings.

6. Avoid self-defeating procrastination. Do unpleasant tasks fast - today! If you still procrastinate, reward yourself with certain things that you enjoy - for example, eating, vacationing, reading and socialising - only *after* you have performed the tasks that you easily avoid. If this won't work, give yourself a severe penalty - such as talking to a boring person for 2 hours or burning a $100 bill - every time that you procrastinate.

7. Show yourself that it is an absorbing challenge and something of an adventure to maintain your emotional health and to keep yourself reasonably happy no matter what kind of misfortunes assail you. Make the uprooting of your misery one of the most important things in your life - something you are utterly determined to steadily work at achieving. Fully acknowledge that you almost always have some choice about how to think, feel and behave: and throw yourself actively into making that choice for yourself.

8. Remember - and use - the three main insights of rational-emotive counselling:

Insight no. 1: you largely *choose* to disturb yourself about the unpleasant events of your life, although you may be encouraged to do so by external happenings and by social learning. You mainly feel the way you think. When obnoxious and frustrating things happen to you at point A (activating events), you consciously or unconsciously *select* rational beliefs that lead you to feel sad and regretful and you also *select* irrational beliefs that lead you to feel anxious, depressed and self-hating.

Insight no. 2: no matter how or when you acquired your irrational beliefs and your self-sabotaging habits, you now, in the present, *choose* to maintain them – and that is why you are now disturbed. Your past history and your present life conditions importantly *affect* you; but they don't *disturb* you. Your present *philosophy* is the main contributor to your *current* disturbance.

Insight no. 3: there is no magical way for you to change your personality and your strong tendencies to needlessly upset yourself. Basic personality change requires persistent *work and practice* – yes, *work and practice* – to enable you to alter your irrational beliefs, your inappropriate feelings and your self-destructive behaviours.

9. Steadily – and unfrantically! – look for personal pleasures and enjoyments – such as reading, entertainment, sports, hobbies, art, science, and other vitally absorbing interests. Take as your major life goal not only the achievement of emotional health but also that of real enjoyment. Try to become involved in a longterm purpose, goal, or interest in which you can remain truly absorbed. For a good, happy life will give you something to live *for*; will distract you from many serious woes; and will encourage you to preserve and to improve your mental health.

10. Try to keep in touch with several other people who know something about RET counselling and who can help go over some of its aspects with you. Tell them about problems that you have difficulty coping with and let them know how you are using rational–emotive principles to overcome these problems. See if they agree with your solutions and can suggest additional and better kinds of disputing methods that you can use to work against your irrational beliefs.

11. Practice using rational–emotive methods with some of your friends, relatives and associates who are willing to let you try to help them with it. The more often you use it with others, and are able to see what their irrational beliefs are and to try to talk them out of these self-defeating ideas, the more you will be able to understand the main principles of RET counselling and to use them with yourself. When you see other people act irrationally and in a disturbed manner, try to figure out – with or without talking to them about it – what their main irrational beliefs probably are and how these could be actively and vigorously disputed.

12. When you are in rational–emotive counselling try to tape record many

of your sessions and listen to these carefully when you are in between sessions, so that some of the rational–emotive ideas that you learned in counselling sink in. After counselling has ended, keep these tape recordings and play them back to yourself from time to time, to remind you how to deal with some of your old problems or new ones that may arise.

13. Keep going back to the rational–emotive reading and audiovisual material from time to time, to keep reminding yourself of some of the main rational–emotive findings and philosophies.

How to deal with backsliding

1. Accept your backsliding as normal – as something that happens to almost all people who at first improve emotionally and who then fall back. See it as part of your human fallibility. Don't feel ashamed when some of your old symptoms return, and don't think that you have to handle them entirely by yourself and that it is wrong or weak for you to seek some additional sessions of counselling and to talk to your friends about your renewed problems.

2. When you backslide look at your self-defeating behaviour as bad and unfortunate, but work very hard at refusing to put yourself down for engaging in this behaviour. Use the highly important rational–emotive principle of refraining from rating *you*, your*self*, or your *being*, but of measuring your *acts*, *deeds* and *traits*. You are always a *person who* acts well or badly – and never a *good person* or a *bad person*. No matter how badly you fall back and bring on your old disturbances again, work at fully accepting yourself with this unfortunate or weak behaviour – and then try, and keep trying, to change your behaviour.

3. Go back to the ABCs of rational–emotive counselling and clearly see what you did to fall back to your old symptoms. At A (activating event), you usually experienced some failure or rejection once again. At rB (rational belief) you probably told yourself that you didn't *like* failing and didn't *want* to be rejected. If you only stayed with these rational beliefs, you would merely feel sorry, regretful, disappointed, or frustrated. But when you felt disturbed again, you probably then went on to some irrational beliefs (iBs) such as 'I *must* not fail! It's *horrible* when I do!' 'I *have to* be accepted, because if I'm not that makes me an *unlovable worthless person*!' Then, after convincing yourself of these iBs, you felt, at C (emotional consequence) once again depressed and self-downing.

4. When you find your irrational beliefs by which you are once again disturbing yourself, just as you originally used disputing (D) to challenge and surrender them, do so again – *immediately* and *persistently*. Thus, you can ask yourself: 'Why *must* I not fail? Is it really *horrible* if I do?' And you can answer: 'There is no reason why I *must* not fail, though I

can think of several reasons why it would be highly undesirable. It's not *horrible* if I do fail – only distinctly *inconvenient*'. You can also dispute your other irrational beliefs by asking yourself, 'Where is it written that I *have* to be accepted? How do I become an *unlovable, worthless person* if I am rejected?' And you can answer: 'I never *have to be* accepted, though I would very much *prefer* to be. If I am rejected, that makes me, alas, a *person who* is rejected this time by this individual under these conditions, but it hardly makes me an *unlovable, worthless person* who will always be rejected by anyone for whom I really care'.

5. Keep looking for, finding and actively and vigorously disputing your irrational beliefs which you have once again revived and that are now making you feel anxious or depressed once more. Keep doing this, over and over, until you build intellectual and emotional muscle (just as you would build physical muscle by learning how to exercise and then by *continuing* to exercise).

6. Don't fool yourself into believing that if you merely change your language you will always change your thinking. If you neurotically tell yourself: 'I *must* succeed and be approved' and you sanely change this self-statement to 'I *prefer* to succeed and be approved', you may still really be convinced: 'But I really *have to* do well and *have got to be* loved'. Before you stop your disputing and before you are satisfied with your answers to it (which in rational–emotive counselling we call E, or an effective philosophy), keep on doing it until you are *really* convinced of your rational answers and until your feelings of disturbance truly disappear. Then do the same thing many, many times – until your new E (effective philosophy) becomes hardened and habitual – which it almost always will if you keep working at arriving at it and re-instituting it.

7. Convincing yourself lightly or 'intellectually' of your new effective philosophy or rational beliefs often won't help very much or persist very long. Do so very *strongly* and *vigorously* and do so many times. Thus, you can *powerfully* convince yourself, until you really *feel* it: 'I do not *need* what I *want*! I never *have* to succeed, no matter how greatly I wish to do so! I *can* stand being rejected by someone I care for. It won't *kill* me – and I *still* can lead a happy life! *No* human is damnable and worthless – including and especially *me*!'

How to generalise from working on one emotional problem to working on other problems

1. Show yourself that your present emotional problem and the ways in which you bring it on are not unique and that virtually all emotional and behavioural difficulties are created by irrational beliefs. Whatever your irrational beliefs are, moreover, you can overcome them by strongly and persistently disputing and acting against these irrational beliefs.

2. Recognise that you tend to have three major kinds of irrational beliefs that lead you to disturb yourself and that the emotional and behavioural problems that you want to relieve fall into one of these three categories:
   (a) 'I *must* do well and *have to* be approved by people whom I find important.' This irrational belief leads you to feel anxious, depressed, and self-hating; and to avoid doing things at which you may fail and avoiding relationships that may not turn out well.
   (b) 'Other people *must* treat me fairly and nicely!' This irrational belief contributes to your feeling angry, furious, violent and over-rebellious.
   (c) 'The conditions under which I live *must* be comfortable and free from major hassles!' This irrational belief tends to create your feelings of low frustration tolerance and self-pity, and sometimes those of anger and depression.
3. Recognise that when you employ one of these absolutist *musts* – or any of the innumerable variations on it that you can easily slide into – you naturally and commonly derive from them other irrational conclusions, such as:
   (a) 'Because I am not doing as well as I *must*, I am an incompetent worthless individual!' (Self-damnation.)
   (b) 'Since I am not being approved by people whom I find important, as I *have to* be, it's *awful* and *terrible*!' (Awfulising.)
   (c) 'Because others are not treating me as fairly and as nicely as they *absolutely should* treat me, they are *utterly rotten people* and deserve to be damned!' (Other-damnation.)
   (d) 'As the conditions under which I live are not that comfortable and as my life has several major hassles, as it *must* not have, I can't stand it! My existence is a horror!' (Can't-stand-it-itis.)
4. Work at seeing that these irrational beliefs are part of your *general* repertoire of thoughts and feelings and that you bring them to many different kinds of situations that are against your desires. Realise that in just about all cases where you feel seriously upset and act in a distinctly self-defeating manner you are consciously or unconsciously sneaking in one or more of these irrational beliefs. Consequently, if you get rid of them in one area and are still emotionally disturbed about something else, you can always use the same rational–emotive principles to discover your irrational beliefs in the new area and to eliminate them there.
5. Repeatedly show yourself that it is almost impossible to disturb yourself and to remain disturbed in any way if you abandon your absolutist, dogmatic *shoulds*, *oughts* and *musts*, and consistently replace them with flexible and unrigid (though still strong) *desires* and *preferences*.
6. Continue to acknowledge that you can change your irrational beliefs by rigorously (not rigidly!) using the scientific method. With scientific thinking, you can show yourself that your irrational beliefs are only

theories or hypotheses – not facts. You can logically and realistically dispute them in many ways, such as these:

(a) you can show yourself that your irrational beliefs are self-defeating – that they interfere with your goals and your happiness. For if you firmly convince yourself: 'I *must* succeed at important tasks and *have to* be approved by all the significant people in my life', you will of course at times fail and be disapproved – and thereby inevitably make yourself anxious and depressed instead of sorry and frustrated;

(b) your irrational beliefs do not conform to reality – and especially do not conform to the facts of human fallibility. If you always *had* to succeed, if the universe commanded that you *must* do so, you obviously *would* always succeed. And of course you often don't! If you invariably *had* to be approved by others, you could never be disapproved. But obviously you frequently are! The universe is clearly not arranged so that you will always get what you demand. So although your desires are often realistic, your god-like commands definitely are not!;

(c) your irrational beliefs are illogical, inconsistent or contradictory. No matter how much you *want* to succeed and to be approved, it never follows that therefore you *must* do well in these (or any other) respects. No matter how desirable justice or politeness is, it never *has to* exist.

Although the scientific method is not infallible or sacred, it efficiently helps you to discover which of your beliefs are irrational and self-defeating, and how to use factual evidence and logical thinking to rid yourself of them. If you keep using scientific analysis, you will avoid dogma and set up your hypotheses about you, other people, and the world around you so that you always keep them open to change.

7. Try to set up some main goals and purposes in life – goals that you would like very much to reach but that you never tell yourself that you absolutely must attain. Keep checking to see how you are coming along with these goals; at times revise them; see how you feel about achieving them; and keep yourself goal-orientated for the rest of your days.

8. If you get bogged down and begin to lead a life that seems too miserable or dull, review the points made here and work at using them. Once again: if you fall back or fail to go forward at the pace you prefer, don't hesitate to return to counselling for some booster sessions.

Encouraging clients to become their own counsellors

During the beginning stage of counselling, the counsellor is quite active-directive with respect to helping the client to learn the ABCs of RET. In the middle stage of counselling this material needs to be reviewed, but the client should be encouraged to take the lead in applying it to problem areas.

Counsellors are advised to be active and directive when first discussing a particular problem area with a client, but to gradually decrease their activity level as a means to promote the client's own efforts and involvement. Here, the overall goal is to help the client to internalise the rational-emotive method for solving emotional problems. The counsellor thus encourages the client's attempts to identify troublesome emotions and behaviours, relate these to particular activating events, and identify operative irrational beliefs. The client would then be encouraged to dispute these irrational beliefs and to develop alternative, rational beliefs that can replace them. It is also important to prompt clients to look for links between problem areas, with the object of identifying and disputing core irrational beliefs.

Counsellors should increasingly utilise the Socratic questioning technique during the middle stage as a means of encouraging clients to do most of the work of counselling. Didactic teaching should be kept to a minimum. Short, probing questions can be used to promote independent thinking, and to decrease client dependence upon the counsellor's problem-solving skills. Thus, when a client discusses her experiences between sessions in dealing with a particular problem area, the counsellor may ask a sequence of questions such as the following:

'How did you feel when that happened?'
'What were you telling yourself to bring on that feeling?'
'How did you dispute that?'
'How did you block yourself from disputing that?'
'What rational belief could you use to replace that must?'
'How is that rational belief more (logical; realistic; helpful) than that irrational belief?'
'If you really believed that, then how would you tend to act?'
'Could you try that during the coming week?', etc.

Some clients may not respond well to a decrease in the counsellor's level of directiveness. A number of individuals may, for instance, be prone to form dependent relationships with their counsellors because they harbour doubts about their ability to function independently as emotional problem-solvers. Counsellors can attempt to deal with these doubts (e.g. by making reference to prior instances when the client in question successfully coped with a particular upset), and can present a rationale for increased independent effort. When a given client appears genuinely stuck with respect to dealing with a particular problem area, the counsellor can temporarily revert back to a more active–directive stance. As work on this problem area proceeds, the counsellor can then gradually return the responsibility for dealing with it back to the client. When clients respond successfully to decreased counsellor directiveness over several sessions, it can be appropriate to begin taking steps to work toward termination.

The Ending Stage

The ending stage of the counselling process involves working towards the termination of regularly scheduled counselling sessions. Termination may be approached either by collaboratively decreasing the frequency of counselling sessions over time, or by setting a definite termination date. Although it is unrealistic to attempt to establish a perfect point at which termination should occur for a given client, it is possible to identify a number of general criteria that can be applied to termination decisions. These criteria are as follows:

1. The client has internalised RET's approach to emotional problem-solving and has made significant, healthy modifications to her personal philosophy.
2. The client has gone beyond dealing with her initial presenting problems such that other significant problem areas have been tackled as well.
3. Core irrational beliefs have been identified and disputed.
4. The client has developed confidence in her capacity to act as her own therapist.
5. Counsellor and client agree that termination is appropriate.

These criteria can be viewed as constituting an 'ideal outcome' within rational-emotive counselling. In reality, however, ideal outcomes are relatively rare and clients may often want to terminate before these criteria have been reached. It is thus important for counsellors to be aware of various sorts of scenario in which premature termination is a possibility, so that they can respond in an effective manner to these situations.

A number of clients will want to terminate counselling before they have made any real progress in identifying and disputing their irrational beliefs. This scenario can occur when clients' troublesome activating events fortuitously change for the better, so that they are no longer experiencing the upsets that may have contributed to their original decision to seek counselling. When clients leave counselling under such circumstances, they will probably be vulnerable to the same sort of upset in the future. Counsellors can make efforts to explain to them that they have not yet dealt with the philosophical underpinnings of their emotional problems, and can encourage them to remain in counselling as a means for militating against a recurrence of their disturbance. Here, it is noted that much useful work can be accomplished within rational–emotive counselling even when clients are not facing any immediate stressors. If clients are unresponsive to the provision of a rationale for continuing in counselling, counsellors can make it clear to them that they may return if their external circumstances take a turn for the worse and they once again create upsets for themselves.

A certain number of clients will state their desire to terminate counselling after having made some initial progress with respect to their original presenting problems. In this scenario a given client may feel that she has accomplished what she set out to accomplish, and she may regard her counselling as having been very helpful. Her counsellor, however, may see that she probably harbours particular core irrational beliefs which have not yet received formal attention within sessions. As such, it may be unlikely that this client will be able to generalise her rational–emotive counselling gains across problems and situations. Again, it would be appropriate for the counsellor to present a rationale for remaining in counselling, as it could still have much to offer this individual. Ellis' (1984c) handout on generalisation and maintenance, reproduced above, could be used to supplement the counsellor's rationale, as it conveys the message that it is possible to make oneself generally less susceptible to emotional and behavioural difficulties. Should the client stand by her preference to discontinue counselling, the counsellor can extend an 'open invitation' to return when she feels that she would like to enhance her treatment gains.

Scenarios also occur in which the client has made some progress in overcoming her emotional problems as per the RET approach, but wishes to terminate formal sessions in order to pursue independent practice of self-counselling. Counsellors will generally want to be supportive of such a preference, although they may wish to engage the client in a discussion concerning the pros and cons of continued counselling contacts. In some instances, such discussion may reveal concerns or issues related to counselling (such as time-scheduling difficulties) that may be easily resolved. If such issues are not a part of the picture and the client maintains her desire to terminate formal contacts, the counsellor may still suggest a limited number of additional sessions that will be focused on facilitating the client's future efforts at self-counselling. The content of these sessions can include recommendations concerning relevant self-help books and audio-tapes, reiteration of rational–emotive strategies for emotional problem-solving, and attempts to help the client anticipate (and hence be better prepared to deal with) activating events that may serve as triggers for future upsets. Whether or not the client agrees to extra sessions, the counsellor can make it clear that it is perfectly appropriate to return for additional contacts when these are viewed as necessary.

In addition to being confronted with situations in which clients may want to terminate prematurely, counsellors will also occasionally encounter individuals who wish to continue counselling sessions beyond an appropriate point. Some clients who have made considerable progress, for instance, may still believe that they need the continued help of their counsellor in order to maintain their counselling gains. Such problems may become manifest when a given client is reluctant either to set a termination date or to decrease the frequency of sessions. When this is the case, the counsellor can work to identify and dispute any irrational beliefs that are in operation (e.g. 'I *must* have the ongoing support of my counsellor; I am incapable of coping on my own'), and can suggest to the client that she attempt an experiment to assess her coping capacity. This could involve helping her to specify the aspects of her life that she thinks she cannot cope with on her own, and then encouraging her to test this out as a homework assignment.

Other clients may be reluctant to terminate counselling because they do not want to lose the special sort of relationship they have developed with their counsellor. Here, it can be appropriate for the counsellor to identify and discuss any feelings of sadness that a client may have about the dissolution of the counselling relationship. It can be emphasised that, while such feelings may be negative in tone, they are an appropriate emotional response to the ending of a significant relationship. If the client believes that she should not have these somewhat painful feelings, the counsellor can encourage her to dispute this irrational belief as a means of helping her to accept this normal part of human experience.

Some counsellors may be unwilling to terminate the counselling relationship with clients who have shown considerable progress. These counsellors may believe that they need to have continued evidence of client progress in order to prove that they are competent practitioners and therefore worthwhile people. Needless to say, it would be highly desirable for such counsellors to identify and challenge their competency needs by using the methods of rational–emotive counselling outlined in this book.

As a final note, counsellors may want to consider building in well spaced out follow-up sessions after regularly scheduled counselling sessions have ended. These follow-up sessions can be used as a means to help clients monitor their future progress. In one respect there is no absolute end to the rational–emotive counselling process, as counsellors would want to encourage their clients to contact them for further assistance when they encounter prolonged difficulties in practising self-counselling.

A Typical Case of Rational–Emotive Counselling

The following account describes a case in which W.D. was the counsellor:

Mrs Haynes (pseudonym), at the time that I saw her, was a 35-year-old professional married woman who had recently discovered that her husband had been having an affair and had decided to leave her for the other woman. There were no children in this marriage. Mrs Haynes was referred to me for counselling by her general practitioner for depression and anxiety. In the initial session she made it clear to me that she did not want to involve her husband in counselling but rather she wanted an opportunity to focus on her own problems. She further did not think that joining a group would give her sufficient time or privacy to discuss her problems in as much depth as she considered to be most productive for her. We thus decided on a course of individual rational–emotive counselling.

In the initial session, I asked Mrs Haynes to describe her prior experiences with counselling. She reported having had a previous spell of individual counselling with a marriage counsellor who, from her description, appeared to practise a kind of non-directive psychoanalytically oriented counselling. She felt that she did not benefit from this approach, mainly because she was confused and put off by the counsellor's passivity and seeming lack of active involvement. I gave her a thumbnail sketch about what she might realistically expect from rational–emotive counselling, and her initial reaction was favourable. We agreed to meet initially for five sessions. I like to make an initial time-limited contract to enable clients to make a more informed decision about whether or not they think that they will benefit from rational–emotive counselling.

Mrs Haynes saw depression as more of a pressing problem for her than anxiety, and it was the one that she chose to make a start on. Her problem list revealed that she was particularly depressed about her own failure to make her marriage work and blamed herself for her husband's preference for another woman. I helped her to see that it was not his preference for another woman that made her depressed, but her belief about the situation which was, 'I must make my marriage work and I am a failure if I don't!' Before proceeding to help her to dispute this belief in the initial session, I worked patiently with her to enable her to see the connections between A, B and C.

I only started to dispute her irrational belief when she said that she saw clearly that it was this belief that caused her depression rather than her husband leaving her, and that in order to overcome her depression she needed to change her belief. While disputing her belief I helped her to develop a list of self-disputes that she could ask herself in the coming week whenever she felt depressed about her presumed failure in marriage. I gave her a copy of *A New Guide to Rational Living* (Ellis and Harper, 1975) and suggested that in particular she read Chapter 2 ('You feel the way you think') and Chapter 11 ('Eradicating dire fears of failure'). I also offered her an opportunity to take away a tape of our session, which she accepted gratefully. She was thus exposed to the idea of working at homework assignments between sessions.

At the beginning of the following session I asked her for her reactions to both the tape and the reading material. It transpired from this that she had a positive response to both the tape and reading material and she commented that she particularly liked the method of bibliotherapy. Her depression had lifted considerably since our first session, and she was able to use her own self-disputes to come up with plausible answers. In order to reinforce her progress I asked her if she would find it helpful to use one of the written self-help forms that exist for this purpose, and showed her three. She decided to start off with the one which I invented (see Figure 7.1). We first worked on an episode of depression – even though she had progressed on that since our initial session – after we had decided that it was better to get closure on her depression before we tackled her anxiety. We spent the rest of session two filling out this form and at the end I gave her a number of these forms and suggested that she read Chapter 15 of *A New Guide to Rational Living* ('Conquering anxiety') and to use such insights to fill in a form whenever she became anxious.

At the beginning of session three, she reported that she benefited from reading the chapter on anxiety, but had experienced some difficulty in zeroing in on the irrational beliefs which underpinned her own anxiety. Using the inference chaining procedure, I helped her to see that she was anxious about ever finding another man again and ending up an old spinster. As is typical in rational–emotive counselling, I encouraged her to assume the worst and to imagine that she was an old spinster and asked her for her feelings about that. Her reply was instructive: 'Oh God, I couldn't stand the thought of living like that'. I disputed her belief that she needed a man in her life in order to be happy and helped her to see that she could in fact gain a fair measure of happiness in her life being single even though she would prefer to be married and have a family. This led on to a discussion of her immediate anxiety, i.e. her feeling that she could not go out on her own because this would be shameful.

Often feelings of shame are related to feelings of anxiety and, assuming this to be the case with Mrs Haynes, I helped her to see that she was saying: 'If I go out on my own then other people will think that I am alone and that would prove that I am worthless'. The rest of the session was spent putting this into A, B, C, D, E form using the self-help form. I then suggested that we try rational–emotive imagery as a bridge between changing her attitude in her mind's eye and putting into practice her new belief: 'I have every right to go out on my own and if other people look down on me, then I refuse to look down on myself'. Mrs Haynes had a great deal of difficulty in using rational–emotive imagery (Ellis's version) in the session, and between sessions three and four.

At the beginning of session four I went over the rational-emotive imagery and suggested instead that she say her new rational belief quite vigorously to herself. She was able to do this, first of all out loud and then internally and felt a mood shift which was much more profound than that she was able to achieve by using Ellis's version of rational-emotive imagery. Let me add that her feelings of depression were no longer considered by her to be a problem since session one.

At the end of session four we negotiated an assignment whereby she would go out socially on her own on two occasions, on one occasion to a local evening class and secondly to a dance hall, while vigorously repeating the rational self-coping statements we developed. This apparently was very helpful to Mrs Haynes, for she reported that she was able to go out on both occasions without undue anxiety. This was our fifth session, the last of our therapeutic contract and I discussed progress with Mrs Haynes and how she wished to proceed in the future. She said that she felt very pleased with her progress and wanted to continue to have sessions every two weeks rather than weekly. Under the circumstances, this appeared to be a reasonable way of approaching termination.

From sessions five to ten Mrs Haynes made great progress. She had a number of dates with men and was able to resist the sexual advances of two of them, which to her was a great stride because in the past she had had great difficulty saying 'No' to men and had for a period prior to her marriage been quite promiscuous, out of desperation rather than out of choice. Between sessions five and ten, I gave her *Why Do I Think I Am Nothing Without A Man* by Penelope Russianoff (1981) and *Living Alone and Liking It* by Lynn Shahan (1981) to read. She also continued to listen to the tapes of her sessions, although I suggested that she review them only once, rather than her accustomed three times, because I wished to encourage her to rely on her own resources rather than to rely on my direction, albeit secondhand, through the tapes. She also continued going out on her own and used vigorous self-disputing to increasingly good effect. It seemed apparent that she was experiencing success in becoming her own counsellor.

As counselling progressed to what I thought would be termination, Mrs Haynes got quite anxious. She said that she felt she had become quite dependent upon my help and was anxious about whether or not she could cope on her own. First of all I disputed her belief that she needed my help, and secondly, I encouraged her to view a break from counselling as an experiment and suggested a 6-week gap between our tenth and eleventh sessions, stressing that she rely more on self-disputing rather than on bibliotherapy. I also suggested that she should not listen to any of the past tapes, so that we could conduct a fair experiment of her inference that she could not cope on her own.

The experiment proved to be a success because she came in and wondered why she even thought that she could not cope on her own, since she had managed the 6-week gap very well. I commented that I was pleased with her progress, to which she replied: 'That's nice to know but even if you weren't, I am. I don't need your approval.' Having been firmly put in my place in this regard, we discussed whether she needed any future sessions and finally agreed that we would have a 6-month follow-up, although I did suggest that she could contact me if she wanted to in the interim, on the condition that she used her own skills for a 2-week period and if she could not cope with any emotional problems which came up in that period then she could contact me.

At the 6-month follow-up session Mrs Haynes had attained and enhanced her therapeutic gains. She was productively involved in many social and voluntary activities and had ongoing casual relationships with three men, one of which included sex out of choice and not out of desperation. Her relationship with her husband was reasonably cordial and they were proceeding towards an amicable divorce. In my keenness to encourage her to cope on her own, I made the error of moving toward termination without helping her to anticipate future problems and encourage her to see that she could use her new coping methods to deal with these problems. Although this was an error at the time, Mrs Haynes was able to do this in the intervening period. In addition, I had to do very little work in helping her set goals for increased satisfaction since she was able to do this on her own.

Appendix I: Possible Reasons for not Completing Self-help Assignments

(To be completed by client)

The following is a list of reasons that various clients have given for not doing their self-help assignments during the course of counselling. Because the speed of improvement depends primarily on the amount of self-help assignments that you are willing to do, it is of great importance to pinpoint any reasons that you may have for not doing this work. It is important to look for these reasons at the time that you feel a reluctance to do your assignment or a desire to put off doing it. Hence, it is best to fill out this questionnaire at that time. If you have any difficulty filling out this form and returning it to the counsellor, it might be best to do it together during a counselling session. (Rate each statement by ringing 'T' (True) 'F' (False). 'T' indicates that you agree with it; 'F' means the statement does not apply at this time.)

1 It seems that nothing can help me so there is no point in trying.   T/F
2 It wasn't clear, I didn't understand what I had to do.   T/F
3 I thought that the particular method the counsellor had suggested would not be helpful. I didn't really see the value of it.   T/F
4 It seemed too hard.   T/F
5 I am willing to do self-help assignments, but I keep forgetting.   T/F
6 I did not have enough time. I was too busy.   T/F
7 If I do something the counsellor suggests I do it's not as good as if I come up with my own ideas.   T/F
8 I don't really believe I can do anything to help myself.   T/F
9 I have the impression the counsellor is trying to boss me around or control me.   T/F
10 I worry about the counsellor's disapproval. I believe that what I do just won't be good enough for him/her.   T/F

11   I felt too bad, sad, nervous, upset (underline the appropriate word(s)) to do it.   T/F

12   It would have upset me to do the homework.   T/F

13   It was too much to do.   T/F

14   It's too much like going back to school again.   T/F

15   It seemed to be mainly for the counsellor's benefit.   T/F

16   Self-help assignments have no place in counselling.   T/F

17   Because of the progress I've made these assignments are likely to be of no further benefit to me.   T/F

18   Because these assignments have not been helpful in the past, I couldn't see the point of doing this one.   T/F

19   I don't agree with this particular approach to counselling.   T/F

20   OTHER REASONS (please write them).   T/F

Chapter 11
Obstacles to Client Progress and How to Overcome Them

Overview

In this chapter we catalogue the major obstacles to client progress in rational-emotive counselling. We deal mainly with common counsellor errors in the practice of rational-emotive counselling as covered in Chapters 6–10. We also briefly discuss client factors, relationship factors and environmental factors that serve as obstacles to client progress. We conclude the chapter by considering how rational-emotive counselling can be individually tailored to the unique requirements of clients.

Sources of Obstacles to Client Progress: Counsellor Factors

In this section we discuss obstacles to client progress that can be attributed to the counsellor. We emphasise errors that are commonly made by counsellors in the beginning phase of rational-emotive counselling (induction and assessment); in attempting to promote intellectual rational insight; in attempting to promote emotional rational insight; and in the general management of cases. It is, of course, desirable for RET counsellors to strive continually to improve their skills by involving themselves in ongoing supervision and training activities (Dryden, 1983; Wessler and Ellis, 1980, 1983).

Finally, we discuss the major irrational beliefs held by counsellors that appear to interfere with the practice of effective rational-emotive counselling.

Beginning rational–emotive counselling

Rational-emotive counsellors can obstruct the progress of their clients by committing the following errors in the induction and assessment stages of beginning counselling:

1. *Failing to explore clients' anticipations and preferences for counselling.* A common result of this failure is that misconceptions that clients have about the process of rational–emotive counselling remain unchecked. Clients may 'resist' the counsellor's interventions when they 'expect' a different type of help from that provided. As such, it is important for counsellors to assess clients' reasons for entering counselling, the types of problems they think counselling will be able to help them deal with, and their views concerning what constitutes 'appropriate' counsellor behaviour. It is good practice to provide clarification for clients concerning the respective roles of counsellor and client within rational–emotive counselling, and to clearly convey that RET seeks to help individuals overcome their psychological problems by identifying and changing dysfunctional personal philosophies.

2. *Failing to assess clients' problems correctly.* This may mean that counsellors proceed to work on 'problems' that clients do not have. This error can be avoided by having clients prepare a problem list, as discussed in the preceding chapter. If necessary, counsellors can work with clients to translate the items on this list into problems that can be dealt with as per the RET approach.

3. *Failing to identify relevant second-order problems (i.e. problems about problems).* When these problems are not identified and assessed clients may not be helped because they may be distracted with their second-order problem when their first-order problems are being discussed. It is advisable for counsellors to be alert to indications that clients may feel ashamed, guilty, anxious or depressed about their primary problems.

4. *Failing to explain why counsellor and client had better work on the secondary problem first.* When this occurs the client often becomes puzzled when the counsellor proceeds to work on the secondary problem without giving an adequate rationale for doing so. This difficulty can be circumvented by providing such a rationale, and by exploring within session the ways in which the secondary problem may interfere with treatment of the primary problem. If the client still insists on dealing with her primary problem at this point, it may be a good idea to honour her preference. To do otherwise could damage the therapeutic alliance.

5. *Failing to identify clearly and specifically negative emotional and behavioural consequences (Cs).* Here counsellors often fail to clarify vague emotional Cs such as 'upset' or 'unhappy' and may thus assume wrongly that these emotions are irrational when they may in fact be rational. We refer readers to Chapter 4 for a full discussion of how to distinguish between irrational and rational emotions.

6. *Failing to help the client understand the dysfunctional nature of his/her self-defeating emotions and behaviours at C.* When this point

is omitted counsellors often assume that their clients will want to change these 'self-defeating problems' when in fact the clients do not necessarily define them as self-defeating (a common example here is irrational anger). Before moving to the disputing stage of counselling it is important that clients are helped to view them as targets for change. Just because particular emotions or actions are deemed irrational by rational–emotive theory does not mean that clients wish to change them. As Golden (1983, p. 34) has shown, clients often 'resist' working on self-defeating Cs if this means confronting a higher-order anxiety, e.g. 'an overweight client fearing that if she lost weight she would then have to deal with her social and sexual anxieties about dating'. Thus higher-order anxieties often need to be assessed in rational–emotive counselling.

7. *Spending too much time listening to irrelevant background data on activating events (As).* When counsellors make this error they unwittingly train their clients to talk about irrelevances and thus practise inefficient counselling. As noted earlier, clients should preferably be encouraged to specify activating events as briefly as possible.

On occasion, counsellors will encounter clients who tend to compulsively provide far more detail on their activating events than is needed. When this becomes a pattern within sessions, it can be tactfully brought to clients' attention and therapeutic exploration can shift to an ABC analysis of the problem. Often, such analysis can reveal that clients harbour irrational beliefs such as the following: 'I *must* provide my counsellor with all the details; otherwise we might miss something of importance and that would have *awful* consequences for my counselling'.

8. *Spending too much time focusing on the historical determinants of clients' problems.* Doing this may encourage clients to believe that such material is very important in understanding their current problems, whereas rational–emotive theory emphasises that it is the client's current beliefs that should ideally be the focus of enquiry. Here, counsellors can convey to clients that identifying the historical determinants of their irrational beliefs will generally have little relevance with respect to the course that treatment will take.

9. *Gaining a total picture of the client's past and present problems before assessing specific problems.* While collecting such data may be helpful, in practice it does not add very much to the assessment of specific problems. Counsellors who make this error often like to place clients in relevant diagnostic categories, believing (wrongly in our opinion) that doing so will aid the treatment process.

10. *Failing to use inference chaining to identify the most relevant inference in the inference chain.* Thus, a man may be angry with his wife for forgetting to collect his suit from the cleaners not because she is

forgetful, but because her forgetfulness will get him into trouble at work, trouble which he dreads. The correct use of inference chaining often helps counsellors to identify significant problems which are not immediately apparent from clients' accounts of their problems. The reader is referred back to Chapters 6 and 9 for material on this procedure.

11. *Failing to show clients that the ideology of their problems is most frequently expressed in the form of devout, absolutist 'musts' or one of the three main derivatives of 'musturbation'.* Inexpert rational-emotive counsellors tend to assume that clients' anti-empirical, or inferentially distorted thinking, 'causes' their emotional and/or behavioural problems. While distorted inferences may be implicated in clients' problems, RET theory holds that they tend to stem from irrational beliefs. Thus, from a therapeutic perspective, it makes sense to focus treatment on identifying and changing the latter.

12. *Failing to uncover clients' relevant irrational beliefs.* Here counsellors may identify irrational beliefs which are either incorrect or too general in nature. An example of the latter occurred when a counsellor identified the general irrational belief 'I must be approved by everyone', whereas the client's actual irrational belief was more specific: 'I must be approved by significant others in my life'. Counsellors are advised to first identify the specific irrational beliefs triggered by particular activating events, and then to look for common themes across the specific beliefs. In this way clients' core irrational beliefs can be identified and dealt with as treatment proceeds.

13. *Failing to explain the B–C connection.* When this explanation is not made clients are often puzzled when their counsellors begin to dispute their irrational beliefs. They cannot fully understand that changing their beliefs will lead to their desired emotional and/or behavioural goals. Chapter 6 presented a teaching dialogue (created by Ellis) that counsellors can employ to convey the B–C connection; other vehicles for accomplishing this task appear throughout the RET practitioners' literature (see, for example, Walen, DiGiuseppe and Wessler, 1980; Wessler and Wessler, 1980).

14. *Failing to assess clients' emotional and behavioural goals.* When counsellors fail to assess their clients' goals, they often assume that clients have goals which they do not in fact have. Here, as elsewhere, rational–emotive counsellors may assume wrongly that their clients will function according to RET theory, e.g. that they will want to be concerned rather than anxious. With respect to setting feasible emotional goals for rational–emotive counselling, counsellors can teach clients the distinctions between rational and irrational feelings (see Chapter 4). In addition, counsellors can work with clients to explore whether their behavioural goals will ultimately prove to be self-defeating.

Promoting intellectual rational insight

The following errors are often committed by inexpert rational–emotive counsellors in this stage of the counselling process.

1. *Assuming that clients will automatically change their irrational beliefs once they have identified them.* Inexpert RET counsellors either fail to dispute irrational beliefs at all or use disputing methods sparingly and with insufficient vigour. It is advisable to persist in disputing clients' irrational beliefs until they are able to acknowledge that such beliefs are illogical, anti-empirical and self-defeating. It is, however, a good idea to change tack when persistence in disputing a particular irrational belief poses a threat to the therapeutic alliance (e.g. as when a client expresses a strong preference to explore a new problem area).

2. *Disputing distorted inferences before disputing irrational beliefs.* Inexpert RET counsellors tend to eschew the preferred rational–emotive strategy of assuming temporarily that distorted inferences are true so that irrational beliefs may be challenged. They tend to dispute distorted inferences because they are distorted, and fail to realise that although such inferential distortions are implicated in clients' problems they are not central to their existence. The danger of disputing distorted inferences before irrational beliefs is that although clients may improve, this improvement is temporary and the ideological evaluative roots of their problems still need to be addressed.

3. *Failing to focus disputing interventions on clients' actual irrational beliefs.* Here counsellors tend to stray from specific irrational beliefs that they correctly assessed earlier. The most common error here is to shift to disputing general beliefs as noted in the previous section. It is generally good practice to dispute specific irrational beliefs first, and then later in the counselling process to work at identifying and disputing core irrational beliefs.

4. *Failing to help clients to understand the difference between rational and irrational beliefs.* Helping clients to understand this difference is important since, in response to questions asking for evidence in favour of their irrational beliefs, they will provide evidence in support of their rational beliefs. Clarifying the distinction between rational and irrational beliefs helps to refocus clients on challenging the latter.

5. *Failing to use Socratic-type disputing with clients who can benefit from this method.* As such, counsellors deprive these clients of the opportunity to think for themselves and impede them from becoming their own future counsellors. Socratic-type disputing is an important part of rational–emotive counselling, as it can provide an in-session model of disputing procedures. Counsellors can attempt to use the Socratic questioning technique on an experimental basis with their

clients, and can make decisions on whether to continue with it based on client response.

6. *Failing to lecture didactically when it is clear that clients do not understand a concept through Socratic disputing.* Although rational-emotive counsellors prefer to use Socratic disputing whenever possible, rigid adherence to this method can be counterproductive. Didactic presentations have their place in rational–emotive counselling and can be fruitfully employed when clients do not benefit from Socratic disputing. When material is presented didactically it is important for counsellors to be concise in their explanations and to check whether or not they have made themselves understood.

7. *Philosophising in an abstract manner.* Although effective rational-emotive counsellors do engage in philosophical discussions with their clients, these debates are focused on clients' actual irrational beliefs and reminders of the relevance of these discussions for the clients' problems at C are provided. Inexpert RET counsellors tend to engage their clients in abstract philosophical discussions divorced from the latter's problems. As such, both counsellor and client lose a productive therapeutic focus. When the client tries to channel discussion to abstract philosophising, the counsellor can explain that this is likely to be non-productive and can attempt to redirect the session to more relevant issues. Some clients may use abstract philosophising as a means of distancing themselves from dealing with their problems; when this appears to be the case, counsellors can approach it as an issue for therapeutic exploration.

8. *Failing to use appropriate examples, metaphors, stories etc., while disputing.* Effective disputing sequences are characterised by a variety of examples, metaphors, stories etc., tailored to the client's own idiosyncratic situation. When these are omitted disputing can lose its desired impact. Counsellors are again referred to the RET literature for a variety of such devices that can be adapted for use with given clients. In addition, they are encouraged to develop their own devices, based on their knowledge of client history, occupation, hobbies, etc.

9. *Failing to remind clients of the dysfunctional consequences of adhering to irrational beliefs.* A good way of encouraging clients to work on relinquishing their irrational beliefs is to provide them with frequent reminders of the dysfunctional consequences of such beliefs. Thus a counsellor may say 'OK, so you keep maintaining that you must achieve your certificate, but where is that belief getting you other than anxious and depressed?'

10. *Failing to counter the illogicalities that clients express during the process of disputing.* Clients often express a variety of illogicalities in defence of their irrational beliefs while responding to the disputing interventions of their counsellors (Edelstein, 1976; Guinagh, 1976).

Ineffective rational–emotive counsellors may not even identify these illogicalities, or when they do identify them they may not address them successfully. Commonly expressed illogical defences include:

(a) *Statements of indifference*. Here clients think that rational alternatives to irrational beliefs are expressive of indifference, e.g. 'I don't care if . . .' rather than, 'I prefer that . . .'. We recommend that counsellors help their clients to distinguish among irrational beliefs, rational beliefs and 'indifferent' beliefs.

(b) *'My belief is true because I feel it to be true'*. This is an example of emotional reasoning (Burns, 1980). Clients should be shown that feeling something to be true is often not a good guide to its validity.

(c) *'I can't change my belief because that's the way I am'*. Here clients wrongly consider that their irrational belief is part of their unalterable identity. Distinctions between thinking and identity should be made, and instances of clients changing important beliefs should be sought to counter this notion.

(d) *Appeals to authority*. Here clients point to respected authorities as the source of irrational beliefs and consider that such beliefs are true because such authorities have credibility, e.g. 'My father taught me that I must do well in life. That's why it's true'. Here clients can be shown that such authorities probably intended to indicate relative rather than absolute values and that, even if absolute values were being taught, such respected authorities probably did not want the clients to have dysfunctional results, e.g. 'Do you think your father wanted you to be miserable? Would he prefer you to be miserable and cling to your belief, or do you think he would want you to give up the exaggerated quality of your belief if it meant you weren't miserable?' It is often not productive, however, to cast the respected authority in a negative light, since counsellors who attempt this may be viewed negatively themselves.

(e) *Evading the issues*. Clients will often evade the issue by changing the subject or by bringing up other problems. They do this to try to distract counsellors from their purpose. Effective rational–emotive counsellors succeed in bringing clients back to the issue at hand while acknowledging that focusing on difficult problems is uncomfortable. In some cases, counsellors may need to dispute clients' LFT beliefs about tolerating the pain of focusing on their problems.

Promoting emotional rational insight

The following errors are often committed by inexpert rational–emotive counsellors while attempting to promote emotional rational insight:

1. *Failing to show clients the differences between intellectual rational insight and emotional rational insight.* It is very important for rational-emotive counsellors to help clients understand that gaining intellectual rational insight is rarely sufficient for them to solve their emotional and behavioural problems. Rather, clients should be shown that they need to challenge their irrational beliefs repeatedly and vigorously using cognitive, emotional and behavioural methods, if they are to achieve lasting change.

2. *Failing to uncover and address clients' blocks to working hard to achieve emotional rational insight.* Clients refuse to work hard to achieve emotional rational insight for a number of reasons. These include: (a) a philosophy of low frustration tolerance (LFT) where clients believe, for example, that 'It's too hard to work to achieve lasting change. Change must not be that hard'; (b) cognitive–emotive dissonance whereby clients feel 'unnatural' as they work towards strengthening their rational beliefs, and believe that they must feel natural at all times (Maultsby, 1984). Grieger and Boyd (1980) note that this phenomenon can take a number of forms: 'I won't be me', whereby clients fear that they will lose their identity if they relinquish their irrational beliefs, and, 'I'll become a robot', whereby clients believe that rationality means becoming devoid of all feeling rather than experiencing appropriate negative emotions, e.g. sadness, regret, etc. (see Chapter 4). It is important for counsellors to monitor clients' efforts to work at counselling between sessions, and to be alert to beliefs that may block them from doing so.

3. *Failing to experiment with a broad range of cognitive, emotional and behavioural techniques.* Clients vary in their response to rational-emotive techniques. It is recommended that counsellors adopt an experimental attitude in attempting to discover which techniques best suit which clients. Counsellors who only employ a limited range of techniques at this stage are generally less effective than counsellors who are willing to use a broad range of techniques.

4. *Insisting that clients employ implosion methods of change.* Rational-emotive theory states that implosive techniques of behavioural change are more effective than gradual methods of behavioural change. Also, Ellis (1979b, 1980a) has argued that many clients perpetuate their problems and deprive themselves of learning experiences because they believe that they *must* be comfortable. Thus rational-emotive counsellors prefer to encourage their clients to fully confront their anxieties, for example, while tolerating their uncomfortable feelings. Although this is a sound strategy, it often needs to be modified for pragmatic purposes, since some clients stubbornly refuse to employ such implosive methods. Rational-emotive counsellors who insist that such clients use these

methods are likely to damage the therapeutic alliance. For example, whereas it may be desirable for a client who is anxious about eating in public to go to an expensive restaurant and challenge her anxiety-creating cognitions in a situation where her worst fears may be realised, many clients will not do this. When we provide a rationale for homework assignments, we do so in a way which incorporates a principle which W.D. has termed 'challenging but not overwhelming' and contrast it with gradual desensitisation and implosion methods (Dryden, 1985b):

> There are three ways you can overcome your fears. The first is like jumping in at the deep end; you expose yourself straightaway to the situation you are most afraid of. The advantage here is that if you can learn that nothing terrible will happen then you will overcome your problems quite quickly. However, the disadvantage is that some people just can't bring themselves to do this and get quite discouraged as a result. The second way is to go very gradually. Here, on the one hand, you only do something that you feel comfortable doing, while on the other you don't really get an opportunity to face putting up with discomfort, which in my opinion is a major feature of your problem. Also treatment will take much longer this way. The third way is what I call 'challenging but not overwhelming'. Here you choose an assignment which is sufficiently challenging for you to make progress, but not one which you feel would be overwhelming for you at any given stage. Here you are likely to make progress more quickly than with the gradual approach, but more slowly than with the 'deep end' approach.

We find that when clients are given an opportunity to choose their own rate of progress, the therapeutic alliance is strengthened. Most clients who will not employ implosive methods of change choose the 'challenging but not overwhelming' approach, and only very rarely do they opt for gradual desensitisation therapy. When they do so we try to dissuade them and frequently succeed. In the final analysis, however, we have not found it productive to insist that clients choose a particular way of tackling problems that is against their preferences.

Case management

The following errors are often committed by inexpert rational–emotive counsellors in general case management:

1. *Focusing too much on the therapeutic relationship in the early stages of counselling.* Although it is important for counsellors to develop a cooperative relationship with their clients, this can often be best achieved through a business-like focus on the clients' problems, the execution of a correct assessment of these problems, and an early start on helping clients to overcome them. We have found that problem-focused counselling is more successful at consolidating the therapeutic relationship than deliberate attempts to develop this relationship in the absence of task activities.

2. *Switching from problem to problem in quick succession.* It is important for rational–emotive counsellors to spend sufficient time on each
of their clients' problems if clients are to benefit from counselling.
Otherwise clients become confused and fail to understand both the
cognitive underpinnings of their problems and how to overcome them.
A particular error here occurs when counsellors switch frequently
from ego to discomfort problems within a given session.

3. *Failing to identify and work with clients' priorities in counselling
sessions.* When counsellors and clients have different priorities concerning what to discuss in sessions, it seems as if they are on parallel
tracks and do not work together as a team. The result is that clients
consider that their counsellors do not understand them, and as such do
not benefit from counselling as much as they would if they perceived
their counsellors as empathic (Truax and Carkhuff, 1967). Utilising a
client problem list and collaborating on session agendas represent
means by which this problem can be avoided.

4. *Failing to work at a pace and using language appropriate to the
learning abilities of clients.* Rational–emotive counselling can perhaps
be best viewed as a psychoeducational approach to counselling. As
such it is important for counsellors to take into account their clients'
learning abilities in executing interventions. Common errors here
include working too fast, or too slowly, for clients and using too
complicated, or too simple, language, with the result that clients are
insufficiently involved in the therapeutic process due to confusion or
boredom. Here again, it is important for practitioners to utilise client
reactions as the vehicle for constructing an optimal learning
environment.

5. *Failing to ensure that clients understand rational concepts.* As
rational–emotive counselling is a psychoeducational approach to
counselling, its practitioners should preferably make frequent checks
that their clients understand rational concepts. It is important that
counsellors do not take clients' verbal assurances, e.g. 'I understand',
and non-verbal assurances, e.g. head-nods, mm-hmms, that they understand and agree with rational concepts at face value. This is particularly
important when counsellors give didactic explanations of these concepts. Good questions to ask include: 'I want to make sure that I am
making myself clear. Can you put into your own words what you think I
said?'; 'What is your reaction to that point?'; 'Do you have any negative
reactions about that?' We have found it particularly valuable to recommend that counsellors ask clients about and deal with their reservations
concerning rational concepts, otherwise their clients may 'resist' their
counsellors' interventions without the latter understanding the source
of the 'resistance'.

6. *Failing to be sufficiently repetitive.* Here counsellors believe falsely

that if client change has occurred at one stage of counselling, then lasting change has taken place. Thinking that once a topic has been discussed in a counselling session the client has thoroughly learned what needs to be learned, such counsellors fail to 'go over old ground' with their clients. In practice, dealing with issues repeatedly is almost always a feature of effective rational–emotive counselling, since one-trial client learning hardly ever occurs.

7. *Failing to determine the basis of client change.* As has been noted in Chapter 3, client change may be inferentially based, behaviourally based or philosophically based. RET counsellors consider that long-term change is rooted in changes in clients' beliefs (i.e. philosophical change). If counsellors do not accurately establish the basis of client change they may miss opportunities of dealing with the philosophical roots of their clients' problems, since clients may terminate counselling, having made progress at the inferential or behavioural level of change. Counsellors are advised to conduct careful enquiries when clients report seemingly positive changes in their usual patterns of feeling and acting. When such enquiries reveal that these changes are not philosophically based, counsellors can present their clients with a rationale for continuing to work at modifying their irrational beliefs.

8. *Failures in the task domain of the therapeutic alliance.* Bordin (1979) has argued that counsellors and clients each have tasks to carry out during the process of counselling, and calls this the task domain of the therapeutic alliance. When obstacles to client progress occur due to problems in the task domain of the alliance the following are common counsellor errors:

   (a) failing to help clients understand what their tasks are in counselling, or if they do understand these, failing to help them understand how executing them will help them achieve their goals;

   (b) failing to identify and deal with clients' doubts about their abilities to execute their tasks;

   (c) failing to help clients understand what their counsellors' tasks are and/or failing to help clients understand the link between their counsellors' tasks and their own tasks and goals;

   (d) encouraging clients to carry out tasks that they cannot realistically execute, e.g. some clients are not intelligent enough to engage in the tasks of Socratic disputing;

   (e) failing to train clients in the appropriate use of their own therapeutic tasks, e.g. clients often need to be trained in the use of rational–emotive imagery if they are to benefit from this procedure;

   (f) executing their own tasks in an unskilled manner;

   (g) employing methods which are not potent enough to promote client change, e.g. disputing irrational beliefs without exposure is unlikely to help clients with phobias.

The reader is referred back back to Chapter 10 for recommendations concerning means of avoiding problems within the task domain of counselling.

9. *Failing to negotiate homework assignments adequately.* In rational-emotive counselling, clients are encouraged to put into practice what they learn in counselling sessions through the execution of a variety of homework assignments. Inexpert counsellors often fail to suggest homework assignments, and when they do suggest such tasks they make the following errors in negotiating assignments with their clients:

(a) failing to provide a persuasive rationale for the importance of homework assignments in rational–emotive counselling. It is desirable to provide such a rationale early on in counselling, and to check whether clients understand it or have any objections to it;

(b) assigning the tasks unilaterally instead of involving clients in the negotiation process. This often occurs when counsellors devote insufficient time to discussion about homework. Devoting adequate time to discussion of homework allows counsellor and client to work together on its design, and provides the counsellor with an opportunity to identify and deal with any concerns the client may have about enacting the assignment;

(c) suggesting assignments which are irrelevant with respect to clients' goals (Golden, 1983). It is important to identify homework that will help clients to approach their goals, and to make sure that clients see the relationship between homework enactment and goal attainment;

(d) suggesting assignments which do not relate to what has been discussed in the counselling session. This can be quite confusing for clients, as it obscures the relationship between homework enactment and goal attainment. As a general rule of thumb, counsellors are advised to promote the design of homework assignments that will help clients to work at disputing and replacing the irrational beliefs that were the focus of a given session. Such assignments may, of course, be cognitive, behavioural or emotive in nature;

(e) negotiating tasks which are vague rather than specific. Clients are more likely to carry out a homework task when they know what to do, when to do it, and where to do it, and when they believe they are capable of doing it;

(f) failing to elicit commitment from clients that they will attempt homework assignments. A simple question (e.g. 'Do you think you'll make an effort to do that this week?') towards the session's end may be all that is required to determine a given client's commitment to doing a particular homework assignment. It is advisable, however, to allow sufficient time to deal with a negative response to this enquiry;

(g) failing to rehearse clients in homework assignments, e.g. in imagery or through role-play methods. Lazarus (1984) has argued that clients will be more likely to carry out homework assignments when they can picture themselves doing them in imagery;

(h) failing to identify and deal with potential obstacles that may prevent clients from carrying out their homework assignments. Here, it is recommended that counsellors be alert to practical as well as psychological obstacles;

(i) suggesting assignments which are too time-consuming for the client (Golden, 1983). Counsellors are advised to bear in mind that the tasks of daily living can impose significant demands on clients' time;

(j) suggesting assignments which are too threatening or anxiety pro-voking for clients at that stage of counselling (Golden, 1983) – see material on the 'challenging but not overwhelming' principle dis-cussed earlier in this chapter.

10. *Failing to check adequately clients' experiences in executing homework assignments.* When clients agree to execute homework assignments it is important that counsellors discuss with them their experiences in carrying them out. This should ideally be done in the following session, although it is not always possible to do this. Common counsellor errors in checking on homework assignments include:

(a) failing to ask clients for a report of their experiences in carrying out assignments;

(b) failing to ask clients for a report of what they learned, or did not learn, from their experiences in carrying out assignments;

(c) failing to reinforce clients' attempts at executing assignments;

(d) failing to correct clients' errors in written homework assignments when these have been completed;

(e) failing to ask for and assess clients' reasons for not attempting, or not completing, their homework assignments;

(f) failing to dispute irrational beliefs (in the domains of ego and/or discomfort disturbance) when these explain why clients did not attempt, or complete, assignments;

(g) failing to reiterate the rationale for assignments when it is clear that clients did not understand them, and thus did not attempt to complete them;

(h) failing to obtain clients' commitment to attempt the assignments again if appropriate.

Guidelines for conducting follow-up on clients' experiences with homework assignments are presented in Chapter 10.

Counsellors' irrational beliefs

Client progress can also be hindered because counsellors may bring their own disturbance to the therapeutic process. Ellis (1983b) has outlined five major irrational beliefs that lead to therapeutic inefficiency:

1. 'I *have* to be successful with all my clients practically all the time.'
2. 'I *must* be an outstanding counsellor, clearly better than other counsellors I know or hear about.'
3. 'I *have* to be greatly respected and loved by all my clients.'
4. 'Since I am doing my best and working so hard as a counsellor, my clients *should* be equally hard working and responsible, *should* listen to me carefully and *should* always push themselves to change.'
5. 'Because I am a person in my own right, I *must* be able to enjoy myself during counselling sessions and to use these sessions to solve my personal problems as much as to help clients with their difficulties.'

In addition, counsellors often fail to dispute clients' irrational beliefs because they share the same beliefs. Thus one of W.D.'s trainees recently did not dispute her client's belief 'I must not die at an early age and it would be awful if I did' because she too believed that it would be awful to die prematurely. Hauck (1966) has called this the 'neurotic agreement' in counselling and psychotherapy.

In such cases, it is recommended that RET counsellors apply RET principles and methods to search for and dispute their own self- and client-defeating beliefs which may (a) impede them from confronting their clients; (b) distract them and their clients from getting the therapeutic job done; (c) foster undue counsellor anxiety and anger; and (d) encourage inappropriate behaviour anathema to the practice of effective and ethical counselling.

Sources of Obstacles to Client Progress: Other Factors

In this section we discuss the following obstacles to client progress: client factors, relationship factors and environmental and other external factors.

Client factors

In order to really benefit from RET counselling clients need to achieve three forms of insight, namely: (1) psychological disturbance is mainly determined by the absolutist beliefs that they hold about themselves, others, and the world; (2) even when people acquired and created their irrational beliefs in their early lives, they perpetuate their disturbance by reindoctrinating themselves in the present with these beliefs; (3) only if they consistently work and practise in the present and future to think, feel and act against these irrational beliefs are they likely to surrender their irrationalities and make themselves significantly less disturbed.

Kempel (1973) has identified a number of client attitudes and feelings which predispose them to terminate counselling prematurely:

1. *'I need to have a very close relationship with my counsellor.'* Such clients may wish to terminate counselling because their RET counsellors generally avoid developing very close therapeutic relationships with them. As outlined in Chapter 5, such relationships are deemed to be countertherapeutic in that they reinforce clients' approval needs.
2. *'Change must be easy.'* Such clients are loath to put in the hard work that change involves and may leave RET counselling to seek a form of counselling that they perceive as less demanding.
3. *'I want changes in A (activating events) not B (beliefs).'* Such clients seek changes in significant others or troublesome events but will neither do anything themselves to try to effect such changes nor work to change their irrational beliefs about these situations. When they realise that RET will not provide them with what they seek, they usually terminate counselling.
4. *'Shame about seeking help.'* Such clients condemn themselves for being weak and not able to solve their own problems. They are thus ambivalent about seeking help and may terminate counselling if their feelings of shame become acute.

Unless counsellors are sensitive to the existence of such client attitudes and feelings, and can identify and deal with relevant irrational beliefs and misconceptions about counselling, clients will not stay in counselling long enough to achieve the three forms of insight outlined above.

Golden (1983) has noted four important client factors that impede client progress. First, some clients may have 'hidden agendas' that could interfere with rational-emotive counselling, e.g. a man who comes into counselling in order to stop his wife filing for a divorce, but who has no intention of seeking personal changes for himself. It is often difficult to identify such agendas, particularly early on in the counselling process and clients are, of course, 'motivated' to keep them hidden. However, if clients are not progressing it is important for counsellors to try and answer the question: 'What has this person to gain from not improving?' and to try and help clients to identify the irrational beliefs and inferential distortions that may underpin any hidden agendas that can be identified. However, it may happen that counsellors never become aware of the presence of such agendas that do in fact exist. This should be accepted as one of the occupational hazards of all forms of counselling.

The second factor discussed by Golden is poor client motivation. This occurs 'when a client does not value the desired outcome of therapy enough to devote the necessary time and effort to change' (Golden, 1983, p. 35). In such cases rational–emotive counsellors would do well to re-negotiate with such clients their goals for change.

Thirdly, some clients demonstrate negative behavioural patterns such as counter-control which may take the form of negativism toward counselling or rebelliousness against the counsellor. In these instances, we have found it helpful to show clients that they have a perfect right to act in such fashion and that the logical consequence of such behaviour is that they will not improve. We then enquire whether this is the outcome from counselling that they seek. It is important for counsellors to disengage themselves from any power struggle with such clients, since the more counsellors try to 'win' such struggles, the more these clients will resist their efforts. Since these clients desperately seek to control situations, they can be calmly shown that they and not their counsellors are in control of whether they improve or not.

Finally, Golden (1983) notes that some clients do not profit from counselling because of neurological and other biological limitations. When counsellors suspect the existence of such factors, referral to and liaison with other professionals is often indicated.

In a study by Ellis (1983d) on the characteristics of clients who 'failed' in RET, the following findings emerged:

1. Clients who did poorly in RET failed to do consistent *cognitive* self-disputation. They were characterised amongst other factors by extreme disturbance, by grandiosity, by lack of organisation, and by plain refusal to do these cognitive assignments.
2. 'Failure' clients, who refused to accept responsibility for their irrational emotions and refused to forcefully and *emotively* change their beliefs and actions, were more clingy, more severely depressed and inactive, more often grandiose and more frequently stubbornly rebellious than clients who benefited from RET.
3. 'Failure' clients who did poorly in the *behavioural* aspects of RET showed 'abysmally low frustration tolerance, had serious behavioural addictions, led disorganised lives, refrained from doing their active homework assignments, were more frequently psychotic and generally refused to work at therapy' (Ellis, 1983d, p. 165).

Thus clients' own extreme level of disturbance is a significant obstacle to their own progress. Although a full discussion of what 'special' therapeutic methods and techniques to employ with such clients is outside the scope of this book (see Ellis, 1985a), counsellors can adopt a number of strategies to enhance therapeutic effectiveness with these 'difficult' clients. Amongst other tactics, counsellors should first be consistently and forcefully encouraging in their therapeutic interactions with these clients, showing them that they can do better if they try. Secondly, counsellors would be wise to keep vigorously showing these clients that they, the counsellors, do in fact unconditionally accept them with all their psychological difficulties and that they can indeed accept themselves in the same way. Thirdly, counsellors can often be successful with such clients by consistently showing them that their refusal to work on their problems will generally lead to bad consequences and needless suffering. Fourthly, counsellors should be flexible in experimenting with a wide range of therapeutic techniques (including some unusual ones!) in their persistent efforts to help their 'difficult' clients. Above all, rational–emotive counsellors should be good representatives of their therapeutic system and accept themselves and tolerate the discomfort of working with 'difficult' clients while sticking to the therapeutic task.

Relationship factors

These can be first attributed to poor counsellor–client matching, which may occur for many reasons. Thus, clients 'may have a therapist who, according to their idiosyncratic tastes or preferences, is too young or too old, too liberal or too conservative, too active or too passive' (Ellis, 1983e, p. 29). If these 'relationship match' obstacles persist, then it is preferable for that client to be transferred to a counsellor with more suitable traits. Other relationship obstacles may occur because the counsellor and client may get on 'too well' and get distracted from the more mundane tasks of counselling. In such cases, the paradox is that if the client improves, the 'life' of the satisfactory relationship is threatened. As a result, collusion may occur between counsellor and client to avoid making counselling as effective an endeavour as it might otherwise be. This problem can be largely overcome if counsellors first help themselves and then their clients to overcome the philosophy of low frustration tolerance implicit in this collusive short-range hedonism.

In previous chapters, we discussed how counsellors should preferably modify their therapeutic style with different clients. In addition, clients may not benefit from counselling when the interpersonal style of their counsellors does not maximise their opportunities for therapeutic learning. In other words the relationship 'milieu' may promote or inhibit client learning. For example, some clients are emotionally overstimulated and hence the therapeutic task for counsellors is to create a learning environment which decreases their emotional tension to a level where they can adequately reflect on their experiences. With these clients counsellors are advised to make use of a lot of cognitive techniques and adopt an interpersonal style which aims to decrease affect. This style may either be formal or informal in character. These strategies are particularly appropriate with clients who have a 'hysterical' style of functioning. On the other hand, other clients require a more emotionally charged learning atmosphere. Such clients often use 'intellectualisation' as a major defence and are used to denying feelings.

With such clients counsellors should preferably endeavour to inject a productive level of affect into the therapeutic session and employ emotive techniques, self-disclosure and a good deal of humour. These 'challenging' strategies are best introduced gradually so as not to 'overwhelm' clients with an environment that they are not accustomed to utilising. However, before deciding upon which interpersonal style to emphasise with clients, counsellors should routinely gain information from them concerning how they best learn. Some clients learn best directly through experience, whereas for others vicarious experiences seem to be more productive. We personally try to develop a learning profile for each of our clients and use this information to help us plan our therapeutic strategies and choose techniques designed to implement these strategies. Care needs to be taken, however, that the counsellor does not use a mode of learning that may perpetuate the client's problems.

Environmental and other external factors

Golden has noted that the following environmental and other external factors can be obstacles to client progress in counselling:

1. Deliberate sabotage from others (for example, threats of rejection or disapproval for being more assertive or successful).
2. Inadvertent sabotage from others such as family members who become 'benevolent saboteurs'. An example is the individual who inadvertently reinforces a family member's agoraphobia by 'chauffering' the phobic person around, thus providing him or her with a 'secondary gain' for being phobic.
3. Other 'secondary gains', such as those from disability and welfare benefits which provide clients with reinforcements for their 'disabilities' (Golden, 1983, p. 35).

To these we would add: organisations, systems and positions that provide limited opportunities for client growth, e.g., unfulfilling jobs, unemployment, prisons, totalitarian states.

In addition to helping clients to change their irrational beliefs about these obstacles, counsellors can use the following strategies to deal with them: when people who serve as willing or unwilling obstacles to client progress are members of the client's family they may be invited to attend for family or marital counselling; when such people cannot be legitimately invited to attend counselling sessons, clients may be specifically helped to deal with them – see Ellis' (1975) *How to live with a neurotic* – or encouraged to distance themselves from them as far as possible; clients may be encouraged to leave situations which inhibit their growth if these situations cannot be modified; and clients may be encouraged to give up the short-term benefits of secondary gains in order to achieve the long-term benefits to their mental health of doing without such 'gains'.

It should be remembered, however, that while environmental and other external factors can limit the client's opportunities for happiness they cannot directly cause their psychological problems, since it is clients' irrational beliefs about these situations which determine their emotional and behavioural responses to these factors.

Notes on Individualising Rational–Emotive Counselling

One of the best ways of minimising obstacles to client progress is to individualise the practice of rational–emotive counselling for each client. In this section we again use Bordin's (1979) concept of the therapeutic alliance as an explanatory framework. Although we cover issues that have already been introduced, we believe that Bordin's ideas provide a fresh way of looking at these issues. As described in Chapter 10, Bordin argues that there are three components of the therapeutic alliance: bonds, goals and tasks. To review: bonds refer to the interpersonal connectedness between counsellors and clients. Goals are the objectives of both counsellors and clients and provide the 'raison d'être' of counselling. Finally, tasks are best viewed as the means by which counsellors and clients attempt to actualise their goals.

It is in the nature of individual RET counselling that, since counsellors are dealing with only one client, they can strive to tailor the practice of counselling with this client free from the concern that a particular style of interaction (and the use of an individually tailored treatment programme) may have an adverse affect on other clients, e.g. in couples counselling, family counselling or group counselling. Thus, as we have shown previously, the counsellor can modify his or her style of participation in individual counselling according to the personality structure of a given client, in order to maximise that client's learning and to minimise the possibility that the client's problems are being unwittingly reinforced. This refers in particular to individualising RET counselling in the bond domain of the therapeutic alliance (Bordin, 1979). Therapeutic bonds in RET counselling may change over time according to the amount of progress that the client makes and according to which bonds the client best responds.

In this latter regard, the counsellor can at the outset attempt to assess what might be a productive bond to form with a particular client, e.g. a formal or informal bond. Thus, as discussed in Chapter 10, the counsellor might ask the client (either on a biographical form or in person) what constitutes helpful and unhelpful counsellor behaviour in the client's mind. The counsellor might also ask the client about the latter's previous experiences of being helped, whether formally or informally, and during this exploration focus on what aspects of the other person's behaviour the client found most helpful and what aspects they found least helpful. It is important, however, to view such information critically because what a client has found helpful in the short term may not have been helpful in the long term. Thus, for example, counsellors can help clients feel better in the short term without helping them to get better in the long term (Ellis, 1972). Although the information that can be obtained from the client about possible helpful ways of intervening with that particular client may be useful, rational–emotive counsellors would be wise to answer by experimentation the question concerning which bond is most productive with this client at this particular time. Thus, the counsellor might try particular ways of interacting with different clients, and observe how these clients respond to these different forms of therapist interaction.

Another way that RET practitioners can individualise counselling for their clients is to ensure that there is congruence between clients' goals and the goals of counselling. Ineffective RET counselling can often occur when clients wish to achieve one goal and their counsellors are working to help them to achieve a different goal. However, we advocate that counsellors do not uncritically accept their clients' goal statements as sacred. Indeed, a good RET counsellor sometimes spends some therapeutic time trying to talk a client out of goals that the client considers to be helpful but which the counsellor considers to be harmful to the long-term welfare of the client. Good RET counselling therefore involves a fair measure of negotiation between counsellor and client concerning the client's goals. It is helpful, however, if the counsellor refrains from dogmatically insisting that a client give up his or her unrealistic or harmful goals, since such insistence may add to the client's problems.

Clients' goals can and often do change over time and counsellors should be sensitive to the changing nature of their clients' aims and attempt to track changes in their goal statements. It is particularly helpful for RET counsellors to understand (and to help their clients understand) what underlies such changes in therapeutic goals. Remember that clients' initial goals are often coloured by the nature of their disturbance and that it is advantageous for counsellors to encourage them to postpone fixing on certain goals until they have achieved a fair measure of success in overcoming their emotional and/or behavioural disturbance. Once this is accomplished, RET counsellors are noted for helping their clients to pursue the latter's own individualised goals, since they believe that a particular client does not *have to* achieve satisfaction in any given way. Thus, clients are encouraged to actualise their potential in their own individualistic way, preferably after having achieved a large measure of freedom from emotional and behavioural disturbance. In general, RET counsellors encourage clients to first work on the goals of overcoming their emotional and/or behavioural disturbance before working to pursue individualistic goals that will bring them happiness.

The third aspect of the therapeutic alliance where rational-emotive counselling can be practised in an individualised way is in the task domain. Bordin (1979) has stressed that every therapeutic system favours particular counsellors' tasks *and* clients' tasks which then become embodied in the practice of that approach to counselling. RET counselling can be practised in an individualised way if the counsellor encourages the client to carry out tasks which are best suited to that particular client and which are likely to encourage that client to achieve his or her therapeutic goals. In this way the practice of RET can be seen as efficient as well as effective (Ellis, 1980b).

Some clients seem to progress better by carrying out techniques which are more cognitive in nature, while other clients seem to benefit more from executing tasks which are more emotive in nature; yet a further group of clients do best by carrying out behavioural tasks. Although a particular therapeutic technique draws upon all three modalities, it is also true that a particular technique may emphasise one modality over others. There are no firm guidelines for RET counsellors to use in determining, before the event, which therapeutic techniques are most appropriate for given clients. However, it may be helpful to explore with clients their past history of effecting productive changes while paying attention to their answers concerning which modalities they spontaneously used, or were encouraged to use. In other words, it may be helpful for RET counsellors to pay attention to a client's prior learning style and modify the practice of rational-emotive counselling accordingly. Once again, perhaps the best indication concerning which techniques clients will benefit from most is experimentation, which is the hallmark of individualising rational-emotive counselling and the scientific method which rational-emotive theory supports. This involves trying out interventions, noting clients' reactions to these, getting clients' feedback on their reactions to these interventions and modifying future interventions accordingly.

Chapter 12
A Client's View of
Rational–Emotive
Counselling

Overview

The rational-emotive counselling literature contains a good number of detailed case descriptions by counsellors and therapists (see, for example, Ellis et al., 1971; Ellis, 1984d, 1990; Dryden, 1987; Dryden and Yankura, 1992). These descriptions can be quite instructive, insofar as they reveal the differing styles of RET practitioners and illustrate the manner in which this form of counselling can be applied to a variety of client problems. It is noted, however, that the RET literature contains few case descriptions from the client's perspective. This could be a significant deficit, as clients' accounts of counselling could shed light on the aspects of RET that they find to be most helpful and beneficial. Conceivably, this in turn could contribute to continued refinements in the theory and practice of rational-emotive counselling.

The present chapter provides a client's written description of her experience in rational-emotive counselling with the first author, W.D. Her account is virtually unedited (except for some very minor modifications in grammar and punctuation), is presented with the client's full permission and is organised in two parts. The first part ('About Myself') offers relevant background data and a description of the problems that led the client to seek counselling. As will be seen, she was troubled by obsessive thoughts, feelings of guilt, shame and depression, and avoidance of situations in which she feared she might act on her 'inappropriate' obsessive thoughts. The second part ('Meeting Dr Dryden') recounts her actual counselling experience. The chapter is concluded with commentary which provides an ABC analysis of the client's problems, as well as a discussion of the various interventions that comprised her treatment.

About Myself

I am 26 years old and was brought up in a rigidly Orthodox Jewish family, although I myself am no longer religiously observant. I did not have any formal sex education, either from my parents or from my school, a strictly Orthodox Jewish girls' school. The source of my knowledge on this subject came almost entirely from teenage friends (who were probably about as ignorant as I was) and the *Encyclopaedia Britannica Book of Health*. Sex was rarely spoken of in my house, except in negative contexts. If the topic *did* arise, my mother would usually say, 'Can we change the subject?' although she did once mention to me that she thought sex was overrated. In addition, she once gave me a long lecture on the importance of preserving one's virginity (and reputation) until marriage. In my family, sex was a secretive, shameful topic governed by defined rules; if these were broken, they would leave one with a burden of guilt. Masturbation was never, *never* mentioned. Homosexuality was only referred to in conjunction with the words 'disgusting' or 'abnormal'. My father is convinced that the aim of male homosexuals is to corrupt young boys. In fact, *male* masturbation and *male* homosexuality are completely forbidden by *halacha* (Jewish ritual law). Of course, female homosexuality and female masturbation are not (though these phenomena certainly do not meet with approval in Orthodox circles). Rather like Queen Victoria, the (male) writers of *halacha* clearly assumed that female homosexuality did not exist, or was unimportant.

My parents, and my peers, always encouraged me to have lots of boy-friends – the assumption being, of course, that one of these relationships would ultimately lead to marriage with a 'suitable' Orthodox, eligible man, whereupon I would settle down and raise a large family. As an attractive woman, I always had my fair share of male admirers. Ever aware of the spectre of the ruined reputation, however, I never allowed sexual relations to go beyond kissing or occasional heavy petting (that is, until the grand age of 24, when I finally lost my virginity). I was fairly naïve and unknowledge-able about sex well into my twenties.

When I was 21, I began to have fairly erotic lesbian dreams. These dreams were always similar: I would see a woman, or women, with fairly large breasts moving about in a state of undress. In my sleep I would become sexually excited and sometimes have an orgasm. (I have difficulty believing that I am writing this so calmly; for years these dreams were a source of unmentionable guilt and shame.) Afterwards, I would wake up and a wave of guilt would crawl over me; how could I, the 'nice Jewish girl', be having such 'disgusting' dreams? At that time, I had absolutely no doubt that they *were* disgusting. I never mentioned these dreams to a soul; I did not know who I could tell. My friends all had disparaging views about homosexuals, whom they regularly referred to as 'poofs' and 'queers'.

Up to that point, I had always been sure that I was 100 per cent heterosexual. After all, I found men attractive, all my waking sexual fantasies concerned men, and I was certain that marriage and motherhood awaited me with all their safe acceptability and guarantees of future happiness. Lacking real knowledge of human sexuality, it never occurred to me that heterosexual people may have homosexual fantasies, or that '100 per cent heterosexuality' does not exist. Here I was, having sexy dreams about women. Never having read anything about adolescent sexual confusion, and desperately afraid to ask in case it confirmed my worst nightmare (that I might be a lesbian), I carried my problem around with me for over 4 years, an unmentionable secret. The question, 'Was I a lesbian?' plagued me without respite. I did not know, and had never met, any openly lesbian women or gay men. The thought of their daughter being a lesbian, would, I am sure, have shocked and horrified my parents.

I did not have any desire to experiment sexually with women; in fact, I viewed such a prospect as the ultimate horror. These contradictory feelings would swim round and round my head without my reaching any resolution; I simply did not understand how I could experience homo-erotic dreams whilst still finding men attractive and having no inclination towards sexual involvement with women. At this stage, an in-depth talk with a suitable counsellor might have resolved much of my confusion and saved me years of useless depression; just knowing that my experience was *normal* would have helped me. But I was afraid to seek help; afraid that, having 'confessed' my awful dreams, I would hear my worst suspicions confirmed: 'Yes, you ARE a lesbian.'

So, I walked around with my problems for 4 years before seeking professional help. At first, I was fairly depressed and convinced that I was completely abnormal. But I did not allow the problem really to interfere with my life. I was at university, working hard, seeing friends. But unshared, unmentionable problems do not solve themselves, as I often wished. They fester and itch, and begin to occupy a disproportionate amount of one's thoughts. I began to be very wary of mixing with women, thinking, in my exaggerated way, that over-interest in female friendship would be mis-interpreted as meaning that I was a lesbian.

Moreover, about 2 years after my lesbian dreams began, a new problem surfaced: unwanted, disturbing (to me) sexual thoughts about women with whom I came into contact. As my worry and confusion over my sexuality grew, so did my desperate attempts to drive the problem from my mind – to absolutely no avail. The first time I had a waking sexual thought about another woman was at a very boring meeting. Sitting next to a woman, a thought suddenly materialised in my head (a thought I tried desperately *not* to think): touching her on her vagina. I was acutely distressed and deeply ashamed. I tried unsuccessfully to drive it from my head, to no avail – the thought was 'thunk'. I called myself disgusting and, as soon as I could, escaped from the room.

I spent the rest of the week either crying or having some sort of anxiety attack – shivering or trembling, feeling nauseous and weak, tense and rigid; I would sweat and my heart would beat rapidly. The sexual thoughts about women multiplied; I could not look at a woman without imagining some sexual thought about her – either touching her vagina or breasts, squeezing her bottom, or lifting up her skirts. I was in an agony of shame and guilt over my 'disgusting' thoughts. I became acutely uncomfortable and tense in the presence of other women, including my mother. I would take every possible precaution not to be present in the same room as other women, or even to sit or stand next to them. You can imagine how difficult this was. If I had no choice but to sit next to another woman, I would clench my fists and squeeze my arms or pinch myself – even recite poetry – in an attempt to drive these thoughts from my head. I never, in fact, succeeded in doing so – I would *invariably* think the thought which I strove not to. I could not relax. I could not read a women's magazine or watch a sexy film in case it inspired the dreaded 'thoughts'. I could not touch other women or kiss them except with great anxiety.

Yet even then, I was not desperate enough to seek help, even though my guilty secret resulted in some odd behaviour patterns (known only to myself, apparently!) over the next 2 years. Outwardly everything appeared normal (I started to work, successfully, at a new job) but *inside* I knew I had an unmentionable problem. I avoided conversation or unnecessary contact with other women. I allowed friendships with women friends to suffer. I have played the piano for many years, yet stopped having piano lessons because this meant sitting next to my piano teacher, a woman. My anxiety increased, and seemingly normal situations (such as parties) were occasions for worry and acute discomfort. My thoughts became more bizarre – including, for example, thoughts of attacking other women. I consistently told myself how disgusting, terrible, and worthless an individual I was. I was terrified that if people discovered what went on in my head, they too would think I was weird and disgusting (though how they would find out, I could not exactly say). And what if I lost control and acted out these thoughts? How awful! My parents would hate me, I'd be ostracised by society, and I'd more than likely be sent to prison for abusing or molesting other women. It was a nightmare.

My original problem – guilt over lesbian dreams – had now been replaced by my guilt over my shameful sexual thoughts. I also began to have problems relating to men. I found sexual contact difficult – despite, or more probably *because* of, my desperate need to appear entirely heterosexual. I wanted to appear comfortable about sexual contact with men, but couldn't because I was continually afraid that the man in question would suspect something 'amiss' about my sexuality. I was confused as hell!

Meeting Dr Dryden

I finally began to see Dr Dryden after confessing my anxiety over my sexuality (leaving out significant details) to a sympathetic boyfriend – possibly the only person I had met during the course of my 4-year depression who I thought would understand (he did). He encouraged me to seek professional counselling. I came into contact with Dr Dryden through a Jewish Counselling Centre, and saw him 12 times over a period of 5 months.

Telling Dr Dryden of my anxiety was an intense relief and immensely cathartic. At last, I could unload my bottled-up depression and reveal my unmentionable problem – which had now, of course, become mentionable. At first, however, it was difficult to be open. I could tell him about my lesbian dreams, but I refused to describe them or tell him that they had resulted in orgasms. I found it extremely difficult to tell him of my shameful thoughts, and it was only after much insistent prompting that I finally did. But he did not judge me in any way. He did not appear embarrassed, did not laugh, explode or condemn.

Dr Dryden helped me to confront a huge series of 'musts' and 'must-nots'. He demonstrated that my insistence that I did not *want* to be a lesbian, to have lesbian dreams, and to think homosexual thoughts, was actually equivalent to saying that I *must not* be a lesbian, *must not* have lesbian dreams and *must not* think homosexual thoughts. When he asked me why I thought that I must not think homosexual thoughts, I replied that I considered these thoughts to be disgusting, and by some kind of derivation, this implied that I myself was disgusting. At this point, Dr Dryden and I discussed the whole issue of homosexuality; whether or not it is disgusting or wrong. Our discussion revealed that although I thought that homosexuality was disgusting (a result, probably, of my education and upbringing), I could not say exactly *why*. There *is* no reason why two people of the same sex, who are attracted sexually and/or emotionally, should not make love together; and there is nothing wrong or disgusting about this. He also told me (and in my naïvete I had not realised this) that it is quite common for adolescents (and sexually I *was* an adolescent) to undergo some confusion about their sexuality and sexual orientation. We unearthed a giant lacuna in my sexual knowledge, which I proceeded to fill with the aid of several books on sex.

Another reason why I did not wish to think these shameful thoughts was because I believed they made me feel depressed. Dr Dryden showed me that it was not the thoughts themselves which depressed me, but *myself*. By continually telling myself what a disgusting, loathsome person I was, I depressed myself. Moreover, by continually telling myself that I *must not* think homosexual thoughts about other women, I actually was thinking them all the time.

Dr Dryden suggested that instead of continually telling myself that I *must not* think sexual thoughts about other women, I should instead say to myself, 'I would prefer not to think sexual thoughts about women, but there is absolutely no reason why I *must not*, and if I do, it does not make me a disgusting or terrible person'. (We discussed whether it was possible for *anyone* to be a totally terrible person, and concluded that it was not; it is clearly impossible for anyone to be an utterly worthless individual.) We also discussed the issue of whether a 'thought' could be considered 'wrong' or 'right'. I decided, or he decided, or we both decided, that it was neither. A thought is simply a series of electrical currents passing across the brain, and has no inherent badness or goodness. Thoughts, unlike actions, are not easy to control, and as most of us know, the less we try and think of something, the more we are guaranteed to end up thinking about it.

Another of my 'must nots' was 'I must not be a lesbian'. Why not? I could not exactly say why, except for the fact that it would incur the heavy disapproval, even rejection, of my family and many of my friends. Dr Dryden encouraged me to confront each of these 'musts' and to show myself why there was absolutely no reason why I must not be a lesbian or think homosexual thoughts, or why I must have the approval of my family. Nevertheless, I could see several reasons why I would *prefer* not to be homosexual; namely, that it's inconvenient to be a lesbian in a society which tends to discriminate against and verbally abuse homosexuals. Continual, unwanted thoughts tend to interfere with more creative thinking; and my family's approval, which I value despite its repressive overtones, is important to me. Dr Dryden showed me that the loss of my family's approval might be unfortunate, but it would certainly not be terrible (for I was continually telling myself that it would be). Being a lesbian might be inconvenient, but I cannot think of one reason why it would be terrible. It might lose me some friends or my family's love, but it certainly would not end my life or ruin my health incurably.

Apart from long discussions aimed at breaking down my self-destructive thinking patterns, Dr Dryden proposed some practical techniques for overcoming my anxiety about mixing with women. He encouraged me to spend as much time as possible with other women. If I thought unwelcome sexual thoughts about them, I should say to myself, 'I prefer not to be thinking these thoughts, but there is absolutely no reason why I *must not* think them, and if I do, it does not make me a disgusting or terrible person'. Or, later, I would simply say to myself, 'It's only a thought'. At first, it was difficult actively to place myself in situations where I would be in close proximity with other women (such as sitting next to them on the tube, standing talking to them face to face), but I persevered and gradually found that the task became easier and easier. I became less tense and anxious; more at ease. Sexual thoughts about women began to surface with less frequency. This process took some time – quite some time, in fact, after I ceased to visit Dr Dryden. But now, nearly 2 years later, it does not even occur to me to avoid the company of other women; these thoughts rarely surface.

Dr Dryden strongly encouraged me to describe the thoughts which I found so shameful. Though deeply embarrassed, after much prompting, I would do so. He was absolutely unperturbed by what I thought were weird or abnormal thoughts. One interesting technique that he used was to record me reciting, repeatedly, one of my most shameful thoughts. This was, 'I thought about having oral sex with a woman I was standing talking to at work'. I had to repeat this about 30 times into a tape recorder. He then gave me the tape, told me to buy myself a personal stereo, and listen to this recording three times over, three times a day, while telling myself that the thought was not disgusting, nor was I a disgusting person for having thought it. This I did. At first I was deeply embarrassed, listening to myself, but gradually I became less so, and eventually became rather bored with the sound of my own voice. I also found that after a while, I was no longer paying attention to the tape, but was thinking of something else. The unbelievable had happened: something which previously had been a source of shame was now merely boring.

Dr Dryden also encouraged me to watch sexy films and was fond of waving pictures of vulvas and vaginas in front of my face.

The whole process was one of confronting my fixated ideas that I must or must not be this or that, or do this or that. Dr Dryden was able to show me that whilst I could build up a case for preferring heterosexuality, I could not prove that I *must* be heterosexual. I could not prove that I must be anything, and therefore the therapy involved breaking down my rigid rules of behaviour and replacing them with preferences. Also, I should try to give up this idea that my actions or thoughts would lead to terrible consequences. I could show that my actions might lead to unfortunate results, but I could not prove that the consequences of my actions would be terrible. For example, I was very afraid that one day I would loss control and 'act out' my sexual thoughts on other women; I might lose control over my hands and suddenly shove them up some unsuspecting woman's skirt as she was bending over. 'How awful!', I reasoned. We first discussed the likelihood of this happening. It seemed rather unlikely; as we agreed, people do have a certain amount of control over their actions (though less over their thoughts). But suppose, just *suppose*, that I did lose control and assault some woman. What would be the result? Well, the woman might scream or act in a horrified manner (she might not!). She might tell other people, and they might demonstrate their shock or disapproval. She might call the police, and I might be arrested. Although all this might prove highly inconvenient or unfortunate, none of the preceding events could be described as terrible, and I would certainly live through them, unless of course I decided to hang myself. Part of the therapy involved repeatedly telling myself that certain events, if they happened, might prove unfortunate, but not terrible.

In fact, here we come to one of the inherent problems (I think) in this form of counselling, RET. By continually wandering around repeating these simple maxims to myself, I gradually became obsessed with thoughts of how to 'conquer' my obsession with my own sexuality. To the exclusion of much else, I now began to continually think of how to finally 'solve' my problem. I found it difficult to concentrate on anything else. Of course, this was part of the problem: I thought that I *had to* find a solution. I had expected, when I began to see Dr Dryden, that I would emerge very soon with some kind of 'magic' or instant cure. This did not happen, and the process of dealing with my problem was a long one.

Moreover, while now prepared to accept that I was not either 100 per cent homosexual or heterosexual, but some combination of the two, I still felt that I had to define my sexuality to the nearest percentage point. (There is, of course, no reason why I must be one or the other, or even some combination.) In my continual 'assessment' of myself, I gradually became more and more confused, until at one point I was probably more confused and distressed than when the therapy began. I discussed this with Dr Dryden and he suggested that I cease looking for some kind of absolute or 'final' solution to my problem. Rather, I should try and accept my confusion (or, accept myself *with* my confusion) and let the future take care of itself; after all, just because I was confused then, it did not mean that I would *always* be confused.

Another area that Dr Dryden and I explored was the uncertainty of the future, and the impossibility of supplying guarantees for the future. At one point in the therapy I became obsessed by the notion that even though I did not appear to be a lesbian at present, I might 'turn into one' in the future. I began to ask Dr Dryden whether this was likely. His reply? 'I think it's 100 per cent likely!' He then went on to explain that he could not provide me with a guarantee of how the future would develop. He showed me that it was my consistently telling myself how awful it would be if I 'turned into' a lesbian that lay at the bottom of my fear. If instead, I told myself that it might be unfortunate if this happened (because, if I chose to publicise it, I might face hostility), but not in any way *dreadful*, I would have less fear of the future. He was right.

We discussed the nature of dreams; what purpose they serve. While no one has come up with any definitive conclusions on the subject, it seems clear that they help us act out our fantasies in a non-threatening environment; a way of experiencing something without incurring any consequences. They may also be a safe way of exploring forbidden territory. Since lesbian experiences were so utterly taboo for me, my dreams were a way of exploring this forbidden realm. Also, the more 'forbidden' something is, the more enticing it becomes; this is one way of explaining why these dreams excited me so much. Indeed, since I have removed this 'ban' on lesbian emotions, these lesbian dreams have become much rarer and less stimulating. Also, I do not feel guilty about having them!

One thing that I discovered from the therapy (which may seem obvious) was the composite and complex nature of human sexuality and emotions. The latter are so complex that they cannot be easily defined or placed in neat square boxes. I realise that I am a complex human being, with a very wide range of emotions and sexual feelings; these have changed over the years and will continue to change. I have no need to define or assess my sexuality.

How do I feel now, nearly 2 years after my last meeting with Dr Dryden? Well, one healthy sign (I think!) is that my interest in the whole topic has declined dramatically! Dealing with my problem left me with a huge amount of energy to be devoted to more interesting subjects, and I realise that I was wasting a good deal of creative energy which could just as easily have been addressed elsewhere. While my sexuality is still mildly interesting, it by no means occupies the gigantic space in my thoughts that it formerly did. There are so many things that interest me more – friends, work, singing, art, music, reading, studying – subjects far more absorbing than my self-centred obsession with my sexuality.

I am no longer afraid to enter a room where women are present; I am no longer anxious about talking with or being close to women – it simply does not occur to me to be nervous of such situations! I have allowed friendships with women friends to develop and flower – indeed, I have rediscovered the beauty of such relationships. I'm now part of a women's peace movement!

I have not had a lesbian affair, nor do I think it very likely at present, since this is not what I desire. But I have not unequivocally ruled out the possibility – it is no longer 'forbidden territory'. As a result, my obsession with 'turning into a lesbian' has subsided and disappeared.

I am no longer anxious about how the future will develop, although I am healthily concerned about it. I am prepared to deal with each new situation as it arises; I do not endlessly imagine hypothetical situations, nor plan detailed responses to future questions.

I think that this form of counselling, RET, was very effective for me. Its emphasis on discussion and 'thinking through' emotional problems appealed to me, as it does not pretend to offer any magic cure. It was also quite important for me that Dr Dryden was Jewish. Although he may not come from an Orthodox family himself, he would certainly understand the pressures and restrictive practices that are involved in growing up in an Orthodox Jewish environment. Knowing this made it easier for me to describe my family and the relationship that I have with them.

I am much more aware of the prejudice and discrimination which exist toward homosexuals, and the need to fight against such attitudes (I now volunteer for a support group for people with AIDS). I am no longer afraid to discuss the issue of homosexuality with friends in an open and honest way; although not prepared to reveal my own confusion over my sexuality, I nevertheless make it clear that I do not consider homosexuality in *any* way wrong or disgusting. As a result, I have found that friends are more open with me regarding their own attitudes toward homosexuality.

I have ceased to search for the ultimate definition of my own sexuality – it does not exist! In fact, I rejoice in my own particular, personal and private, unique, individual and undefinable brand of sexuality!!!

Commentary

This client was experiencing recurrent, intrusive dreams and waking thoughts with homosexual content, perhaps related to her upbringing in a household in which sex and homosexuality were treated as taboo subjects. She apparently had only the most basic sexual knowledge prior to entering counselling, and seemed to accept without question her family's (and religious tradition's) belief that homosexuality is wrong. Her account suggests that she had no friends or family members with whom she could share her problems; even if such individuals had been available, it is quite likely that her feelings of guilt and shame would have presented obstacles to frank discussion of sexual issues.

It is interesting to note that the client's attempts to deal with her problems on her own seemed to contribute to an unwanted exacerbation of her 'inappropriate' thoughts. She describes her desperate efforts to drive such thoughts from her mind, with the effect that the 'sexual thoughts about women multiplied'. She relates how she took to avoiding contact with other women, such that she terminated her piano lessons with her female instructor and allowed friendships with female friends to suffer.

It seems evident that prior to counselling, this client defined her problems in terms of the fact that she was having 'lesbian thoughts' and the possibility that she might indeed be a lesbian. From the RET perspective, however, these aspects of her problems merely represented activating events. The irrational beliefs that she brought to bear upon these activating events were actually more central to her difficulties, as they resulted in the variety of inappropriate negative emotions she experienced and contributed to the development of her avoidance behaviour.

More specifically, in terms of the ABC model (where A refers to activating events, B stands for beliefs, and C connotes emotional and behavioural consequences), this client's problems can be analysed and understood as follows:

1. With respect to identifying relevant activating events, it is noted that the client experienced unwanted waking thoughts and dreams with homosexual content. She inferred from these dreams and thoughts that she might be a lesbian, and that she might act on these in some inappropriate way. She predicted that such actions would result in her being subjected to the disapproval and rejection of friends, family, and society at large. Thus, her activating events consisted not only of an actual 'event' (i.e. the occurrence of a lesbian thought or dream), but also (and more importantly from a clinical view) of her inferences about this event.

2. With respect to her beliefs, she first held the rational belief 'I do not *want* to have lesbian thoughts or be a lesbian, because I think that this is wrong and being a lesbian would result in a number of unfortunate

consequences for me'. This belief, according to RET theory, is considered rational since it only reflects the individual's preferences and values. The client, however, escalates this statement of preference to the level of an absolutistic command: 'I *must not* have lesbian thoughts or be a lesbian!' This irrational belief represents a premise from which certain irrational derivatives tend to follow: (a) 'If I have lesbian thoughts, it proves I am a *disgusting person*;' (b) 'If I am a lesbian, people will reject me and that will be *awful*'. In the present case, these irrational derivatives constitute global negative self-rating and awfulising, respectively.

3. With respect to her emotional and behavioural consequences, the client appears to experience feelings of guilt, shame and depression in relation to her global negative self-rating. Her awfulising probably results in anxiety about the negative future outcomes she associates with being a lesbian; this anxiety, in turn, contributes to the action tendency to avoid contacts with other women.

As per the rational–emotive approach to counselling, identification and disputation of this client's irrational beliefs would represent the most important element of her treatment. The client's account, however, reveals that her treatment was multifaceted and touched upon a number of issues and areas. In fact, W.D.'s therapeutic interventions in this particular case can be seen to include the following:

1. Unconditional acceptance of the client with her problems.
2. Exploration of values with respect to the issue of homosexuality.
3. Education on human sexuality and the nature and meaning of dreams.
4. Disputing of distorted inferences.
5. Disputing of irrational beliefs and construction of alternative rational beliefs.
6. Exposure exercises designed to assist the client in internalising a new, rational philosophy.

Each of these components of treatment will be discussed separately.

With respect to the first, the reader will recall that, at the time she entered counselling, the client was deeply ashamed of herself for having her inappropriate thoughts and dreams. It appears that W.D.'s non-judgmental response to her descriptions of her problems helped her to eventually feel comfortable with full self-disclosure. In addition, it could be conjectured that his lack of a condemning response could have indirectly communicated the message that it was unnecessary for the client to engage in self-condemnation.

Values exploration was aimed at the issue of whether or not it is wrong for two individuals of the same sex to share a sexual relationship. Although the client began counselling with the attitude that homosexuality is disgusting and wrong, in-session discussion led her to see that she could not provide any sound rationale to support this position. As a result she came to adopt a more accepting view of homosexuality, which may have further helped her to refrain from negative self-rating with respect to her own homosexual thoughts and dreams.

Education on human sexuality and the nature and meaning of dreams also proved to be an important intervention for this client. She describes a 'giant lacuna' in her sexual knowledge that was filled in part through in-session discussions, as well as through a number of books on human sexuality that were recommended by W.D. Over time, she developed an appreciation of the 'composite and complex nature of human sexuality', and ceased trying to define herself as either exclusively heterosexual or homosexual. Her discussions with W.D. on dreams helped her to place her so-called lesbian dreams in proper perspective. Here, it is interesting to note the client's observation that removal of her musts concerning her sexuality seemed to lead to a decrease in the frequency and stimulating properties of such dreams.

Disputing interventions with this client were focused upon both her distorted inferences and her irrational beliefs. With regard to the former, W.D. helped her to conduct a realistic appraisal of the probability that she would some day lose control of her behaviour and act on her lesbian thoughts (e.g. by shoving her hands 'up some unsuspecting woman's skirt'). As a result of this inferential disputing, the client was able to see that human beings are generally able to exert greater control over their actions than over their thoughts.

Although rational–emotive counsellors may conduct disputing at the inferential level with their clients, they focus more of their efforts on disputing clients' irrational beliefs. This is because irrational beliefs are regarded by RET theory as being the cause of inappropriate negative emotions and the 'source' of distorted inferences. Throughout the client's account of her counselling, numerous references are made to the process of identifying and disputing the irrational beliefs she subscribed to with respect to her sexuality, behaviour and relationships with significant others. She does, in fact, note that the discussion she had with W.D. concerning the likelihood that she might act on her lesbian thoughts did not terminate with the conclusion that this was a low-probability event. Instead, she and W.D. went on to consider the possible outcomes that might accrue if she did act on her thoughts (e.g. the disapproval of her family; being arrested by the police), and then worked together on de-awfulising these outcomes. As the client stated: 'Part of the therapy involved repeatedly telling myself that certain events, if they happened, might prove unfortunate, but not terrible'. Disputing was also focused upon the negative self-rating in which the client engaged, such that she was able to conclude that it is impossible for any human being to be rated as an utterly worthless individual.

In addition to disputing irrational beliefs, rational–emotive counselling also places an emphasis on helping clients to construct and apply alternative rational beliefs. It is apparent that this component of treatment was an integral part of this particular client's counselling experience, as she in several places makes reference to rational self-statements (suggested to her by W.D.) that could be used to counter her irrational beliefs. As she stated, 'the therapy involved breaking down my rigid rules of behaviour and replacing them with preferences'.

In order to assist the client in moving from intellectual to emotional rational insight (and thus gain conviction in her alternative rational beliefs), a variety of exposure exercises were utilised. Basically, these exercises entailed exposure to stimuli (i.e. activating events) that served to trigger the client's irrational beliefs. As such, W.D. encouraged her to increase her contacts with other women, and to actively dispute her shoulds and musts if she found herself experiencing unwanted sexual thoughts about them. He also prompted her to make an audio recording of one of her 'most shameful' sexual thoughts, so that by reviewing the tape she could expose herself to a problematic activating event at will. Here again, she was instructed to counter the irrational beliefs that were triggered by this exposure exercise. She was also encouraged to see 'sexy films' (as these could serve as yet another stimulus for homosexual thoughts), and describes the in-session exposure she received by way of W.D.'s 'waving pictures of vulvas and vaginas in front of my face'.

The client states that her rational–emotive counselling proved very effective for her, and attributes a wide variety of positive changes to it. She notes that, over time, she ceased to engage in anxious avoidance of other women, and experienced sexual thoughts about them with less and less frequency. She reports that she is no longer ashamed of such thoughts, and is able to comfortably discuss the issue of homosexuality when it arises in conversations with friends. She has given up her efforts to rate the 'degree' to which she is either heterosexual or homosexual.

It is interesting to note, however, that the work of counselling was not completed at the time of the client's last scheduled session with W.D. By her account, she found it necessary to devote continued time and effort to the goal of feeling comfortable when in contact with other females. This observation serves to highlight an important feature of rational–emotive counselling: the practitioner attempts to prepare the client to function as her own counsellor. This does not always mean that the client's presenting problems will be completely resolved by the time that counselling contacts have ended; rather, it can mean that the client has reached a point where she feels competent to practise self-counselling on an independent basis. Clients who encounter difficulties with self-counselling can, of course, request additional 'refresher' or problem-solving sessions with their counsellor.

The present client offers only one criticism of her rational–emotive counselling: she notes that it contributed to her becoming obsessed with finding an absolute solution to her problems. Here, it is possible to speculate that she was subscribing to the irrational belief, 'I *must* find the means to swiftly resolve the difficulties I'm experiencing; I *can't stand* having these problems'. It is not uncommon for clients in RET to develop such musts at some point in treatment, and rational–emotive counsellors attempt to remain alert to this possibility. Frequently, in fact, they may try to take pre-emptive action by warning clients in advance that applying irrational beliefs to their counselling progress will probably result in additional upsets. It does not appear that W.D. took such pre-emptive action in his work with this particular client; he was, however, able to respond effectively when the client broached the issue herself. He encouraged her to surrender the idea that she *had to* find a final solution to her problems, and suggested that she could accept herself *with* her confusion over her sexuality. Although it might have been better from a therapeutic perspective if W.D. had been able to anticipate the client's self-created need for a 'magic cure', we trust that the reader will refrain from globally rating him as a 'bad therapist'!

Chapter 13
The Distinctive Features of Rational–Emotive Counselling: A Review

Overview

In this final chapter, we review the distinctive features of rational–emotive counselling and contrast these with other approaches to cognitive-behavioural counselling. We conclude the chapter and the book by outlining techniques that are generally avoided in rational–emotive counselling.

Introduction

The major goal of rational–emotive counselling is an ambitious one: *to encourage clients to make a profound philosophical change in the two main areas of ego disturbance and discomfort disturbance.* This involves helping clients, as far as is humanly possible, to give up their irrational beliefs and to replace these with rational beliefs as discussed in Chapter 3.

In rational–emotive counselling the major goals are to help clients pursue their long-range basic goals and purposes and to help them to do so as effectively as possible by fully accepting themselves and tolerating unchangeable uncomfortable life conditions. Rational–emotive practitioners further strive to help clients obtain the skills which they can use to prevent the development of future disturbance. In encouraging clients to achieve and maintain this profound philosophical change, rational–emotive counsellors implement the following strategies. They help their clients see that:

1. Emotional and behavioural disturbances have cognitive antecedents and that these cognitions normally take the form of absolutist devout evaluations. RET counsellors train their clients to observe their own psychological disturbances and to trace these back to their ideological roots.
2. People have a distinct measure of self-determination and can thus *decide* to work at undisturbing themselves. Thus, clients are shown that they are not slaves to their biologically based irrational thinking processes.

3. People can implement their choices and maximise their freedom by actively working at changing their irrational beliefs. This is best achieved by employing cognitive, emotive and behavioural methods – often in quite a forceful and vigorous manner (Ellis, 1979d).

With the majority of clients, from the first session onward, RET counsellors are likely to use strategies designed to effect profound philosophic change. The counsellor begins the process with the hypothesis that this particular client may be able to achieve such change and thus begins to implement rational–emotive methods which he or she will abandon only after collecting sufficient data to reject this initial hypothesis. Rational–emotive practitioners regularly implement this viewpoint, which is based on the notion that the client's response to counselling is the best indicator of his or her prognosis.

When it is clear that the client is not able to achieve philosophic change, either on a particular issue or in general (despite repeated and varied attempts at philosophical disputing), the counsellor may decide to effect a therapeutic 'compromise' (Dryden, 1991) by utilising methods intended to bring about inferentially and behaviourally based change. Inferentially based change occurs when the client experiences some degree of improvement as a result of correcting distorted inferences such as negative predictions and overly negative interpretations of events and others' actions. Behaviourally based change occurs when clients improve by effecting constructive changes in particular aspects of their behaviour, as with skills-training approaches. As another type of compromise, the counsellor may attempt to help the client to directly alter her problematic activating events in a positive fashion, so that they no longer serve to trigger her irrational beliefs. Such changes in tack can be appropriate when persistent efforts to conduct philosophical disputing would imperil the therapeutic alliance.

A good example of this change in strategy is one often reported by a counsellor of our acquaintance. He was working with a middle-aged married woman who reported feeling furious every time her ageing father would telephone her and enquire 'Noo, what's doing?' She inferred that this was a gross invasion of her privacy and absolutistically insisted that he had no right to do so. The counsellor initially intervened with the usual rational–emotive strategy by attempting to dispute this client's dogmatic belief, and tried to help her see that there was no law in the universe which stated that he *must* not do such a thing. Meeting initial resistance, the counsellor persisted with different variations of this theme, all to no avail. Changing tack, he began to implement a different strategy designed to help the client question her inference that her father was actually invading her privacy. Given her father's age, the counsellor inquired, was it not more likely that his question represented his usual manner of beginning telephone conversations rather than an intense desire to pry into her affairs? This enquiry proved successful in that the client's rage subsided because she began to reinterpret her father's motives. Interestingly enough, although he returned to disputing her irrational belief later, the counsellor never succeeded in helping this client to give up this irrational belief!

However, some clients are more amenable to re-evaluating their irrational beliefs *after* they have been helped to correct distorted inferences. We should do research on this topic if we are to answer the question: 'Which strategy is most appropriate for which clients at which stage in counselling?' Meanwhile, it is important to note that RET counsellors, if they follow this lead, are unique in that they are more likely to challenge their client's irrational beliefs and to dispute them much earlier in the therapeutic process than are other cognitive-behavioural counsellors. Further differences between rational-emotive counselling and other approaches to cognitive-behavioural counselling are listed below. Although it should be noted that rational-emotive counsellors do use strategies derived from other cognitive-behavioural approaches, we want to reiterate that the focus in the previous chapters has been on strategies and techniques that are mainly associated with rational-emotive counselling.

Differences between rational–emotive counselling and other forms of cognitive–behavioural counselling

As opposed to other approaches to cognitive-behavioural counselling, rational-emotive counselling:

1. Has a distinct philosophical emphasis, which is one of its central features and which other forms of cognitive-behavioural counselling appear to omit. Thus, it stresses that humans appraise themselves, others and the world in terms of: (a) rational, preferential, flexible and tolerant philosophies, and (b) irrational, musturbatory, rigid, intolerant and absolutist philosophies.

2. Has an existential-humanistic outlook which is intrinsic to it and which is omitted by most other approaches to cognitive-behavioural counselling. Thus, it sees people 'as holistic, goal-directed individuals who have importance in the world just because they are human and alive; it unconditionally focuses upon their experiences and values, including their self-actualising potentialities' (Ellis, 1980c, p. 327). It also shares the views of ethical humanism by encouraging people to emphasise human interest (self and social) over the interests of deities, material objects and lower animals.

3. Favours striving for pervasive and long-lasting, philosophically based change, rather than symptomatic change.

4. Attempts to help humans eliminate all self-ratings and views self-esteem as a self-defeating concept which encourages them to make conditional

evaluations of self. Instead, it teaches people *un*conditional self-acceptance (Ellis, 1972).

5. Considers psychological disturbance to reflect an attitude of taking life 'too' seriously and thus advocates the appropriate use of various humorous therapeutic methods (Ellis, 1977a, 1977b, 1981c).

6. Stresses the use of antimusturbatory rather than anti-empirical disputing methods. As it considers that inferential distortions often stem from dogmatic musts, shoulds etc., rational–emotive counselling favours going to the philosophic core of emotional disturbance and disputing the irrational beliefs at this core rather than merely disputing anti-empirical inferences, which are more peripheral. Also, rational–emotive counselling favours the use of forceful logico-empirical disputing of irrational beliefs whenever possible, rather than the employment of rationally oriented, coping self-statements. When feasible, rational–emotive counselling teaches clients how to become their own scientists instead of parroting counsellor-inculcated rational beliefs.

7. Employs, but only mildly encourages, the use of palliative cognitive methods that serve to distract people from their disturbed philosophies, e.g. relaxation methods. Rational–emotive counselling holds that such techniques may help clients in the short term, but do not encourage them to identify, challenge and change in the long term the devout philosophies that underpin their psychological problems. Indeed, these palliative methods may make it harder for people to engage in philosophic disputing, since they may be less likely to do this when they are calm and relaxed than when they are motivated by their emotional distress. For these reasons, rational–emotive counselling also employs problem-solving and skill-training methods, along with, but not instead of, teaching people to work at understanding and changing their irrational beliefs.

8. Gives a more central explanatory role to the concept of discomfort anxiety in psychological disturbance than do other cognitive-behavioural approaches to counselling. Discomfort anxiety is defined as 'emotional hypertension that arises when people feel that their life or comfort is threatened; that they *must* not feel uncomfortable and *have to* feel at ease; and that it is awful or catastrophic (rather than merely inconvenient or disadvantageous) when they don't get what they supposedly must' (Ellis, 1980c, p. 331). While other cognitive-behavioural approaches to counselling recognise specific instances of discomfort anxieties, e.g. 'fear of fear' (Mackay, 1984) they tend not to regard discomfort disturbance to be as centrally implicated in psychological problems as does rational–emotive counselling.

9. Emphasises, more than other approaches to cognitive-behavioural counselling, that humans frequently make themselves disturbed about

their original disturbances. Thus, rational–emotive counsellors actively look for secondary symptoms of disturbances and encourage clients to work on overcoming these before addressing themselves to the primary disturbance.

10. Has clear-cut theories of disturbance and its treatment, but is eclectic or multimodal in its techniques. However, it favours some techniques, e.g. active disputing over others such as cognitive distraction, and strives for profound or elegant philosophic change where feasible.

11. Discriminates between 'rational' and 'irrational' negative emotions. Rational–emotive theory considers such negative emotions as sadness, annoyance, concern, regret and disappointment as 'rational' affective responses to thwarted desires based on a non-devout philosophy of desire. Further, it views them as healthy when they do not needlessly interfere with people's goals and purposes. However, it sees depression, anger, anxiety, guilt, shame/embarrassment, self-pity and feelings of inadequacy usually as 'irrational' emotions based on absolutist demands about thwarted desires. Rational–emotive counselling considers these latter feelings as symptoms of disturbance because they very frequently, but not always, sabotage people from pursuing constructively their goals and purposes. Other approaches to cognitive–behavioural counselling do not make such fine discriminations between 'rational' and 'irrational' negative emotions.

12. Advocates counsellors giving unconditional acceptance rather than giving warmth or approval to clients. Other cognitive–behavioural approaches to counselling tend not to make this distinction. Rational–emotive counselling holds that counsellor warmth and approval have their distinct dangers in that they may unwittingly encourage clients to strengthen their dire needs for love and approval. When RET counsellors unconditionally accept their clients they also serve as good role models, in that they also help clients to unconditionally accept themselves.

13. Stresses the importance of the use of vigour and force in counteracting irrational philosophies and behaviours (Ellis, 1979d; Dryden, 1984c). Rational–emotive counselling is alone among cognitive–behavioural approaches to counselling in stressing that humans are, for the most part, biologically predisposed to originate and perpetuate their disturbances and often experience great difficulty in changing the ideological roots of these problems. Since it holds this view it urges both counsellors and clients to use considerable force and vigour in interrupting clients' irrationalities.

14. Is more selective than most other cognitive–behavioural approaches to counselling in choosing behavioural change methods. Thus, it favours the use of penalisation in encouraging resistant clients to change. Often these clients will not change to obtain positive reinforcements, but may

be encouraged to change to avoid stiff penalties. Furthermore, rational-emotive practitioners have reservations concerning the use of social reinforcement in counselling. They consider that humans are too reinforceable and that they often do the right thing for the wrong reason. Thus, they may change to please their socially reinforcing counsellors, but in doing so they have not been encouraged to think and act for their own sake. RET counsellors aim to help clients become maximally non-conformist, non-dependent and individualistic and would thus use social reinforcement techniques sparingly. Finally, rational-emotive counselling favours the use of in vivo desensitisation techniques, since it argues that the former procedures best help clients to raise their level of frustration tolerance (Ellis, 1983c).

Whilst RET counsellors prefer to use these distinctive features of rational-emotive counselling wherever feasible, they do not dogmatically insist that they be employed. When, on pragmatic grounds, they employ other cognitive–behavioural methods their therapeutic practice is frequently indistinguishable from that of other cognitive–behavioural counsellors.

Sources of other cognitive–behavioural methods

We have mentioned that rational-emotive counsellors use other cognitive-behavioural methods when rational-emotive methods are insufficient to help the client. Since this book focuses on the distinctive features of rational-emotive counselling, we have not discussed these other methods here. However, we recommend the following as resource material on these methods: disputing distorted inferences (Beck et al., 1979; Beck and Emery, 1985); decision therapy (Greenwald, 1973; Wessler and Hankin-Wessler, 1986); self-instructional training (Meichenbaum, 1977, 1985); problem-solving therapy (D'Zurilla and Goldfried, 1971; Spivack, Platt and Shure, 1976); imagery methods (Lazarus, 1984); skills training (Lange and Jakubowski, 1976; Trower, Bryant and Argyle, 1978). Finally, a good general text on cognitive–behavioural counselling has been written by Cormier and Cormier (1985).

Techniques that are avoided in rational–emotive counselling

By now it will be clear that rational-emotive counselling is a multimodal form of counselling and advocates the employment of techniques in the cognitive, emotive and behavioural modalities. However, because the choice of therapeutic techniques is inspired by rational-emotive theory, the following available therapeutic techniques are avoided, or used sparingly in the practice of rational-emotive counselling (Ellis, 1979c, 1983c, 1984b):

1. Techniques that help people become more dependent, e.g. undue

counsellor warmth as a strong reinforcement and the creation and analysis of a transference neurosis.
2. Techniques that encourage people to become more gullible and suggestible, e.g. pollyannaish positive thinking.
3. Techniques that are long-winded and inefficient, e.g. psychoanalytic methods in general and free association in particular; encouraging clients to give lengthy descriptions of activating experiences at A.
4. Methods that help people feel better in the short term rather than get better in the long term (Ellis, 1972), e.g. some experiental techniques like fully expressing one's feelings in a dramatic, cathartic and abreactive manner, i.e. some gestalt methods and primal techniques. The danger here is that such methods may encourage people to practise irrational philosophies underlying such emotions as anger.
5. Techniques that distract clients from working on their irrational philosophies, e.g. relaxation methods, yoga and other cognitive distraction methods. These methods may be employed, however, *along with* cognitive disputing designed to yield some philosophical change.
6. Methods that may unwittingly reinforce clients' philosophy of low frustration tolerance, e.g. gradual desensitisation.
7. Techniques that include an antiscientific philosophy, e.g. faith healing and mysticism.
8. Techniques that attempt to change activating events (A) before or without showing clients how to change their irrational beliefs (B), e.g. some strategic family systems techniques.
9. Techniques that have dubious validity, e.g. neurolinguistic programming.

Finally, to reiterate, RET counsellors do not avoid using the above methods in any absolute sense. They may, on certain restricted occasions with certain clients, utilise such techniques, particularly for pragmatic purposes. For example, if faith healing is the only method that will prevent some clients from harming themselves, then RET counsellors might either employ it themselves or, more probably, refer such clients to a faith healer (Ellis, 1985a).

References

ADLER, A. (1927). *Understanding Human Nature.* New York: Garden City.

ADLER, A. (1964). *Social Interest: A Challenge to Mankind.* New York: Capricorn.

ANCHIN, J. C. and KIESLER, D. J. (1982). *Handbook of Interpersonal Psychotherapy.* New York: Pergamon.

BANDURA, A. (1969). *Principles of Behavior Modification.* New York: Holt, Rinehart & Winston.

BANDURA, A. (1977). *Social Learning Theory.* Englewood Cliffs, NJ: Prentice-Hall.

BANDURA, A. (1986). *Social Foundations of Thought and Action: A social cognitive theory.* Englewood Cliffs, NJ: Prentice-Hall.

BARD, J. A. (1973). Rational proselytizing. *Rational Living,* **12**(1), 2-6.

BARD, J. A. (1980). *Rational-Emotive Therapy in Practice.* Champaign, IL: Research Press.

BECK, A. T. (1976). *Cognitive Therapy and the Emotional Disorders.* New York: International Universities Press.

BECK, A. T. and EMERY, G. (1985). *Anxiety Disorders and Phobias: A Cognitive Perspective.* New York: Basic Books.

BECK, A. T., RUSH, A. J., SHAW, B. F. and EMERY, G. (1979). *Cognitive Therapy of Depression.* New York: Guilford.

BEUTLER, L. E. (1983). *Eclectic Psychotherapy: A Systematic Approach.* New York: Pergamon.

BORDIN, E. S. (1979). The generalizability of the psychoanalytic concept of the working alliance. *Psychotherapy: Theory, Research and Practice,* **16**, 252-260.

BURNS, D. D. (1980). *Feeling Good: The New Mood Therapy.* New York: Morrow.

CHESNEY, M. A. and ROSENMAN, R. H. (Eds.) (1985). *Anger and Hostility in Cardiovascular and Behavioral Disorders.* Washington: Hemisphere.

CLARK, D. M., SALKOVSKIS, P. M. and CHALKLEY, A. J. (1985). Respiratory control as a treatment for panic attacks. *Journal of Behavior Therapy and Experimental Psychiatry,* **16**, 23-30.

CORMIER, W. H. and CORMIER, L. S. (1985). *Interviewing Strategies for Helpers: Fundamental Skills and Cognitive-Behavioral Interventions,* 2nd ed. Monterey, CA: Brooks/Cole.

DIES, R. R. (1973). Group therapist self-disclosure: An evaluation by clients. *Journal of Counseling Psychology,* **20**, 344-348.

DIGIUSEPPE, R. (1984). Thinking what to feel. *British Journal of Cognitive Psychotherapy*, **2**(1), 27–33.

DIGIUSEPPE, R. (1991). Comprehensive cognitive disputing in rational-emotive therapy. In: M. Bernard (Ed.), *Using Rational-Emotive Therapy Effectively*. New York: Plenum.

DRYDEN, W. (1982). *A Guide for Solving Your Emotional and Behavioural Problems by Re-examining Your Self-defeating Thoughts and Attitudes*. London: Institute for RET (UK).

DRYDEN, W. (1983). Audiotape supervision by mail: a rational-emotive approach. *British Journal of Cognitive Psychotherapy*, **1**(1), 57–64.

DRYDEN, W. (1984a). Rational-emotive therapy. In: W. Dryden (Ed.), *Individual Therapy in Britain*. London: Harper & Row.

DRYDEN, W. (1984b). Therapeutic arenas. In: W. Dryden (Ed.), *Individual Therapy in Britain*. London: Harper & Row.

DRYDEN, W. (1984c). *Rational-Emotive Therapy: Fundamentals and Innovations*. Beckenham, Kent: Croom-Helm.

DRYDEN, W. (1985a). Marital therapy: The rational-emotive approach. In: W. Dryden (Ed.). *Marital Therapy in Britain. Volume 1: Context and Therapeutic Approaches*. London: Harper & Row.

DRYDEN, W. (1985b). Challenging but not overwhelming: A compromise in negotiating homework assignments. *British Journal of Cognitive Psychotherapy*, **3**(1), 77–80.

DRYDEN, W. (1986). Language and meaning in rational-emotive therapy. In: W. Dryden and P. Trower (Eds.), *Rational-Emotive Therapy: Recent Developments in Theory and Practice*. Bristol: Institute for RET (UK).

DRYDEN, W. (1987). Theoretically consistent eclecticism: Humanizing a computer 'addict'. In: J. C. Norcross (Ed.), *Casebook of Eclectic Psychotherapy*. New York: Brunner/Mazel.

DRYDEN, W. (1991). *Reason and Therapeutic Change*. London: Whurr.

DRYDEN, W., FERGUSON, J. and CLARK, T. (1989). Beliefs and inferences – a test of a rational-emotive hypothesis: Performing in an academic seminar. *Journal of Rational-Emotive and Cognitive-Behaviour Therapy*, **7**(3), 119–129.

DRYDEN, W., FERGUSON, J. and HYLTON, B. (1989). Beliefs and inferences – a test of a rational-emotive hypothesis: 3. On expectations about enjoying a party. *British Journal of Guidance and Counselling*, **17**(1), 68–75.

DRYDEN, W., FERGUSON, J. and MCTEAGUE, S. (1989). Beliefs and inferences – a test of a rational-emotive hypothesis: 2. On the prospect of seeing a spider. *Psychological Reports*, **64**, 115–123.

DRYDEN, W. and GOLDEN, W. L. (Eds.) (1986). *Cognitive-Behavioural Approaches to Psychotherapy*. London: Harper & Row.

DRYDEN, W. and GORDON, J. (1990). *Think Your Way to Happiness*. London: Sheldon Press.

DRYDEN, W. and YANKURA, J. (1992). *Daring to be Myself: A case study in rational-emotive therapy*. Buckingham: Open University Press.

DUCK, S. (1986). *Human Relationships: An Introduction to Social psychology*. London: Sage.

DUCKRO, P., BEAL, D. and GEORGE, C. (1979). Research on the effects of disconfirmed client role expectations in psychotherapy: A critical review. *Psychological Bulletin*, **86**, 260–275.

DUNLAP, K. (1932). *Habits: Their Making and Unmaking*. New York: Liveright.

D'ZURILLA, T. J. and GOLDFRIED, M. R. (1971). Problem-solving and behavior modification. *Journal of Abnormal Psychology*, **78**, 107–126.

EDELSTEIN, M. R. (1976). The ABCs of rational-emotive therapy: Pitfalls of going from D to E. *Rational Living*, **11**(1), 12–13.

ELLIS, A. (1958). Rational psychotherapy. *Journal of General Psychology*, **59**, 35–49.

ELLIS, A. (1962). *Reason and Emotion in Psychotherapy*. Secaucus, NJ: Lyle Stuart.

ELLIS, A. (1968a). *Is Objectivism a Religion?*. New York: Lyle Stuart.

ELLIS, A. (1968b). *Personality Data Form*. New York: Institute for RET.

ELLIS, A. (1972). Helping people get better: Rather than merely feel better. *Rational Living*, **7**(2), 2–9.

ELLIS, A. (1973). *Humanistic Psychotherapy: The Rational-Emotive Approach*. New York: McGraw-Hill.

ELLIS, A. (1975). *How to Live with a Neurotic: At Home and at Work*, Rev. ed. New York: Crown.

ELLIS, A. (1976). The biological basis of human irrationality. *Journal of Individual Psychology*, **32**, 145–168.

ELLIS, A. (1977a). Fun as psychotherapy. *Rational Living*, **12**(1), 2–6.

ELLIS, A. (Speaker, cassette recording). (1977b). *A Garland of Rational Humorous Songs*. New York: Institute for RET.

ELLIS, A. (1977c). Intimacy in psychotherapy. *Rational Living*, **12**(2), 13–19.

ELLIS, A. (1978). Personality characteristics of rational-emotive therapists and other kinds of therapists. *Psychotherapy: Theory, Research and Practice*, **15**, 329–332.

ELLIS, A. (1979a). The theory of rational-emotive therapy. In: A. Ellis and J. M. Whiteley (Eds.), *Theoretical and Empirical Foundations of Rational-Emotive Therapy*. Monterey, CA: Brooks/Cole.

ELLIS, A. (1979b). Discomfort anxiety: A new cognitive behavioral construct. Part 1. *Rational Living*, **14**(2), 3–8.

ELLIS, A. (1979c). The practice of rational-emotive therapy. In: A. Ellis and J. M. Whiteley (Eds.), *Theoretical and Empirical Foundations of Rational-Emotive Therapy*. Monterey, CA: Brooks/Cole.

ELLIS, A. (1979d). The issue of force and energy in behavioral change. *Journal of Contemporary Psychotherapy*, **10**(2), 83–97.

ELLIS, A. (1980a). Discomfort anxiety: A new cognitive behavioral construct. Part 2. *Rational Living*, **15**(1), 25–30.

ELLIS, A. (1980b). The value of efficiency in psychotherapy. *Psychotherapy: Theory, Research and Practice*, **17**, 414–418.

ELLIS, A. (1980c). Rational-emotive therapy and cognitive behavior therapy: Similarities and differences. *Cognitive Therapy and Research*, **4**, 325–340.

ELLIS, A. (1981a). The place of Immanuel Kant in cognitive psychotherapy. *Rational Living*, **16**(2), 13–16.

ELLIS, A. (1981b, Sept.). *New Developments in Rational-Emotive Therapy*. Address given at the First European Conference on the Cognitive-Behavioral Therapies, Lisbon, Portugal.

ELLIS, A. (1981c). The use of rational humorous songs in psychotherapy. *Voices*, **16**(4), 29–36.

ELLIS, A. (1982a). The treatment of alcohol and drug abuse: The rational-emotive approach. *Rational Living*, **17**(2), 13–16.

ELLIS, A. (1982b). Intimacy in rational-emotive therapy. In: M. Fisher and G. Striker (Eds), *Intimacy*. New York: Plenum.

ELLIS, A. (1982c). Must most psychotherapists remain as incompetent as they now are? *Journal of Contemporary Psychotherapy*, **13**(1), 17–28.

ELLIS, A. (1983a). *The Case against Religiosity.* New York: Institute for RET.

ELLIS, A. (1983b). How to deal with your most difficult client: You. *Journal of Rational-Emotive Therapy*, **1**(1), 3–8.

ELLIS, A. (1983c). The philosophic implications and dangers of some popular behavior therapy techniques. In: M. Rosenbaum, C. M. Franks and Y. Jaffe (Eds), *Perspectives in Behavior Therapy in the Eighties.* New York: Springer.

ELLIS, A. (1983d). Failures in rational-emotive therapy. In: E. B. Foa and P. M. G. Emmelkamp (Eds.). *Failures in Behavior Therapy.* New York: Wiley.

ELLIS, A. (1983e). Rational-emotive therapy (RET) approaches to overcoming resistance. 1: Common forms of resistance. *British Journal of Cognitive Psychotherapy*, **1**(1), 28–38.

ELLIS, A. (1984a). The essence of RET - 1984. *Journal of Rational-Emotive Therapy*, **2**(1), 19–25.

ELLIS, A. (1984b). Rational-emotive therapy. In: R. J. Corsini (Ed.), *Current Psychotherapies.* (2nd ed.). Itasca, IL: Peacock.

ELLIS, A. (1984c). *How to Maintain and Enhance your Rational-Emotive Therapy Gains.* New York: Institute for RET.

ELLIS, A. (1984d). Treating the abrasive client with rational-emotive therapy (RET). *Psychotherapy Patient*, **1**(1), 21–25.

ELLIS, A. (1985a). *Overcoming Resistance: Rational-Emotive Therapy with Difficult Clients.* New York: Springer.

ELLIS, A. (1985b). Expanding the ABCs of rational-emotive therapy. In: M. J. Mahoney and A. Freeman (Eds.), *Cognition and Psychotherapy.* New York: Plenum.

ELLIS, A. (1985c). Jealousy: Its etiology and treatment. In: D. C. Goldberg (Ed.), *Contemporary Marriage: Special Issues in Couples Therapy.* Homewood, IL: Dorsey.

ELLIS, A. (1985d). Dilemmas in giving warmth or love to clients: An interview with Windy Dryden. In: W. Dryden, *Therapists' Dilemmas.* London: Harper & Row.

ELLIS, A. (1987). The use of rational humorous songs in psychotherapy. In: W. F. Fry Jr and W. A. Salameh (Eds), *Handbook of Humor in Psychotherapy: Advances in the Clinical Use of Humor.* Sarasota, FL: Professional Resource Exchange, Inc.

ELLIS, A. (1990). Treating the widowed client with rational-emotive therapy (RET). *Psychotherapy Patient*, **6**(3), 105–111.

ELLIS, A., ARD, B., GEIS, H. J., GULLO, J., HAUCK, P. and MAULTSBY, M. (1971). *Growth Through Reason: Verbatim Cases in Rational-Emotive Therapy.* North Hollywood, CA: Wilshire Book Co.

ELLIS, A. and BECKER, I. (1982). *A Guide to Personal Happiness.* No. Hollywood, CA: Wilshire.

ELLIS, A. and BERNARD, M. E. (1985). *Clinical Applications of Rational-Emotive Therapy.* New York: Plenum.

ELLIS, A. and DRYDEN, W. (1987). *The Practice of Rational-Emotive Therapy.* New York: Springer.

ELLIS, A. and HARPER, R. A. (1975). *A New Guide to Rational Living.* No. Hollywood, CA: Wilshire.

ESCHENROEDER, C. (1979). Different therapeutic styles in rational-emotive therapy. *Rational Living*, **14**(1), 3–7.

FESTINGER, L. (1957). *A Theory of Cognitive Dissonance.* Evanston, IL: Row, Peterson.

FRANSELLA, F. (1985). Resistance. *British Journal of Cognitive Psychotherapy*, **3**(1), 1-11.

FREUD, A. (1937). *The Ego and the Mechanisms of Defense*. London: Hogarth.

FREEMAN, A. (1981). Dreams and imagery in cognitive therapy. In: G. Emery, S. D. Hollon and R. C. Bedrosian (Eds.), *New Directions in Cognitive Therapy*. New York: Guilford.

GARCIA, E. J. (1977). Working on the E in RET. In: J. L. Wolfe and E. Brand (Eds.), *Twenty Years of Rational Therapy*. New York: Institute for RET.

GENDLIN, E. T. (1978). *Focusing*. New York: Everest House.

GOLDEN, W. L. (1983). Resistance in cognitive-behaviour therapy. *British Journal of Cognitive Psychotherapy*, **1**(2), 33-42.

GOLDFRIED, M. and DAVISON, G. (1976). *Clinical Behavior Therapy*. New York: Holt, Rinehart & Wilson.

GREENWALD, H. (1973). *Direct Decision Therapy*. San Diego: Edits.

GREGORY, R. L. (1966). *Eye and Brain*. London: Weidenfeld & Nicholson.

GRIEGER, R. M. (1985). The process of rational-emotive therapy. *Journal of Rational-Emotive Therapy*, **3**(2), 138-148.

GRIEGER, R. M. and BOYD, J. (1980). *Rational-Emotive Therapy: A Skills-based Approach*. New York: Van Nostrand Reinhold.

GUIDANO, V. F. (1988). A systems, process-oriented approach to cognitive therapy. In: K. S. Dobson (Ed.), *Handbook of the Cognitive-Behavioral Therapies*, pp. 307-356. New York: Guilford.

GUINAGH, B. (1976). Disputing clients' logical fallacies. *Rational Living*, **11**(2), 15-18.

GURMAN, A. S. and KNISKERN, D. P. (1978). Research in marital and family therapy. In: S. L. Garfield and A. E. Bergin (Eds.), *Handbook of Psychotherapy and Behavior Change*, 2nd edn. New York: Wiley.

HAUCK, P. A. (1966). The neurotic agreement in psychotherapy. *Rational Living*, **1**(1), 31-34.

HAUCK, P. A. (1971). A RET theory of depression. *Rational Living*, **6**(2), 32-35.

HAUCK, P. A. (1972). *Reason in Pastoral Counseling*. Philadelphia: Westminster.

HEIDEGGER, M. (1949). *Existence and Being*. Chicago: Henry Regnery.

HORNEY, K. (1950). *Neurosis and Human Growth*. New York: Norton.

JANIS, I. L. (1983). *Short-Term Counseling*. New Haven, CT: Yale University Press.

JONES, M. C. (1924). A laboratory study of fear: The case of Peter. *Journal of Genetic Psychology*, **31**, 308-315.

JONES, R. A. (1977). *Self-Fulfilling Prophecies: Social, Psychological and Physiological Effects of Expectancies*. Hillside, NJ: LEA.

KASSINOVE, H. and DIGIUSEPPE, R. (1975). Rational role reversal. *Rational Living*, **10**(1), 44-45.

KELLY, G. A. (1955). *The Psychology of Personal Constructs*. New York: Norton.

KEMPEL, L. T. (1973). Identifying and confronting ways of prematurely terminating therapy. *Rational Living*, **8**(1), 6-9.

KNAUS, W. and WESSLER, R. L. (1976). Rational-emotive problem simulation. *Rational Living*, **11**(2), 8-11.

KORZYBSKI, A. (1933). *Science and Society*. San Francisco: ISGS.

KRANZLER, G. D. (1974). *You Can Change How You Feel: A Rational-Emotive Approach*. Eugene, OR: RETC Press.

KUHN, T. (1970). *The Structure of Scientific Revolutions*, 2nd edn. Chicago: University of Chicago Press.

LANGE, A. J. and JAKUBOWSKI, P. (1976). *Responsible Assertive Behavior: Cognitive-Behavioral Procedures for Trainers*. Champaign, IL: Research Press.

LAZARUS, A. A. (1977). Toward an egoless state of being. In: A. Ellis and R. Grieger (Eds.), *Handbook of Rational-Emotive Therapy*. New York: Springer.

LAZARUS, A. A. (1981). *The Practice of Multimodal Therapy*. New York: McGraw-Hill.

LAZARUS, A. A. (1984). *In the Mind's Eye*. New York: Guilford.

LAZARUS, A. A. (1989). The practice of rational-emotive therapy. In: M. E. Bernard and R. DiGiuseppe (Eds.), *Inside Rational-Emotive Therapy: A Critical Appraisal of the Theory and Therapy of Albert Ellis*. New York: Academic Press.

MACASKILL, N. D. and MACASKILL, A. (1983). Preparing patients for psychotherapy. *British Journal of Clinical and Social Psychiatry*, **2**, 80-84.

MACKAY, D. (1984). Behavioural psychotherapy. In: W. Dryden (Ed.), *Individual Therapy in Britain*. London: Harper & Row.

MAHONEY, M. (1977). Personal science: A cognitive learning theory. In: A. Ellis and R. Grieger (Eds.), *Handbook of Rational-Emotive Therapy*. New York: Springer.

MAHONEY, M. J. (1988). The cognitive sciences and psychotherapy: Patterns in a developing relationship. In: K. S. Dobson (Ed.), *Handbook of the Cognitive-Behavioral Therapies*, pp. 357-386. New York: Guilford.

MAULTSBY, M. C. Jr (1975). *Help Yourself to Happiness: Through Rational Self-counseling*. New York: Institute for RET.

MAULTSBY, M. C. Jr (1984). *Rational Behavior Therapy*. Englewood Cliffs, NJ: Prentice-Hall.

MEICHENBAUM, D. (1977). *Cognitive-Behavior Modification*. New York: Plenum.

MEICHENBAUM, D. (1985). *Stress Inoculation Training*. New York: Pergamon.

MOORE, R. H. (1983). Inference as "A" in RET. *British Journal of Cognitive Psychotherapy*, **1**(2), 17-23.

NEUMAN, F. (Leader). (1982). *An Eight-week Treatment Group for Phobics*. (Series of eight cassette recordings). White Plains, NY: F. Neuman.

NORCROSS, J. C., DRYDEN, W. and BRUST, A. M. (1992). British clinical psychologists: I. A national survey of the BPS Clinical Division. *Clinical Psychology Forum*, **40**, 19-24.

NORCROSS, J. C. and PROCHASKA, J. O. (1982). A national survey of clinical psychologists: Characteristics and activities. *The Clinical Psychologist*, **35**, 1-8.

PASSONS, W. R. (1975). *Gestalt Approaches in Counseling*. New York: Holt Rinehart and Winston.

PERSONS, J. B., BURNS, D. D. and PERLOFF, J. M. (1988). Predictors of dropout and outcome in cognitive therapy for depression in a private practice setting. *Cognitive Therapy and Research*, **12**, 557-575.

PHADKE, K. M. (1982). Some innovations in RET theory and practice. *Rational Living*, **17**(2), 25-30.

PLATT, J. J., PROUT, M. F. and METZGER, D. (1986). Interpersonal cognitive problem-solving (ICPS). In: W. Dryden and W. L. Golden (Eds.), *Cognitive-Behavioural Approaches to Psychotherapy*. London: Harper & Row.

POPPER, K. R. (1959). *The Logic of Scientific Discovery*. New York: Harper & Bros.

POPPER, K. R. (1963). *Conjectures and Refutations*. New York: Harper & Bros.

POWELL, J. (1976). *Fully Human, Fully Alive*. Niles, IL: Argus.

PROCHASKA, J. O. and NORCROSS, J. C. (1983). Contemporary psychotherapists: A national survey of characteristics, practices, orientations, and attitudes. *Psychotherapy: Theory, Research and Practice*, **20**, 161-173.

RAVID, R. (1969). Effect of group therapy on long-term individual therapy. *Dissertation Abstracts International*, **30**, 2427B.

REICHENBACH, H.S (1953). *The Rise of Scientific Philosophy.* Berkeley, CA: University of California Press.

ROGERS, C. R. (1957). The necessary and sufficient conditions of therapeutic personality change. *Journal of Consulting Psychology*, **21**, 95-103.

RUSSELL, B.S (1930). *The Conquest of Happiness.* New York: New American Library.

RUSSELL, B. (1965). *The Basic Writings of Bertrand Russell.* New York: Simon & Schuster.

RUSSIANOFF, P. (1981). *Why Do I Think I Am Nothing Without a Man?* New York: Bantam.

SACCO, W. P. (1981). Cognitive therapy *in vivo.* In: G. Emery, S. D. Hollon and R. C. Bedrosian (Eds.), *New Directions in Cognitive Therapy.* New York: Guilford.

SHAHAN, L. (1981). *Living Alone and Liking It.* New York: Warner.

SICHEL, J. and ELLIS, A. (1984). *RET Self-Help Form.* New York: Institute for RET.

SNYDER, C. R. and SMITH, T. W. (1982). Symptoms as self-handicapping strategies: The virtues of old wine in a new bottle. In: G. Weary and H. L. Mirels (Eds.), *Integration of Clinical and Social Psychology.* New York: Oxford University Press.

SPIVACK, G., PLATT, J. J. and SHURE, M. B. (1976). *The Problem-solving Approach to Adjustment.* San Francisco: Jossey-Bass.

TEASDALE, J. D. (1985). Psychological treatments for depression: How do they work? *Behaviour Research and Therapy*, **23**, 157-165.

TILLICH, P. (1977). *The Courage to Be.* New York: Fountain.

TREXLER, L. D. (1976). Frustration is a fact, not a feeling. *Rational Living*, **11**(2), 19-22.

TROWER, P., BRYANT, B. and ARGYLE, M. (1978). *Social Skills and Mental Health.* London: Methuen.

TRUAX, C. B. and CARKHUFF, R. R. (1967). *Toward Effective Counseling and Psychotherapy: Training and practice.* Chicago: Aldine.

WACHTEL, P. L. (1977). *Psychoanalysis and Behavior Therapy: Toward an Integration.* New York: Basic Books.

WALEN, S. R., DIGIUSEPPE, R. and WESSLER, R. L. (1980). *A Practitioner's Guide to Rational-Emotive Therapy.* New York: Oxford University Press.

WATSON, J. B. and RAYNER, R. (1920). Conditioned emotional reactions. *Journal of Experimental Psychology*, **3**, 1-14.

WERNER, E. E. and SMITH, R. S. (1982). *Vulnerable but Invincible: A Study of Resilient Children.* New York: McGraw-Hill.

WESSLER, R. A. and WESSLER, R. L. (1980). *The Principles and Practice of Rational-Emotive Therapy.* San Francisco: Jossey-Bass.

WESSLER, R. L. (1984). Alternative conceptions of rational-emotive therapy: Toward a philosophically neutral psychotherapy. In: M. A. Reda and M. J. Mahoney (Eds.), *Cognitive Psychotherapies: Recent Developments in Theory, Research and Practice.* Cambridge, MA: Ballinger.

WESSLER, R. L. and ELLIS, A. (1980). Supervision in rational-emotive therapy. In: A. K. Hess (Ed.), *Psychotherapy Supervision.* New York: Wiley.

WESSLER, R. L. and ELLIS, A. (1983). Supervision in counseling: Rational-emotive therapy. *The Counseling Psychologist*, **11**, 43-49.

WESSLER, R. L. and HANKIN-WESSLER, S. W. R. (1986). Cognitive appraisal therapy (CAT). In: W. Dryden and W. L. Golden (Eds.), *Cognitive-Behavioural Approaches to Psychotherapy.* London: Harper & Row.

WEXLER, D. A. and BUTLER, J. M. (1976). Therapist modification of client expressiveness in client-centred therapy. *Journal of Consulting and Clinical Psychology*, **44**, 261-265.

YANKURA, J. and DRYDEN, W. (1990). *Doing RET: Albert Ellis in Action.* New York: Springer.

YOUNG, H. S. (1974). *A Rational Counseling Primer.* New York: Institute for RET.

YOUNG, H. S. (1977). Counseling strategies with working class adolescents. In: J. L. Wolfe and E. Brand (Eds.), *Twenty Years of Rational Therapy.* New York: Institute for RET.

YOUNG, H. S. (1984a). Practising RET with lower-class clients. *British Journal of Cognitive Psychotherapy*, **2**(2), 33–59.

YOUNG, H. S. (1984b). Teaching rational self-value concepts to tough customers. *British Journal of Cognitive Psychotherapy*, **2**(2), 77–97.

Author index

Subject index